A Death Undeserved

For Bella

A shining light taken from this world too soon.

A Death Undeserved

Andrew Clark

First published in Great Britain in 2026 by
Pen & Sword Crime
An imprint of
Pen & Sword Books Ltd
Yorkshire - Philadelphia

ISBN 978 1 03618 309 7

A CIP catalogue record for this book is available from the British Library

Typeset in INDIA by IMPEC eSolutions
Printed and bound in the UK by CPI Group (UK) Ltd, Croydon, CRO 4YY

The Publisher's authorised representative in the EU for product safety is
Authorised Rep Compliance Ltd., Ground Floor, 71 Lower Baggot Street,
Dublin D02 P593, Ireland.
www.arccompliance.com

For a complete list of Pen & Sword titles please contact

PEN & SWORD BOOKS LIMITED
47 Church Street, Barnsley, South Yorkshire S70 2AS, United Kingdom
E-mail: enquiries@pen-and-sword.co.uk
Website: www.pen-and-sword.co.uk

or

PEN AND SWORD BOOKS
1950 Lawrence Rd, Havertown, PA 19083, USA
E-mail: Uspen-and-sword@casematepublishers.com
Website: www.penandswordbooks.com

Chapter 1

Sir David Fanshaw gently positioned the barrel of a shotgun underneath his chin. The coolness of the metal rested under his fragile jowls, his friable skin tearing as he adjusted his head. His finger sought the trigger, and once locating it, it froze. Eyes locked forward, he stared at the photograph of his wife on the mantelpiece. *She would never forgive me,* he thought.

With an agonising scream, Sir David tore the muzzle away, spittle flying from his lips. He stood up, his face twisted with self-loathing, and threw the weapon at the hearth, resulting in a thunderous explosion, which rattled as a cartridge struck fiery logs, blasting glowing cinders from the grate. Sir David cowered, then uncurled in the deafening silence. Tears ran down his cheeks as the bright coals singed the rug and as they cooled, left pitted black craters in their stead. Their life was extinguished, as his daughters had been twenty years before, leaving him with the residue of grief in his life and on his face. Sir David removed a monogrammed pocket handkerchief from his silk robe and dabbed his tears. Leaning heavily on the chair arms he stood and slid a slippered foot forward, extinguishing the last dying ember. He reached for the shotgun and broke it, then placed it gently down on a side table.

"What a bloody mess," he mumbled.

Smoothing the front of his robe and tucking the kerchief away, he listened but heard no other sounds in the house. No one had been disturbed. He turned to the mantle, the newly pockmarked stone clear to see, and observed that the remains of the fire still burned slowly. The note now lay under his chair, its edge poking out, reminding him of its presence, goading him with its message. He picked it up, folded it and placed it in his breast pocket. *Tomorrow. I'll deal with it tomorrow.*

***

Sir David walked out onto the upstairs landing from his bedroom. The house felt calm with morning sun rays banishing the insidious shadows of the night before. The beams highlighted a bust of Darwin which held pride of place on a marble plinth at the base of the stairs. A curved bannister led him towards the ground floor where oak panels absorbed the sun's warmth. Sitting upon a veneered side table was the morning paper which Fanshaw collected before entering his dining room. He walked towards one of the bay windows and enjoyed the view of his estate grounds.

Although his twilight years encroached, Fanshaw still commanded the room, unfazed by the opulence of his surroundings. He wore neatly pressed trousers, a shirt and tie, comfortable brogues and a buttoned cardigan. His hair, though now white, was still thick, combed neatly to the right and held in position by a touch of Brylcreem. Tucking the newspaper under one arm he reached into his cardigan pocket and withdrew a wooden pipe and his spectacles. He turned to the table, which had a place setting for one, and absently placed the empty pipe in his mouth, donned his glasses and viewed the day's news. The dining room door opened.

"Coffee, Sir?" asked a man dressed in a dark suit and carrying a tray holding a coffee jug.

"Thank you, yes." replied Sir David, "Place it down. I'll pour."

"Naturally, Sir." The silver-coloured pot was placed gently upon a leather trivet within reach of Fanshaw. "Breakfast, Sir?"

"Toast please, Fletcher."

"I'll advise the cook, Sir." Fletcher stood quietly to Fanshaw's left. Fanshaw glanced towards him.

"Was there anything else, Fletcher?" The butler cleared his throat nervously before speaking.

"Only one small thing, Sir. I hope you don't mind but I took the liberty of returning your gun to the cabinet. Needless to say, I cleaned it thoroughly first. Safer in there, Sir." Fletcher had a worried look on his face.

"Oh, yes," replied Fanshaw. "I had it out last night. I was thinking about joining the shoot next week. I thought that I'd give it a once over."

"Certainly, Sir." Fletcher moved towards the door.

"And Fletcher," spoke Fanshaw, turning to look at his butler. Fletcher reached for the door handle and halted, turning towards Sir David. "Thank you." Fletcher nodded and exited the room leaving Fanshaw to read his paper.

***

Two hours later Fanshaw walked out of the front of his house, closing the large entrance door behind him. He descended the stone steps from the house to the gravel drive, where his feet crunched against the gravel parking area as he walked towards his gleaming Land Rover Discovery. He climbed into the driver's seat, started the engine, and drove slowly forward, enjoying the views of his estate as he headed towards the gatehouse and the road leading to Sterndale.

The grounds were in good condition. Luscious lawns led out towards an open pasture where a herd of deer grazed within a fenced paddock. Sir David drove sedately along the drive, now with a walled garden to his right and topiary bushes to his left. His calm demeanor did not betray his inner turmoil but as he reached to indicate direction at the gatehouse, his hands trembled. He turned left onto the main road and headed out, his mind determined to seek answers. Pastor Melthrop raised a hand in greeting as Sir David passed by the village church. Sir David nodded in response and slowly accelerated as he headed away from the hall.

Half an hour later Sir David pulled up outside Sterndale Police Station, parked over double yellow lines and placed a disabled parking permit on his dashboard. Switching the engine off he looked into the rear view mirror seeing tired bloodshot eyes looking back at him.

"Come on, man. Get a grip of yourself." He took a deep breath, patted his breast pocket and set his shoulders. As he climbed out of the vehicle and walked towards the main entrance of the station, a feeling of deja vu descended upon him. After a short walk up the path he straightened his posture, and with an air of confidence, strode into the front counter of the station.

"Good morning, madam." Behind the glass-fronted counter sat a lady staring avidly at a computer screen, her hands upon a keyboard.

"Wait a second, love," the lady squinted at the screen, "I need to quickly send this," her fingers moved swiftly across the keys. Sir David waited patiently, watching the second hand of a wall clock travel around its dial. The sound of typing finished, and with a flourish, the lady hit send and turned to address Sir David.

"Right, sir. What can I do for you?"

"Well, madam, I would like to see DC Kaur please."

"DC Kaur," the lady repeated, writing down the name. "Have you got an appointment?"

"No, I'm afraid not." Sir David watched as the lady wrote 'no appointment' on the scrap piece of paper.

"And why do you wish to see DC Kaur, love?"

"It's a private matter of the most importance." The words were scribbled onto the paper.

"Can you call him for me, please?" The receptionist looked at Sir David.

"Well, I could try and find him for you, but no DC Kaur works here."

"Yes he does, you silly woman. I've spoken to him before. Now kindly get him."

"No need to raise your voice, sir, I'm only trying to help."

"Can I help?" interrupted a police officer who had approached the counter.

"This gentleman," replied the receptionist looking Fanshaw up and down, her eyes clearly disagreeing with her voice, "is looking for a detective."

"It's Mr Fanshaw isn't it?" said the constable, smiling at Sir David.

"Yes, constable it is. I need to see DC Kaur."

"I've told him we have no DC Kaur," interjected the receptionist.

"He means Jamal, Jamal Kaur. The Detective Inspector."

"Oh, I didn't know that was his surname," giggled the lady.

"He's had a couple of promotions, sir," explained the constable. "What's it about, if I may ask?"

"Information about my daughter, young man."

"Aagh, I see. Let me see if I can locate him for you. If you push on that door," the officer pointed to an internal door, "then I'll buzz you in and you can wait in an interview room." Sir David walked to the door and on hearing a buzzer pushed, entered and waited. The officer walked around from the reception and showed Sir David into a small room containing a table and two chairs.

"Take a seat, sir."

"Thank you, Officer."

"It's Rob, sir. I'll be back in a couple of minutes." Rob walked out of the room, closing the door behind him.

"Thanks, Constable Rob," replied Sir David to the closed door. A few minutes later, Jamal Kaur walked in.

"Sir David. How are you doing? What can I do for you?" Sir David, now standing, grabbed Kaur's extended hand and shook it gently.

"I'm fine, thank you, Detective Kaur. Thank goodness you are working. I came in on the off chance but I wasn't sure that you'd be here. That lady behind the desk didn't even seem to know that you worked here. Constable Rob knew it was you though." Kaur gestured towards a seat and guided Sir David to it.

"Well, I am here, so that's good. If you'd like to take a seat and catch your breath then I'll try to help. You seem anxious. Rob's getting us a cup of tea." As if on cue there was a knock on the door. Kaur reached for the door handle and allowed Rob in. Rob carried two tea mugs, with 'Crimestoppers' emblazoned on the side, and placed them on the table.

"That's kind of you, Constable Rob. You'll go far," said Sir David, reaching for the drink and raising it in 'cheers' to Rob.

"Thank you, sir," replied Rob, closing the door as he left the room.

"Sir David. What can I do for you?" said Kaur. Fanshaw looked at Kaur, noting his shiny black shoes, pristinely ironed shirt, patterned tie and dark intelligent eyes, which watched him expectantly. Kaur's black framed spectacles and silvered hair were the only clear signs of ageing since Sir David had seen him last. *Possibly a bit tired around the eyes,* thought Sir David.

"I know it's been a long time, Detective, but it is about Victoria." Kaur's shoulders visibly dropped. "Now, I know what you think. Here's this silly old bastard coming to bother me again." Kaur raised his hands as if in defence.

"Now I would never…"

"Wait a minute. I've got something new. Some new evidence. Something for you to have a look at," interrupted Fanshaw, reaching towards his pocket.

"Sir David, I would never insult you, and you are not wasting my time, but as you know we have been here before. The case has been investigated and investigated and reinvestigated. I've turned over every stone. Please believe me." Kaur watched as Sir David withdrew a folded piece of paper from his pocket.

"See, here it is. I received this two days ago. It was found within the mail when Fletcher collected it from the front door." Sir David opened up the piece of paper displaying the message to Kaur.

WE KNOW SHE WAS MURDERED

"Sir David," Kaur leaned forward, hands clasped together, and spoke gently. "You know we saw a similar note during the original investigation. I know it's hard but we investigated every avenue that we could and we still got nowhere."

"But this is new evidence, dammit," Sir David's hand slammed on the table. "It's new. You have to do something."

"We have tried, Sir. It's a piece of paper. No envelope and a typed message again. It could have come from anywhere, from anybody. Some crank playing a sick trick on you. We'll never know."

"What about fingerprints? Surely you'll check for them?"

"If I did it would have Fletcher's and your prints all over it. The previous message had no one else's on. It won't help, Sir David, and I'm afraid that it's not enough to reopen the investigation. Especially an investigation that has been investigated as thoroughly as Victoria's has. I'm sorry, Sir David, truly I am."

Fanshaw's posture slumped. He was defeated. Kaur felt guilty but knew that he was right. This wasn't a significant step forward in the case. The enquiry had been investigated by two separate SIOs and also reviewed by the cold case team. They had all come up with nothing. The Force had higher priorities and though he could never tell Sir David that, it was the reality of policing. Kaur stood up and opened the door.

"Rob," he yelled. Rob appeared from the front office.

"Sir."

"Can you show Sir David out when he is ready please?"

"Yes, sir." Kaur turned to Sir David who was placing the note back in his pocket.

"I'm sorry that this is not what you wanted to hear. I wish I could do more." Sir David's elderly face looked at him, tears brimming in his eyes. *A broken man*, thought Jamal. He reached into his pocket, pulled out his wallet and produced a business card from it.

"I don't need that," said Sir David, "you're no use to me." He looked away. Kaur placed it on the table.

"It's not mine. Look, it may get you nowhere but give that person a call. They may be able to help you." With that, Kaur took his leave.

***

"Subject exits the vehicle and walks towards the farm entrance. The vehicle drives away from the area."

"Let the vehicle go. I have it technically. Stay with the subject," said Rachel, her instruction clear, over the radio airwaves.

"Received," replied Sarah.

"Tom's ahead with a view of the stables and riding arena," said Tom.

"Loud and clear," replied Sarah, who continued driving along the road, then pulled into a woodland parking area not far from the farm entrance. "Sarah stays with Tom," she transmitted, reassuring the team that Tom had someone to support him should it be required. She took out her iPad and rechecked the maps, ensuring that she knew where Tom was hidden.

"Rachel to the team."

"Go ahead," replied Tom.

"Technical shows that the vehicle has left the area, heading in the general direction of the workplace."

"Received," replied Tom.

Tom Fairbank was sitting within a copse of trees on farmland near a livery stable. He was camouflaged to blend in with his surroundings and had built a hide for himself within the shrubbery. Sarah had dropped him off at midnight last night and he had made his way to his chosen location under the cover of darkness. He had completed a recce of the area the previous week and had gone through his plans meticulously with the team. Although they all didn't have his expertise in this type of work he valued their thoughts and ideas on how to achieve objectives, limit compromises, and keep everybody safe.

It had been chilly last night when he deployed, but the day was starting to warm as the sun climbed in the sky. Now at ten o'clock, he was ready. A camouflaged camera and tripod was positioned before him, pointing in the direction of the stables. He leaned forward and looked through the telescopic lens.

"Tom has eyes on the subject." He looked at a forty-year-old lady, with long blonde hair tied back in a ponytail, and watched as she placed a riding helmet on her head.

"Subject places a riding helmet on and approaches a horse. The horse is being held by a stable hand." Tom depressed the camera trigger. "She pats the horse and reaches to the saddle. Subject climbs the mounting steps and throws her leg over the saddle. Subject mounted. Reins in hand. She manoeuvres to the dressage arena. Photographs obtained."

Rachel remained in the office chair as she listened to Tom describing the subject controlling the horse in the arena before taking it over some jumps. *Another one in the bag,* she thought as she walked to a small kitchen area and flicked on the kettle.

Work was going well. It had turned out that working for insurance companies was proving lucrative for the team. The subject, whom Tom and Sarah were watching today, had been off sick from work for three months with a back injury, which she claimed to have received when lifting a chair whilst at work. Still collecting full pay she had advised the company that she remained unfit to work in any role for them. Tom's footage would be enough to disprove her continued injury and allow the company to challenge her claim. The subject's partner, who worked for the same company, had dropped her off in his company car before going to work himself. He would likely be treading in some deep water too. The team had also managed to obtain video footage of him dropping her off last week.

"How's the file going, Ron?"

"About done, Rach," replied Ronnie Cuthbertson, retired detective. "It's a straightforward one. Jim gave me a spreadsheet of all the movements of the car. Tom and Sarah have evidenced their photography and today's work should have nailed it."

"Yep. That woman is likely to be forced to resign and her partner will be lucky to get away with a good bollocking," replied Rachel.

"It's all money in our pockets, Rach. We'll save that company thousands in lost income and a potential medical payout."

"I know, Ron but it's not —"

"Making you happy? Covering the bills?"

"No, that's all going fine."

"You are not happy with the team?" Ron leaned back in his chair and put his feet on his desk, having accepted a coffee that Rachel had made him.

"No, Ron," she perched on the edge of his desk, "The team is great. I couldn't have wished for better."

"What then?" Ron slurped from his mug, his eyes bulging as it scolded his mouth. Feet dropping to the ground he spat it back in the cup, coffee residue sprinkling his beard. "Christ, that's hot," said Ron, sucking in cool air and wiping at a spillage on his T-shirt. Rachel stood up ignoring his exclamation.

"It's not exciting, Ron. There's nothing to get my teeth into. No challenge. It's easy."

"Easy suits me." Ron, now recovered, took a gentle sip from the cup he'd spat into. "We've done our time. Given our service. Especially you. Time for others to step into the breach."

"Maybe, maybe," replied Rachel. "Anyway," Rachel snapped out of her reverie. "What are the rest of them up to today?"

"They should all be landing fairly soon. Jim's been out looking at some new equipment with some old contacts of his. Matt and Joe have been doing some research on some of the locations for the Bridewell's job. They should be back soon too."

"Good," replied Rachel returning to the comms desk where the radio base station was positioned in front of an array of computer screens and TV monitors.

"All footage obtained," reported Tom's voice over the airwaves. "I'm gonna pack up and shift out if that's in order, Rach?"

"Yes, Tom. Sarah will collect you."

***

Tom removed his camera from its tripod and started packing his gear away. He produced a plain blue hiker's backpack from within his camouflaged pack and placed the camouflaged pack within it, secreting items within. He would extract in daylight and wanted to give the impression of a daywalker as he did so. Fifty metres away he knew that an ordnance survey map recorded a public footpath. Although little used it gave him an excuse to be there. He would be careful exiting the woods and move to the agreed rendezvous point with Sarah. Insertion and extraction were the riskiest part of this job, as they were the most likely times of compromise.

Now packed, Tom swept the area where he had lived for the day, ensuring that he left no sign that he had been there. The likelihood of anyone else ever coming to this location was remote but Tom believed in practising good habits. *Keep it professional and keep it safe.* He checked the woods for unnatural noise and movement and, on detecting neither, moved carefully towards the footpath.

"Tom is extracting and moving to the RV point."

"Loud and clear," replied Sarah. "Moving forwards to meet you."

The path now in view, Tom crouched and listened. Woodland birdsong resonated amongst the trees and he could faintly hear what he presumed to be a tractor in the distance. He checked the track either way and, believing it clear, stepped out, adjusting the zip on his flies as he did so. *If anyone's seen me stepping out they'll think I've been for a piss.* He checked both ways and with no one present, placed on a cap and walked in the direction of the RV point.

"Towards you now, Sarah."

"Pulling in now," came her reply.

"All clear here," said Sarah. "I have Tom in view."

"Loud and clear." Rachel transmitted.

Tom waved to Sarah, who responded likewise, looking like she had come to collect him from a walk. Tom climbed into the vehicle.

"Job done," he said to Sarah, "let's head back to the office."

***

Joe ran back to the car where Matt was waiting to collect him.

"Any joy?" asked Matt as Joe jumped into the passenger seat.

"Well, I got us a couple of pasties if that helps?" replied Joe, throwing a white paper sandwich bag to Matt.

"Cheers," replied Matt, pulling away from the kerbside and into the flow of traffic. "How about the reason that we are here?"

"Oh, that. Think I've got us something," mumbled Joe, through a mouthful of a Greggs cheesy bean bake. "Boy, these are great." He looked at the bean slice in reverence. "Whoever invented these must be worth a fortune. They should be knighted."

"Joe?"

"Sorry, mate. I think he's gambling."

"Gambling?"

"Yep."

"Go on."

"Around the corner from where you were waiting is a private car park. I've had a look around and it looks like the car park for one of the local casinos. A bit more exclusive than most but I'd bet my paycheck that he's going there."

"It would account for his wife's concern about his expenditure."

"Yes, and for the late nights out and his tiredness. We only need to check his attendance pattern and then bing bang, we get him in the casino." Matt started laughing, knowing where this was heading.

"And how do we get him inside there?" he asked Joe.

"Simple, my old friend. I go in as well. Get me a dapper suit and I'll blend in fine. Take me to the closest tailor."

"Not so fast, Bond. We'll head back to the office and report in. Decide how to move forward as a team." Joe grabbed Matt's arm.

"Come on, man. You know it makes sense. I'll make the team a fortune." They both laughed aloud. Matt looked at Joe and smiled before looking back to the road. *It worked mate. We got you out of that hole and look at you now.*

"I'll ring Rach. Let her know we'll be back soon." Matt dialled her on the car's hands-free as they headed back to the office.

***

Matt turned right into the road leading to the industrial estate, checking his rearview mirror before doing so. He wasn't professionally trained in surveillance, like Tom and Sarah, but the whole team had been provided ad hoc training by them both. The training was ongoing and all had been asked to continually practise to improve their skills. On their trip back to the station they had both been commentating on vehicles preceding them, describing their movement on the road, speed, indications and such like for when it may be needed to follow a live vehicle.

"No car behind us as we entered, Joe."

"Good stuff." Matt pulled towards the works compound as Joe triggered the switch to open the electronic gates and they moved to a parking area behind the main building. The gate closed automatically behind them. Ronnie stood at the rear of the building smoking a cigarette and waved to them in greeting.

"They're not doing him any good," said Matthew as he parked the vehicle.

"Nor me," replied Joe, jumping out of the vehicle and sparking up a roll-up as he approached Ron. Matthew climbed out.

"Everyone here?" asked Matt.

"Yes," replied Ron, "4 x 4 is tucked away in the garage."

"How's Rachel?"

"She's good, mate. A bit restless but good."

"Then let's hope the team meeting settles her down." Matt entered the building and nipped up the two flights of stairs through the garage to the main office above. The room was split into half office, and half relaxation area. Rachel was sitting behind her desk peering at a computer screen, Jim and Tom looked to be downloading camera footage and Sarah lay sprawled across one of the sofas reading a bikers magazine.

"Hi all," Matt piped. A series of grunts and raised hands were his reply. He walked over to Rachel. "Busy?"

"As always," she replied, completing some typing on the screen. *Quiet today*, thought Matt.

"I'll stick the kettle on. Anyone for a coffee?" All hands were raised. *Well, this looks like it will be a fun meeting. Hope we can get more than a grunt or sign language from them.* He smiled. "Great, I'll get on with it then."

Ten minutes later the team were sitting on sofas and chairs, cups in hand, conducting a debrief of their current work. Matt needn't have worried, as everyone appeared to be enthusiastic and positive. Rachel remained subdued but joined in where needed.

"That's the stable job complete?" she asked Tom.

"From our side, yes. We've got photos of her clearly riding with no evidence of any injury. Once the package is complete I simply need to have their company car for two minutes to remove our equipment."

"I've downloaded the imagery and sent it to Ron," said Jim. "I've also switched our equipment off at the moment. We don't need to know the patterns now. I can switch it back on if there are any problems finding the car when we need to retrieve the tracker."

"Thanks, Jim. Hopefully, that won't be a problem. I'm sure the company director will allow us to have the car when we need it."

"The file will be complete this afternoon, Rach. Then it's free for you to hand it to them," stated Ron.

"How'd you get on this morning, Jim?" asked Rachel.

"I've had a look at a range of covert listening devices that I think could be of use to us," he replied. "I've also bought a good quality wildlife cam that we can play with. It may be something we could use in the future."

"Good. Matt, Joe?"

"We've researched some of the locations. The one of most interest is behind a casino. The guy may be gambling and not having an affair as the wife suspected."

"Not sure which is worse," said Jim.

"Both sound like a bit of fun to me," said Ron, rubbing his hands together.

"And that could be why you are single," said Sarah, digging Ron in the ribs. The rest of the team laughed. Matt continued.

"We simply need to come up with a plan to evidence if he is there. Joe's keen to go gambling on behalf of the team." He placed his hand on Joe's shoulder as he spoke.

"I bet he bloody is. With whose money?" said Tom. Joe leaned forward.

"Well, I thought we could all pull a bit together and then maybe top it up from company funds. Get me some new threads to look the part and …" He looked around at the team who were staring at him. "What?" He asked, his face a picture of innocence. Rachel looked at him with one eyebrow raised. "Well, it was worth a shot." He slumped back in his seat with a sulky look on his face.

"Nice try," Matt shoved him gently. Joe smiled. *Nothing ventured*, he thought.

"Anything from you, Rach?" asked Jim. All eyes turned to Rachel.

"Well, there's possibly a couple of new clients for more insurance jobs. Much the same as we have been doing. Nothing meaty though. Nothing to challenge or grip us." Her face showed her disappointment.

"That's maybe not a bad thing," interjected Matt, as Rachel's phone rang. She looked at the screen, not recognising the number.

"Let me get this. Two minutes." Rachel stood up and walked towards her desk. Matt noticed her slight limp where her leg would have stiffened up from sitting for a while.

"Hello, Rachel Barnes," she said.

"Hello, Detective Barnes," said a male voice. "I believe that you may be able to help me. My name is Sir David Fanshaw."

Chapter 2

Rachel drove steadily towards the entrance gates to Evesham House, enjoying the freedom of the road in an automatic car that had been adapted with a twin flip pedal to enable her to drive safely. The technology helped her to use her left foot for acceleration and braking, allowing her weakened right side to rest while she was driving. She had entered the village from the main road and now followed a minor road.

A large stone estate wall dominated her right-hand side and to her left side, open fields. The call she had received in the office intrigued her. Sir David Fanshaw had given little away, apart from informing her that her number had been supplied to him by the police and that he had been advised that she could help him with an investigation. The only other snippet he had provided was that it was all related to a historical murder investigation that the police had shelved. Sir David had requested a personal meeting at his estate, not wishing to divulge any further information over the phone. Rachel had agreed to meet with him the following day and had spent the previous afternoon researching his background.

David Fanshaw had grown up in Evesham within the family home. Having attended private school and gained a degree at university, he had returned to settle back at Evesham House to take over the running of the estate. Comprising both arable and livestock farming, it also boasted a pheasant shoot and a well-maintained estate house. In an attempt to compete with modern times, the estate grounds were open to the public and the house itself was accessible to visitors on escorted visits. A farm shop selling local produce and a small cafe rounded up the enterprise, which seemed to be thriving in the modern economic climate. Rachel had surmised that though Fanshaw headed the estate, he had gathered a good team behind him to be making a success of the business.

Evesham village was a small community comprising a church, village hall and a pub, but little else. The housing was both original stock and old council housing, but had not yet succumbed to any new housing development. Its stolid resistance to new build encroachment was admirable, but possibly destined to fail. The population was a mixture of old and young, retired and employed.

She had arranged to meet Sir David at the entrance to the cafe and expected him to be waiting there for her arrival. Rachel had deliberately not delved too deeply into his general family past. She was aware that there had been an investigation into his missing daughter many years ago. Rachel had not even been in the force when this had occurred. She wanted to speak to him objectively, unaffected by any press or police views as much as she could, as both could be equally biased and opinionated. This matter may not even relate to the daughter, though she suspected it would.

Rachel approached the large entrance, where black wrought iron gates were open, and a signpost directed the way to the car park. Turning right and then immediately left, she negotiated some wooden bollards and parked her car within a red gravelled area. Large oak trees provided shelter from the climbing sun as Rachel opened her door and slowly manoeuvred her legs out of the vehicle. She reached back to the passenger side, retrieving her walking stick and laptop bag, before slowly standing and gaining balance. Rachel was looking well, and although her leg still caused her issues, her mobility was vastly improved. The adaption to the accelerator of the car was a godsend. Breathing in the warming fresh air and straightening her shoulders, she set off slowly towards the cafe entrance, which she could see beyond the beech hedge in the foreground.

Rachel wore a light-coloured suit and had her hair tied back in a ponytail, showing a tanned complexion. She felt good and ready to face the day. Passing the hedge, she spotted the cafe entrance where an elderly gentleman was talking with a vicar. The man wore the green and browns of a country gent and a pale fedora, which protected his face from the sun. Rachel recognised David Fanshaw from his image on the internet and walked towards him with a welcoming smile. Sir David glanced up and sighted Rachel. A slight frown creased his brow but on seeing the recognition on her face he parted company with the vicar and approached her.

"Ms Barnes?" he asked.

"Rachel. Nice to meet you, Sir David," she replied, stopping as she transferred her walking stick to the left, and reached out with her right hand to take his bony, yet firm, grip in an introductory handshake. "I hope I haven't disturbed your conversation."

"Not at all. That was only Pastor Melthrop doing his rounds. Inspecting his flock. You're here now and – not what I expected," replied Sir David, whose frown disappeared to be replaced by a gentle smile.

"Well, I'll take that as a compliment," replied Rachel. Sir David looked at her and chortled.

"Very good, very good." His smile widened and he gestured with his hand towards the cafe entrance. "Shall we?" Rachel stepped forward as they walked towards the cafe. The doors opened automatically and Sir David held back, allowing Rachel to enter first.

"We'll cut through the cafe if you don't mind," said Sir David. "I'd prefer to discuss things at the house where things are more private."

"Naturally," said Rachel. They walked towards a rear patio door, onto an outdoor seating area. Although the cafe was quiet at the moment, it was prepared for visitors with an array of fruit scones, cheesecakes and pastries adorning the pristine delicatessen cabinets. The aroma of freshly brewed coffee and baked goods wafted through the air. Rachel's taste buds responded in harmony as she fought temptation.

"I may have to buy some cakes when I leave."

"Tempting, aren't they?" replied Sir David. "All cooked on site from as much of our produce as possible. The team does an amazing job. Let's head down here." Sir David directed her to a graduated walkway, which led to a small golf buggy waiting on the road behind the cafe. "Great fun this. I'll drive." Sir David stepped spritely round to the driver's side with a grin on his face. Rachel could see the excitement of a young man reflected in his face and she couldn't help but smile herself. She climbed in slowly and the vehicle pulled away gently onto the small road that led to the house.

"I'll quickly show you around the grounds, as I suspect that you will be spending some time here." Rachel raised an eyebrow, which was spotted by Sir David. "I'm confident that you'll want to help me, you see," he clarified. The road swept to the right and Sir David pointed to the walled garden to the left, and as they passed topiary bushes on the right, the majestic house came into view.

"It's beautiful," said Rachel.

"I never tire of the sight or forget how privileged I am to live here."

"Do you own it all?"

"I do. However, I see myself as the caretaker of the estate. You know, preserving it for future generations. It's been hard work but we're getting there." The buggy trundled past the house and descended the road which cut through an expansive grassed area beyond the formal lawns. Two great oak trees stood solemnly surveying the surroundings, their great bows creating natural shelter for wildlife and guests. Small pathways had been cut through longer grasses, creating natural walkways, and in the distance, Rachel could see a herd of deer grazing. Sir David halted the buggy and looked at Rachel as she absorbed her surroundings.

"I wanted you to feel it, Rachel. The happiness, and the natural beauty of the estate. It's important that you understand. Understand that this was all taken away from my daughter. A life that she would have loved, would have thrived in. She wouldn't have chosen to leave this," he indicated with his arms spread wide. "Some bastard took her from this." She saw the flash of anger in his eyes, swiftly followed by deep sorrow.

"OK, Sir David —"

"David, please," he interjected.

"You've got me hooked."

***

"See you tonight, love." Jamie closed the front door behind him and walked towards his Silver Golf GTI, which was parked on the driveway of his house in Evesham village. Opening the passenger door, he threw in his kitbag, walked around to the driver's side and climbed in.

The old detached estate house stood within a lawned garden, its natural stone blending with the environment. Jamie had lived in the village for most of his adult life and had done all right for himself. Dressed in black trousers, shirt and commando boots, he was heading off to start his shift at Fenchurch Police Station. He revved the engine, swiftly reversed the vehicle onto the road and pulled away from the house, barely noticing his wife waving to him from the kitchen window.

Jamie loved his car but despite his occupation, he had little regard for speed limits within the village. He fastened his seatbelt as he ascended the hill and raised a hand to a resident descending the path with her dog leashed tightly to her side. On approaching the main road, he positioned to turn left and, despite the approaching lorry from the right, pulled out, flooring the accelerator as he did so. He noted the vehicle flash its headlights at him.

"Prick," said Jamie aloud.

Twenty minutes later Jamie pulled into the rear car park of Fenchurch Police Station. He parked his car over two bays, thereby ensuring that it couldn't get knocked by any adjacent car owners opening their doors. Jamie grabbed his kit bag and strolled towards the designated smoking shelter, lighting a Regal cigarette as he did so.

"Now then," he greeted John Longshaw. John was rolling a cigarette.

"Jamie," he replied. "They must be costing you a fortune." John indicated towards the Regal cigarette. "I can't afford straights."

"Well, I know someone, mate. I get them on the cheap."

"You wanna be careful."

"I am, Longy. They don't give a shit." He nodded towards the main police station. "They've got bigger fish to fry. What've we got on today?"

"Doing a warrant?"

"Looking for what?"

"Drug squad's around so it'll be the usual." Jamie looked towards the upper floor of the building.

"His nibs is watching us?" John looked up to the window to see the station commander looking down from his top-floor office. He checked his watch.

"Best be moving then." John pinched the end of his roll-up and placed it back within his Golden Virginia tobacco pouch. Jamie smiled up to the top floor, took a further drag and walked towards the building, flicking his butt end towards the cigarette bin as he did so.

Both men entered the changing rooms and opened their respective lockers. Jamie grabbed his stab vest, with a kit belt attached, and shrugged it on. Its comfortable weight settled on his shoulders. He walked out with John following behind, and on entering the parade room, grabbed two batteries for his radio. Jamie fitted one on the radio and waited for it to connect as he placed the spare in his vest pocket. The voices of colleagues were transmitted over the radio.

He pressed a button on his own, which informed the control room that he was on duty.

The parade room had been prepped for a briefing with two rows of chairs facing towards a smartboard. The team sergeant was speaking to a plainclothes officer at the front of the room, whilst the rest of Jamie's team were sitting chatting. The sergeant looked over to Jamie and John.

"Nice of you to join us, lads," he said, checking his wristwatch. "Right, we'll get started. Grab a seat, gents." John grabbed a chair and Jamie propped himself on an empty desk. The plainclothes officer commenced his briefing, whilst Jamie checked his phone for any messages.

"Thanks for coming, guys. Though I know you had no choice." A couple of officers quietly laughed. "This afternoon we are going to execute a warrant at this address." The image on the smart screen altered showing a residential premises in one of Fenchurch's suburbs. Jamie continued texting on his phone. "Intelligence indicates that this address is controlled by a criminal network specialising in the cultivation and distribution of cannabis, utilising Asian workers living at the house." Jamie's fingers stopped on his screen and he looked up. *Now this could be interesting,* he thought. The briefing officer continued, letting everyone know their roles and responsibilities for the job ahead. The briefing took about twenty minutes and concluded with open questions. Jamie allowed his colleagues to ask theirs and then raised his hand.

"Yes, mate?" asked the plainclothes officer.

"Where's the intelligence coming from?"

"There's always one," said the shift sergeant.

"It's all recorded on the system, ehm —" stated plainclothes waiting for a name.

"Jamie."

"Jamie," continued plainclothes, "All graded correctly. Any sources of information are hidden on the system, as you would expect."

"Informant led then," stated Jamie with a big grin on his face, looking around at his colleagues. A couple of the crew smiled back.

"Not necessarily," replied plainclothes. The sergeant interrupted,

"You should know better than to ask." He looked admonishingly at Jamie. "Right, that's the briefing completed. Everyone go and check your kit. You know your roles. We'll meet in the backyard in ten." The group exited the room and headed off in various directions.

"Why have you always gotta push it?" murmured Longy to Jamie, as they left the room.

"Always worth asking," replied Jamie. "Drug Squad swan around here like they own the place but, when it comes to the proper police graft of putting doors in and arresting people, it's always us lot that get it done. They're lazy gits with easy jobs. I like to get under their skin."

"It's only another role, Jamie. They're still our colleagues."

"Well, I wish someone would give me an easy job like them, mate. Roles like that never land my way. Let's grab our kit. We can get a quick fag in before we go." Jamie strode towards the rear door of the station grabbing his kit bag as he did so, Longy left in his wake. *You don't look as if you're doing too bad to me mate, with your flash car and nice cottage in the country,* thought Longy, trailing along behind him.

***

Ten minutes later a marked police van exited the station car park, followed by a police car, and headed out through the streets of Fenchurch, towards their destination. Each officer was primed for their role. Ahead and waiting at the premises, the drug squad had the house under observation. The vehicles travelled through Fenchurch before pulling off the main route onto a housing estate. Although going about their daily business, members of the community noticed their passing. Dog walkers halted, and youths pulled out their phones. It was obvious to the locals that something was going to happen. The van approached a pedestrian crossing. An elderly woman stepped off the kerb, pulling a trolley shopping bag and scruffy terrier behind her. The van stopped and waited, with the driver tapping his steering wheel.

"Come on, love. We haven't got all day," he murmured to himself as he watched the dog tangle its lead within the trolley wheel. The lady stopped, seemingly oblivious to the van, or even of being in the middle of the road. "For fuck's sake. Someone get out and help her." A group of teens had gathered outside the shops nearby and were laughing at the situation. One of the group, hoody up and face covered, gestured obscenely at the 'coppers' but on seeing the side door of the van open, scarpered quickly into a side street. Longy stepped out and approached the woman.

"Hello, madam, can I help you?" She looked at him in confusion.

"Well, why would you do that?"

"I'm a police officer, madame. You look like you've got a bit tied up." She looked Longy up and down indignantly and then her face altered as she recognised his uniform.

"Well indeed you can, young man. That's why I pay your wages." She handed him the trolley and then the dog continued over the crossing, stopping at the far kerb. She turned to Longy.

"Hurry along now. I haven't got all day." The driver of the van's head was now resting on the steering wheel as the crew giggled in the back, having heard the interaction. Longy untangled the dog and swiftly pulled the trolley and dog across the road. He turned to cross back to the van. At the other side of the road, a youth stood, bent forward, with his hand resting on his back.

"Officer, officer," he called loudly, "please could you help me across, I've hurt me back." The youths' friends were all standing laughing.

"Get lost," responded the van driver, window now wound down. "Get in, Longy." He revved the engine as Longy jumped in, to applause from the crew. Longy pulled the door closed and the convoy once again set off.

"That's the strike team moving towards the cul-de-sac," transmitted the team sergeant, who rode in the squad car behind the van.

"Loud and clear," from the obs van. "No movement at the house. We believe it to be occupied. You can move forward."

"Sergeant to the team. STRIKE, STRIKE, STRIKE."

The van moved into the cul-de-sac at speed and halted in front of the house. The driver shouted. "GO, GO, GO." Side doors opened and officers leapt out. Three towards the front door and two to the back. One of the three held a heavy metal door enforcer. One tried the door handle. It was locked.

"POLICE, POLICE, POLICE. STAND BACK." The enforcer hit the door and the wood splintered. A second hit and it came off its hinges. "IN, IN, IN." Jamie led the charge, running into the house. Before him in the corridor, an Asian female held a baby in her arms. He shouldered past, heading for the stairs, and two officers followed him as three more headed to clear the ground floor. Jamie pounded up the stairs. The sweet smell of cannabis was already pungent in the air. He pushed on a door, which flew open, revealing a bedroom containing six bunk beds.

"CLEAR," he shouted, indicating that the room was empty of occupants.

"BACK HERE," shouted his colleague. Jamie turned towards the hall, where he could see his colleague with a male who he had detained. "The loft," said his colleague, indicating with his head towards a set of retractable ladders, which were extended downwards. Jamie drew out his asp and held it above him as he poked his head through the open loft hatch.

"Clear," he called to his colleague, "but there's a shit load of plants up here," he continued with a smile on his face. As he climbed back down the ladder, his colleague transmitted on his radio. "One detained on the first floor."

"Seven detained, ground floor," came in reply. *Seven,* thought Jamie, *they're packed in like sardines.*

"No runners out the back," transmitted a further voice.

"Premises secure," came the resonant tones of the shift sergeant over the airwaves.

"What we got up there then?"

"Full blown grow," replied Jamie, "all lined out. Full of plants that are all budding. Hydroponics, the lot. Better get him downstairs," Jamie gestured towards the Asian male. "I'll stay up here."

"OK, cheers." The officer led the detained male towards and down the stairs. *I'll take a quick snoop,* thought Jamie.

Within the further bedroom, a large cannabis plant stood within a plant pot, heavy with leaves. Mid-grade plants stood within an elaborate system which allowed them to be grown hydroponically, with false lights and a watering system. The plants looked healthy and covered the whole floor of the room with only a small central walkway in view. The walls had been lined with foil and the window blacked out, creating a warm atmosphere with an intense smell emanating from the plants. Cooling fans were placed strategically around the room. Jamie knew that the loft reflected this setup but that the plants were in a later stage of growth and looked like they would soon be ready to crop. The buds contained the highest concentration of tetrahydrocannabinol (THC) and would therefore be the most marketable product from the plant. This household knew what they were doing. He checked out the further bedroom.

Six bunk beds were crammed into the double-sized room, each bunk an individual's own living space. Each had a laptop thereon, some with headphones attached. Little rucksacks were stowed at the end of each bed but no other possessions were visible. *Poor bastards probably have nothing*, thought Jamie. Each bottom bunk appeared to have a wired rail and curtain attached, which probably offered a small degree of privacy to that bunk.

He peered into one of the bags, seeing some cigarette cartons. Jamie reached in, pulling out two packs of Regal. He checked the boxes over. *Snide,* he thought, secreting them in the pockets of his stab vest, *Won't be missed though*. The bunk also had a notebook laid upon it. Jamie picked it up and, on examining it, saw that it contained a list of telephone numbers and email addresses. He heard movement on the stairs.

"You OK, mate?" asked the colleague who he had raided the top floor with.

"Fine," replied Jamie, swiftly shoving the discovered notebook into the cargo pocket of his police trousers. "Fine, I was only having a quick look around before the squad and Scenes of Crime come trampling all over the place." Jamie walked out of the bedroom.

"Sergeant says not to touch owt until the electrician arrives. Looks like they've bypassed the meter, and with all this water around it could be dangerous."

"Fine by me, we'll wait up here." Jamie got one of his own cigarettes out and offered his colleague one. They both sparked up, waiting for further instructions.

"It's a bloody good set-up."

"They always are," replied Jamie. "They know what they are doing alright."

"There's seven of them downstairs in the kitchen. Two of them were cooking up a stir fry. How do they live like this?"

"They have no choice. Half of them are trafficked in and made to do this to pay off their debts. Look in the room there," Jamie indicated towards the one used bedroom.

"Bloody hell, all crammed into here?"

"Yep. All with their own bed."

"What do they do all day?"

"One of the lads here will be the main 'gardener'. He'll know how to tend the plants and instruct the others on their upkeep. There are a couple of chefs. Others will go out and shop when needed, move drugs around, and collect any equipment. They'll travel miles to collect stuff. They will be told the places where they have to shop for their own food and also where to buy equipment for the grow."

"Well they could buy stuff down the road at the Co-Op or B&Q." Jamie laughed.

"Not unless they want a slap they won't. It's all organised crime, mate. Buy equipment in London, shop in Manchester, travel here, travel there and stay cooped up all day, surfing the internet and betting on crappy two-bit football matches."

"Poor sods."

"Must be better than home," continued Jamie. "You stay here. I'm gonna ask to be released. I've got a couple of jobs that I could be getting on with." Jamie stubbed out his cigarette on the stair newel and headed downstairs.

***

Police Constable Emily Dutton closed the door to her flat, walked to her car and climbed in. She'd finished a night shift at six this morning and, following a couple of hours of sleep, had forced herself out of bed to try and make the most of her two days off. Emily was single and with no kids or pets only had herself to look after. Her night shifts had passed slowly, in the rural beat area in which she worked, with no major jobs reported.

She had spent much of her shift patrolling for 'lampers' in conjunction with farm watch. A scourge to farmers, lampers would trespass on their land, with high-powered torches and lurcher dogs, and hunt down indigenous wildlife for sport. No instances had been reported. Although she had covered a lot of ground, Emily felt that she had achieved little. *Still getting paid though*, she thought, driving into the local supermarket car park and negotiating its one-way system before selecting a parking spot. She climbed out and headed towards the store.

Tonight the shift was going out for a few beers so she intended to grab a bottle to have a drink at her friend's house before they went to the pub. Emily grabbed a trolley and, pushing it forward, negotiated a barrier as the cart travelled in its own direction with the obligatory broken wheel. The shop was quiet as she headed to the food aisle where items which had been reduced in price were stocked. She managed to get a couple of cheap ready meals and also some dubious-looking sushi with the date expiring today. *Oh well, it's cheap and won't kill me.*

Emily wandered the aisles, grabbing various items before heading to the alcohol aisle. She examined the prosecco options and grabbed a bottle on offer. An experienced shopper at this store, Emily compared the bottle label to the shelf label.

"What a surprise," she said aloud. *I wonder how many people fall for this?* In her experience, Emily had noted that the incorrect placement of more expensive products within cheaper areas was a regular occurrence in this store. A tactic of supermarkets to fool customers who never questioned at the tills? A result of laxness and reduced staffing levels which every business was going through? Or a genuine error? Emily would never know, but what she did know was that the insidious activity infuriated her. She placed the bottle back with disgust and turned the shelf price label around so that no other customers would fall for the ruse. A member of staff approached her.

"Can I help you, madam?"

"Wrong bottles with the wrong price label, mate," she replied, pointing to the guilty shelf.

"Oh, sorry. Someone must have made a mistake." The man retrieved the shelf label. "I'll get another one printed. Sorry about that." He walked off towards the rear of the store.

"I'm sure you are," mumbled Emily under her breath, selecting a different bottle and heading to the checkout. She walked up to a self-serve till, placing the prosecco through first, knowing that it would need to be approved. The red light flashed on the light bar as she waited to scan her food products. A female member of staff wearing a Cher microphone and headset shuffled across to her. Emily stepped back, allowing the lady access to the screen.

"You could have waited until you had scanned everything and done the bottle last," advised the staff member looking at Emily.

"You looked free. I was only trying to help."

"You could have waited." The woman looked at Emily as if she was stupid. "I'll have to authorise it now. I could have approved it all at the end you see." The headphones seemed to impair the woman's awareness of her own volume, as she spoke loudly.

"OK," replied Emily. *Does this woman think I'm an idiot?*

"I'll do it now though. It will save you waiting once you've scanned it all in, you see."

"OK," replied Emily with a frown on her face. *What a bizarre conversation.* The woman walked away, having approved Emily's alcohol.

"I'm coming, I'm coming," the assistant bellowed at customers waiting. Emily's phone vibrated in her pocket. She retrieved it and, noting the text notification, opened it.

We need to meet. Ring me.

"Bloody hell. That's all I need." Emily shoved her shopping into her bag and walked out of the shop towards her car. With her shopping in the boot, she climbed into the driver's seat and, leaving the ignition off, dialled a number. There's no way that she wished this conversation to be overheard over the hands-free system of the car. The ringing tone sounded in her ear and, following a couple of clicks, a male voice spoke.

"Hello,"

"Hi, it's me."

"Nice one, Heather. Thanks for getting back to me so quickly."

"No problem." Emily's tone belied her feelings.

"We need to meet today or tomorrow. When are you free?"

"I'm busy today, so it will have to be tomorrow."

"OK. If it's tomorrow it will have to be in the morning. We're busy all afternoon. I'll need you for about an hour to an hour-and-a-half."

"Why so long?"

"I'll explain tomorrow. New pick-up point. Hanson's Park. You know where it is?"

"Yes."

"Usual precautions. Take a good long walk in, keep your wits about you and we'll talk you in. Nine o'clock?"

"Too early. I'm out tonight."

"How about ten thirty then?"

"Fine, but I can't guarantee what state I'll be in."

"As long as you are there."

"I will be." Emily pulled the phone away from her ear but heard the male continue. "What was that?" she asked.

"Enjoy your night."

"Will do." She terminated the call. "Wanker," she mumbled at the phone as she chucked it on the dashboard. Emily started the car engine and drove out of the car park, heading for home.

Shopping put away, prosecco chilling and having completed a thirty-minute workout, Emily climbed out of the shower and after drying off wrapped herself in her dressing gown. She took a seat on her bed whilst looking begrudgingly at her mobile phone.

The call had played on her mind throughout the morning and was sure to ruin her 'relaxing' two days off. They had her exactly where they wanted her and she knew that she could do nothing about it. She loved her job, and now six years in, felt able to deal with most situations. Unfortunately, this was a situation that she couldn't walk away from and one that she would regret forever.

Chapter 3

"Morning guys," called out Emily, as she walked into the intelligence office with a big smile on her face. Having served two years in the police she had completed her probationary period and after six months on the beat, had requested an attachment to the Intelligence Unit.

Supported by her shift sergeant, the request had been granted, and now three weeks in she was loving it. The police service ran on intelligence. Whether incidents were reported by members of the public, given by informants, or extrapolated from data by analysts, intelligence was the 'bread and butter' of all police work. The work interested Emily and she felt happy to be at work. If only she could say the same about her home life.

Emily had now been dating a man for six months. Jason was a good laugh and she liked him but there was something underlying about him that she wasn't sure of. They had great fun when they went out together as a couple but he was never keen to meet any of her mates, even for a quick drink. No pressure, only a couple of friends, but he always refused. God forbid, she'd never take him out on a full work social do, as that would be so unfair on him. He wasn't a copper, which meant he wasn't in the club. It was clear that he would feel uncomfortable around the cops but, more interestingly, they would feel uncomfortable around him. She'd seen it before on nights out with a civilian daring to enter the police drinking posse. The questions would start, the blokes would become protective, almost possessive, over the female cops and at some point, the interrogation of the civilian would begin. Almost aggressive in nature, attempts would be made to wheedle out any information which may be perceived as a threat to the police community. Emily didn't wish to put Jason through that.

Simply to take Jason around to a friend's house though, one on one, would be fine but he didn't want it. Jason saw Emily when he wanted to, rang her when he wanted to and otherwise his own thing. Two weeks ago at home, she'd nipped to the loo, leaving her mobile phone on the lounge floor where she had been sitting, and noticed on returning to the lounge that it had been moved. Jason was sitting there innocently, watching the television. She'd said nothing.

Last week he'd asked her to quickly check a car out for him at work as he was thinking of buying it. Emily realised that, in reality, she knew little about him. He was around to have a good time and that was it. The relationship ran on his terms and it was making her unhappy. She hadn't checked the car out for him but had a look for herself to see why he was interested. There was nothing obvious to her. A quick check on the intelligence system on Jason revealed nothing either. His phone number appeared on no police systems. On the face of it, he was fine. She'd decided that he was purely self-centred and chauvinistic, and that the relationship was doomed. However, that was not going to blight her day today.

"What have we got on?" she asked.

"The kettle would be great for starters," said Becky, one of the field intelligence officers. Other hands raised in the room in response to Becky's suggestion.

"Fine," replied Emily, "I suppose I walked into that one."

"Sure did," Becky smiled, handing Emily her coffee mug. Emily gathered cups from around the office, took them to the kitchen, and then filled the sink to wash them. She looked up as the unit's sergeant walked in. "Morning Pete. Coffee?"

"In a bit. Dry your hands, Emily, and come with me?" She looked at him in confusion. "Just a quick job that I need you to do downstairs for me," he clarified. Pete turned and walked from the kitchen, expecting Emily to follow, which she did.

"Where are we heading, Pete?"

"Super's office." He led the way to the office with Emily in tow. The door was closed. Pete knocked.

"Come in." Pete opened the door, indicating that Emily should enter first. Emily stepped forward, feeling worried, and was confronted by two men wearing suits as she entered.

"PC Dutton. I am Inspector John Trimble of the Police Professional Standards and Complaints Unit. You can take a seat." Emily heard the office door close behind her. Pete had remained outside. Her legs weakened and she reached for the chair to steady herself before sitting down. *Oh shit!*

"Are you OK, Emily? You look a bit shaken."

"I am." A glass of water was positioned on the desk in front of her. "May I?" She pointed to the glass.

"You may." Trimble smiled at Emily with a look she didn't trust. Predatory. With grey thinning hair combed back, square-rimmed gold spectacles and a moustache gripping his upper lip, Trimble portrayed the image of an officer from a bygone era. His name was known throughout the service. A good thief taker in his time, he was now an inspector in the 'rubber heel squad' and not a man to be trusted.

"Take a seat, Bob." The second officer settled into one of two seats at the desk. Positioned on the desk were a lined notepad, a pen and a voice recording machine. Trimble slowly removed his suit jacket, placed it carefully on the back of the last empty chair, lowered himself into it, and checked his watch. He looked at Emily. She looked back, her stomach churning as she did so. The room remained silent. She placed the glass down, the sound of its base against wood cutting the air, then silence. The gap extended, with the tension in the air palpable.

"Have I done something wrong? Do I need a friend? A solicitor?" Trimble smiled and then looked at Bob. Bob switched the machine's power on in readiness.

"I don't think so, Emily. We're only here to discuss a couple of matters. Things that you probably already know about. We'll record it, you know, for your record and ours. This isn't a formal interview at this stage, so I don't think you need to worry." Emily was sitting bolt upright, hands clasped, knuckles white. Bob pressed the record button on the machine. "Now, tell us about Jason." Emily's stomach flipped. *What have I got myself into?*

An hour later the officers knew everything about Jason that she knew. How she'd met him, places they had visited, the little she knew of his family. They had asked little but encouraged her to expand when needed. She blabbed out everything, confident that she had nothing to hide.

Trimble cleared his throat, "Emily, the crux of why we are here. Misuse of the police computer system." Emily's eyes widened in shock. *That's what they've got.* "Now think carefully before you answer," he continued. "Have you ever checked Jason out on any of the police computers?" Emily took a steady breath in. *This could be the end of my career. They know. If I lie they'll know. If I tell the truth then I may lose my job.* She made her decision.

"Yes, I have." Trimble looked at Bob. His gaze returned to Emily.

"Can you explain why and which systems?" Emily leant forward. Trimble raised his hand, halting her reply. "Can I advise you to make sure that you are totally honest, Emily? I am sure that you are aware of how important this is." She nodded.

"The intelligence system only. I searched for him there. I didn't know anything about him. I was worried. Trying to protect myself." She pleaded. Trimble raised his hand. Emily went quiet.

"PC Dutton, for clarification, you are aware that use of any police system for personal reasons is a breach of the Police Conduct Codes and potentially a dismissable offence."

"Yes." Emily grabbed the chair seat to stop her hands trembling as her eyes filled with tears. Trimble looked at Bob.

"Interview concluded," stated Bob, switching off the tape machine. Emily looked at them, shellshocked.

"Is that it? I've lost my job?" Tears began rolling down her cheeks.

"That ball, PC Dutton, is now well and truly in your hands," stated Trimble.

"What do you mean?"

"We've done our research, Emily." The shark's grin returned. "You're a good cop. Never been in trouble. You've got potential. You've been honest with us, which counts for a lot. We've also discussed your case with the boss."

"The boss?"

"You don't need to know. The important thing is that I am in a position to make you an offer."

"An offer?" Emily's head was spinning.

"Yes, an offer. We have recorded on that machine," he pointed to the machine that Bob was now placing in a black briefcase, "your full confession to misuse of the police intelligence system for personal reasons. We already knew that you had done that. We needed clarification as to why you did it and your admission of doing so. In light of everything, the boss may be persuaded to see it as a minor indiscretion or treat it as a dismissable offence." Emily felt herself starting to get annoyed.

"Can you tell me what's happening?"

"To put it simply, Emily, we either sack you or you keep your job and continue working for the police."

"But I already work for the police?" Trimble leaned forward looking Emily directly in the eyes.

"As a police officer and as a police informant," he clarified. The penny began to drop.

"Informing on who?"

"Your colleagues, people within our service, anyone that we want you to." *Bollocks,* thought Emily.

"Do I have any choice?"

"Not if you want to keep your job." This situation was out of Emily's control. She then made a decision which would affect her forever.

***

Rachel placed her teacup down carefully onto its saucer and looked at her notepad, in which she had taken copious notes. Sir David had reentered the room following a comfort break. Rachel moved to stand.

"No need, no need," said Sir David, indicating that Rachel should remain seated, "though the gesture is appreciated." He also now carried a thick file in his hands. "Some of the items you have requested and some other bits which may be of use." He handed the dossier to Rachel.

"Thank you, David." Rachel took hold of the green cardboard file and placed it on her lap. She opened the front cover and looked at a photograph of Victoria smiling back at her. Dark eyed, auburn hair parted to one side, and a mischievous smile upon her face. Rachel could see a young woman of both strength and character.

"She's stunning."

"She was undeniably," replied Sir David, "and with a beautiful soul to match." He was standing, looking out of the lounge window towards the grounds, clearly attempting to control his feelings. Rachel's heart ached for him but she was here as a professional and that was what was needed. She flicked through the paperwork. Newspaper clippings from the time (one featuring DC Kaur as a young man), correspondence that Sir David had received from friends, family and workers from his estate. Copies of extracts of Victoria's diaries, address books and a couple of handwritten letters. The paperwork was extensive.

"Did she have a laptop or mobile phone?" Sir David turned around, shaken from his trance.

"Oh, yes. The police took them. I think that they downloaded everything."

"Mmm, could be a bit tricky. I could do with them. I could do with anything that they have."

"Well you shall have it," stated Sir David.

"It may not be that easy."

"It bloody well will be. They've found nothing. Detective Kaur more or less told me to contact you. I'll tell them that you need it all and if you don't get it then I'll …"

"Calm down, David. I know Jamal. I'll contact him. See what he says."

"Well if he refuses, you let me know. I mean, they're sick of me asking them to reinvestigate. I'm confident that they want you to help?"

"We'll see." Sir David leaned on a chair and slowly lowered himself into it. He was breathing heavily following his verbal explosion.

"Is there a map of the estate here? Ah yes, got it." A labelled document became apparent in the back of the file. Rachel unfolded and examined it. "This clearly shows the estate-owned houses, rentals, private and council houses. It doesn't show current occupants though."

"Well, they are not all occupied. Some of the estate rentals are empty. I can sit with Fletcher and sort out who lives in each house now though."

"That would help. Also, I know it may be harder, but I could do with another list detailing who lived in the village on the day of Rachel's disappearance."

"We can do that too, though it may take a bit longer."

"Terrific."

"Are you willing to take it on?" Rachel looked Sir David in the eyes.

"Yes." He smiled. "I can't promise anything though. It's been a long time and the police so far have gotten nowhere with it." Sir David leaned forward grasping Rachel's hand.

"I know you will though. I can feel it."

"It may be —"

"Costly." Sir David finished Rachel's sentence. "Don't worry about that, I'm not short of a few bob." Rachel gently stood, gaining her balance, and took hold of her walking stick. Sir David stood also. "I'll drive you back up to the gate."

"If it's OK, I'd prefer to walk. It's been a long meeting and I could do with giving my legs a stretch. I also want to get a feel for the estate."

"Of course you do." Sir David smiled as he led Rachel towards the hallway. He opened the door for her.

"Whilst I am thinking about it, Sir David, you said that some of your estate houses are empty at the moment."

"Yes, they are. No tenants in them."

"That may be of use. I'll let you know." They both walked down the hallway, where Sir David opened the front door for her. Rachel walked out onto the steps leading to the drive. "I'll be in contact soon." She negotiated the steps and slowly walked away from the house, hearing the large door close gently behind her. *Who'd have believed it? Something to challenge me at last. Something to challenge the team.*

She stopped and turned to look back at the building. Within the lounge window stood the solitary figure of Sir David, who raised a hand in farewell. Rachel raised her hand in return and, on turning, caught a second figure looking down in her direction from an upstairs window. The figure quickly ducked from view. She remained looking at the majesty of the building as she began formulating some initial plans. The figure did not reappear.

***

"Hi, this is Tanya. I can't take your call right now but if you leave me a message I'll call you back ASAP." Jamie waited for a tone and then spoke.

"Hi love, you must be busy. I'm gonna be a little late. Don't worry about tea. I'll bring us a takeaway." Jamie had ended his afternoon liaising with the Crime Prosecution Service about one of his cases and had now finished his shift.

Now in his car, he broke the seal on his newly-acquired cigarettes and lit one, inhaled, and started coughing as the acrid smoke assaulted his lungs. Eyes now watering, he examined the cigarette. *A bit rough but they'll do.* His left hand tapped his pocket, reassuring himself that he still held the notepad in his cargo pants, He looked up and, on seeing the rest of the shift crossing in front of him, he maneuvered his vehicle, exited the parking bay and negotiated through the car park. Longy waved a 'goodbye' as Jamie drove past. Jamie pipped his horn and, after checking his rearview mirror, raised his right arm out of the window, flicking Longy the bird as he did so.

Driving towards the rear of the station, Jamie spotted the superintendent watching him. He quickly grabbed his cig from his mouth and held it near his lap as he passed by him.

"Sir," said Jamie, winking at the boss as he drove by. He received no reply. *Jumped up tosser,* thought Jamie, as he increased speed and headed to the exit.

***

Thirty minutes later and now changed into civilian clothes (always kept in the car in case needed), Jamie parked outside a delicatessen and walked towards his destination.

Cheung Li's Chinese takeaway's public entrance was closed at the moment but was due to open in ten minutes. The wonderful aroma of stir fry filled the air in the vicinity of the shop, stimulating Jamie's senses. Next door was an off-licence. Jamie walked around to the back of the takeaway where a stable door was situated, bottom half wood, top half grilled. The door opened into the kitchen area where Jamie could see the chefs industriously preparing the menu for the night. He knocked on the wooden part of the door. An Asian male looked up, and on recognising Jamie, held his finger up indicating 'one minute'. The chef disappeared into the building and reappeared followed by an Asian female. She opened the top grill.

"Jamie, can I help you?" Jamie held up the notebook.

"This may be of interest. I found it lying about in a grow in Fenchurch this morning." The woman took the book from Jamie and placed it in the front pocket of her hoody.

"Thank you. I'll pass it on. I'm sure they'll be in contact." She closed the grill and walked away. Jamie turned and walked back to the front of the shop, entered the off-licence and grabbed a fridge pack of Stella. Back at the car he broke the pack, pulled out a can, and released its ring pull. Checking that no one was around, he took a quick swig, set the car in motion and headed to a takeaway closer to home. *Job done. They should be happy with that*, he thought.

***

Emily walked into her bedroom and lay down on her bed to dry her hair with the sounds of Dance Monkey booming out loud. She was looking forward to her night out. The shift hadn't hit the pubs for ages and following their set of shifts, the team would be ready to let its hair down.

She took a sip from a can of lager positioned on her side table and checked her hair in the mirror. *My roots are starting to show*. She placed the can down and parted her hair centrally, looking at the darkness encroaching upon the blonde. *Time to book the hairdresser's again. Oh well, it'll have to do for tonight*. Emily grabbed her hair dryer and dipped her head forward, allowing the warm air to evaporate the water from her hair. With her left hand tousling through her fronds it didn't take long. Now that it was almost dry, she scrunched some product in, and placed on a loose Alice band to hold it back so that she could apply her makeup.

Emily looked at her bare reflection and, although happy with her look, always felt that a little bit of makeup helped. Jason had always liked her to look immaculate, which for him meant her hair needed to be perfect, her makeup flawless and her nails manicured. That was in the past now. She had come to realise what a controlling man he had been and, following her brush with police complaints, had ditched him straight away. Professional Standards had reassured her that they had no concerns about him and that he had no police record. However, she felt happier without him. Emily now recognised that he had dominated her. Despite her being in an assertive profession she realised that any person could inadvertently allow themselves to be controlled. *Not any more*, she reassured herself once more, as she applied her eyeliner. *You're in control now.* She laughed out loud.

"Unless you class being a police informant as being in control, Emily," she said to her reflection. She knew that she was being used but at least this time she knew it. She also knew that it was partially on her terms too. She could leave the job, walk away from it all or, take her wage, work for the good of the organisation, and help get rid of the 'bad apples'.

So far, the unit had been looking after her and she had no complaints. Corruption wasn't high at her nick and to date, she'd spent most of her time completing small tasks, which were inconsequential to her, but apparently helped with the 'bigger picture'.

Lipstick now applied, Emily thought that she was looking okay. She checked her watch.

"Shit. Time to go. Alexa, stop." The loud music halted. Emily finished her lager, tidied her lipstick and grabbed the rest of her booze from the kitchen before heading out the door.

***

"Subject's vehicle is approaching the car park." Ronnie was sitting at Rachel's desk looking at a monitor which displayed a street mapping system. A blue dot, representing their subject's car, moved slowly along one of the small streets within the city. Ronnie's task was to monitor and commentate on its movement in order to assist the deployed ground team.

"Loud and clear, Ronnie," replied Tom, who was commanding tonight's operation. Rachel and Matthew had taken the evening off and had arranged to meet everyone in the office the following morning.

"Approaching the entrance to the car park."

"Entering the casino now," said Jim. Joe looked on despondently as Jim walked towards the front entrance doors to the casino, dressed in a smart suit. The door was opened by a doorman who had greeted him as he approached. He had smiled politely and was now in the reception.

Unbeknownst to Joe, Jim was already a member of the Grosvenor Casino chain and so entry to the venue had been no problem for him. Joe's dreams of being a pseudo Bond had quickly been vanquished by the team, who thought that his 'look' was better suited to other roles. Wearing shorts and a T-shirt and pushing along a shitty bicycle, he had on his back a large green square cool bag. People often see what they expect and, on this occasion, Joe gave the appearence of a Deliveroo delivery man. Despite not displaying any livery, most people would assume that he was one.

"That's Jim within the building now," said Joe over the radio. He turned into the side street where the subject's vehicle had approached the car park.

"Jim with a radio check."

"Background noise but clear enough," replied Tom. Joe stopped on the pavement in the side street, hanging his bag from his front handlebars. He faced towards the path which led from the car park. He reached for his bike chain, disconnected it from the cogs, and waited. Within the cool bag was positioned a small battery and pinhole camera, the lens of the camera pointing to where the subject should appear.

"Joe in position," transmitted Joe, as he retrieved some bike tools from under his saddle. "Sighting of the subject. I can confirm it's him." Joe started fiddling with his bike chain as a chubby and balding middle-aged man wearing a suit walked towards him. The male walked beyond Joe, barely taking any notice. "Towards you, Tom." Tom was sitting within a line of parked cars with a view of the entrance to the casino, Sarah was behind him with a telescopic lens, resting on the seat above Tom's shoulder, pointed towards the casino doors.

"Tom has control." Tom paused as Sarah depressed the camera button and the shutters sounded. "Images obtained," he continued. Back at the office, Ronnie recorded the commentary on behalf of the team. "Towards the entrance and you, Jim."

"Received," replied Jim.

"Towards the doorman. Door opened and into the casino."

"Jim has control," said Jim's voice on the radio. Tom and Sarah relaxed in the car.

"Looks like we'll have this sorted tonight," said Sarah.

"Seems so," replied Tom. "I'll give Joe a ring and tell him he can go. We'll sit tight and support Jim."

"Cool," replied Sarah, sitting back and placing the camera next to her on the seat. "I'm gonna grab forty winks." Tom's mobile vibrated.

Greeted by name. Obs known here. Settling down at the tables.

Tom had received the text from Jim and transmitted the information over the radio on Jim's behalf. Now for the boring part of surveillance. The long wait doing nothing as their subject enjoyed himself. *Good little earner for our team though*, thought Tom. He dialled Joe.

"Free to go, mate. We'll take it from here. See you at the office meeting in the morning."

***

"That's Rach and Matt entered the compound now," said Sarah looking at a computer screen which displayed CCTV covering the gate. Ronnie peeled himself from the team sofa, extricating himself from his natural habitat whilst leaving half a digestive biscuit in his imprint.

"Oops, the one that got away." He reached back, collecting the biscuit, which he then popped into his mouth. "All for a drink?" The team answered in the affirmative. "I'll stick the kettle on and nip for a quick smoke before we get started. You coming, Joe?" Crumbs from the biscuit decorated Ronnie's beard as he spoke.

"Yes, mate." Joe stood up and removed a packet of roll-up tobacco from his pocket.

"I'll sub you a straight," said Ronnie, holding out his packet of Regals.

"Don't mind if I do." Joe reached for the packet, removing a cigarette as both males walked towards the stairs leading to the garage.

"I'll wash up," said Jim, collecting discarded mugs from around the office. Ronnie and Joe descended the metal stairs.

"He'll have them made by the time we return," said Ronnie.

"What made?" asked Rachel, who was now slowly walking through the garage.

"Morning, boss," said Ronnie, smiling. "Jim's said he's making the coffee now that you've got here. We're having a quick cig and we'll be back upstairs."

"Great. Briefing will be in about fifteen minutes." Rachel looked at Matthew and handed him a bag that she was carrying. He took the item and watched as Rachel adjusted her stick and, using the handrail, started climbing the stairs. Matthew held back before climbing, knowing that Rachel would take longer to ascend. He watched both the men leave the building, chatting to each other as if they'd known each other for years.

Fifteen minutes later the team were all sitting within the office. Rachel had already received updates about the casino job. She had spent last night preparing her briefing for today's meeting. The team all took turns in planning the jobs that came in. Matthew and Joe took a lesser role in the planning, having never worked with the briefing models and templates used to organise and plan their work.

"OK everyone, let's get down to business," she started. "New job for us. It's a bit out of our norm, but as you know I've been looking for a job that we can sink our teeth into. I think that this is the one. As always, everyone's views, ideas, and concerns are important, so get your minds working on it. Nothing is off-limits. If you're thinking it, then share it." She looked around at everyone. She had their attention. Rachel pressed a button on her laptop. The smart screen on the wall displayed a photograph of Victoria Fanshaw smiling at the camera.

"Miss Victoria Fanshaw, aged 19 years, daughter of Sir David Fanshaw. Victoria has been missing since 18th June 1997 and is presumed dead. No corpse has ever been located and Sir David believes that she was murdered. He wishes our team to reinvestigate the incident and see if we can establish what happened to Victoria." Rachel looked around the faces staring back at her. Joe was sitting forward in his chair, his interest peaked. Sarah and Tom looked at each other slightly confused. Jim studiously wrote some notes in a book and Ronnie looked shocked, coffee in hand, with his mouth wide open like a carp.

The silent bubble burst as everyone spoke at once. Rachel raised her hands to calm them. "I know, I know. It's a big ask but we do have free reign. The police haven't got anywhere with it; they referred Sir David on to us. It's a big opportunity. Sir David's holding the purse strings and as I said, anything is on the table." The team started talking aloud again. Rachel's hands raised again, and the team quietened. "Let me tell you what I know and we'll go from there." The image on the smart screen changed to a photograph of the note that Sir David had received at home.

WE KNOW SHE WAS MURDERED

Chapter 4

17th June 1997 – Preceding 24 hours

Victoria stretched her arms above her head, yawning loudly before pushing her hair gently away from her face. Morning sunshine seeped through the gap in the bedroom curtains, warming her right leg, which poked out from underneath the duvet. Her alarm clock displayed nine am as she grabbed her cigarettes and lighter. Drawing a cigarette out, before lighting it and inhaling deeply.

Her father disapproved of her smoking in the house but this was her bedroom, which was, in her opinion, her private domain. A space where she could be herself and suffer no others' judgement. She opened her bedside drawer, placing a small bag of herbal cannabis that she had recently acquired beneath some notelets. There was no need to be too blatant as the cleaner would see it and gossip with the other house staff.

Pulling the duvet back, cigarette balanced in her mouth, she straightened her pyjamas and walked across to the window. With hair tousled, last night's makeup in place and wearing her comfiest sleepwear, Victoria still looked stunning and naturally radiated self confidence.

She drew the curtains, allowing the sunlight to flood the room, and on looking out, hastily removed the cigarette from her mouth, secreting it behind her back. An automatic reaction on seeing her father, who was standing on the lawns beyond the patio, as he turned to face the house. The curtain movement must have caught his eye. He raised a hand to Victoria in greeting, to which she responded with her free hand and a wide smile.

Her father was speaking to Danny, one of the groundsmen. Danny had looked towards her window as well but had quickly looked away again. Victoria liked Danny. She liked his gentle soul, his muscular build and good looks, which didn't go amiss on her. She sighed, turned from the window, and taking a last inhalation, stubbed out her half cigarette in an ashtray.

"Time for a shower." She entered her en suite bathroom, stripping as she did so, and switched on the shower. Victoria checked her face in the mirror. Running her tongue over her teeth, she grimaced at the smoky taste of the cigarette and quickly grabbed her toothbrush and toothpaste to alleviate the suffering of her mouth. Selecting some lotion, she swiftly removed her makeup and, clicking the radio on, stepped into the shower listening to R Kelly's voice ringing out.

***

Now dressed in jeans and a plain white T-shirt, Victoria descended the central staircase and headed towards the kitchen. Breakfast would have been cleared from the dining room by now and, though she could have had it brought to her, she didn't wish to put the house staff out of their routine. She strolled into the kitchen with a bright smile.

"Morning, Annie. How are you today?" Annie, the house cook, was standing in an apron, bullying some pastry with a rolling pin.

"Morning, Miss. I'm well thank you. Do you need some breakfast?"

"Don't worry yourself," said Victoria as she opened the fridge door, looking for inspiration. "You're busy baking. What's the occasion?"

"Sir David is holding a small dinner party this evening."

"Oh, yes. I'd forgotten. The Fothergills and their awful son." Victoria removed a jug of fresh orange juice and an apple from the fridge. She placed the jug down and took a bite from the apple.

"They're not so bad," replied Annie. "Young Charles is a bit of a looker and he will do well for himself. He has prospects."

"But he's so boring," mumbled Annie through her mouthful of food.

"Excitement isn't everything, dear. I think Sir David expects you to be there tonight." Annie handed Victoria a freshly brewed coffee.

"Everyone needs some fun though, Annie. Life's not worth living without a bit of a thrill." She took the cup from Annie. "Thank you." Victoria swept out of the kitchen, leaving Annie to her duties, and headed to the day lounge.

The lounge was situated off the main hallway and was used by the family as a place to relax. Its generous windows provided a clear view of the grounds to the east of the house and maximised the morning sunshine which bathed the building. Two large comfortable couches encompassed a central oak coffee table. Upon the table were a selection of magazines and the morning newspapers. A writing desk was positioned in the left corner of the room with blotter, pens and paper at the ready. At the other corner stood the cocktails table with a selection of spirits, mixers and glasses available. Beautiful oak flooring covered with a large Persian rug, framed by crisp white walls on three sides, and a dominant Inglenook inset opposite the windowed side finished the room.

This was the heart of the home. Deliberately untouched by modern fetishism, the family attempted to preserve the past. Victoria loved the lounge, a room that had remained unchanged throughout her life and cuddled her every time that she entered. She placed her cup down on the coffee table, retrieved a newspaper and relaxed back on the sofa. She browsed the pages noting the continued coverage of Naomi Campbell's hospitalisation and further speculation as to how Rusedski would perform at Wimbledon. The lounge door flew open, startling Victoria, as her brother marched into the room.

"There you are," said Jonathan.

"Oh, it's you," she replied, looking back at her paper.

"Sitting on your arse doing nothing as usual."

"Piss off."

"I'm not joking, Victoria." Jonathan walked towards Victoria positioning himself behind her and looking down at her. "Seriously, you do nothing except flounce around the house, party, or chat up the blokes from the village in the pub while I'm busting my gut trying to support our father's business." Victoria ignored him. Clenching his fists in exasperation, Jonathan suddenly reached forward and snatched the newspaper from Victoria's hands.

"What the hell do you —" she yelled, standing up and turning towards him.

"Oh shut up, you lazy cow," he interrupted. Jonathan's face was scarlet, a sneer twisting his face. "You're a waste of space." He stood there bristling with anger and threw the paper onto the floor. "It's time you either got a job or made some sort of effort around here."

"Who the hell are you to tell me what to do?" she screamed.

"The bloody man who will eventually inherit this place."

"You're welcome to it, you tosser. I don't need it." Victoria stormed towards the door.

"Don't you dare walk away from me," shouted Jonathan.

"Or what?" replied Victoria, having reached the open door. She strode out, slamming the door in her wake, leaving behind her a muffled bellow from Jonathan.

"I could bloody kill you." Victoria continued walking and then ran up the stairs, tears barely held back as she entered her room.

In the lounge, Jonathan stood seething. Since their mother had died he had felt responsible for supporting his father and, consequently, the estate. Victoria had done little to assist but had always managed to wheedle her way around their father. Jonathan had been devastated by their loss but knew that life had to move on. He stared out of the window towards the walled garden. *Dinner party tonight*, he thought.

Draconian as it seemed, Jonathan would support a marriage between Victoria and Fothergill. *If she's no good for work then she can get married and have babies.* Jonathan knew that his father wouldn't live forever and with Victoria syphoned away, the estate would be Jonathan's in its entirety. He could run things as he pleased and provide her with a yearly dowry to keep her quiet.

"That's if I don't kill her first," he mumbled, straightening his tweeds and heading to the room containing the gun cabinet. Jonathan had been invited to a local shoot tomorrow and wished to give the shotgun a once over so that it was ready for tomorrow. Opening the cabinet he smiled as he looked at the immaculate Purdey and Westley Richards standing side by side. The door to the room opened as Fletcher entered.

"Sorry, Sir. I didn't realise that you were in here."

"That's fine, Fletcher. Simply checking the guns for tomorrow."

"I went over them yesterday," replied Fletcher.

"You're a good man. Have we enough ammunition?"

"Yes, Sir. I checked that this morning. I'll have everything ready for you in the morning."

"Splendid. I may take the HW out later and get my eye in on some rabbits."

"Right, you are, Sir. I'll leave you to it." Fletcher left the room, closing the door behind him, leaving Jonathan wondering as to what caused Fletcher to enter the room in the first place.

***

Victoria walked across the front of the building to where her Mercedes SLK was waiting for her. Abandoned there yesterday evening, it was now neatly parked, bonnet facing out, with the keys in the ignition. She climbed in and switched it on, enjoying the purring of the engine. Still fuming with Jonathan, she revved the engine before swiftly pulling away, oblivious of the tyres firing gravel towards the house.

Victoria was off to visit her friend Tanya who lived in a shepherd's cottage at the bottom of the village. Both women had grown close since turning seventeen, having initially met in the village pub. Tanya wasn't working today so she was confident that she would be at home and would patiently sit and listen to Victoria's grumbling. She drove her SLK out of the main gates and headed downhill towards the small village green.

Tanya's car was parked outside of her cottage and the living room window was open. Victoria parked in front of Tanya's Corsa and walked up the small lane to the back gate and door. She knocked once on the door and opened it.

"Hi Tan, only me." A muffled response was yelled from upstairs as Victoria entered and switched the kettle on. The cottage was rented from the estate and was small but quaint. A tiny kitchen led into a living room which had space for a two-seater settee, a side table and a coffee table. The front door led directly into the lounge and a real fire grate was positioned in the largest wall with homemade bookcases set in alcoves to either side. The walls were painted in a plain cream and a staircase led from one corner to upstairs where there were two bedrooms and a bathroom. The bookshelves were filled with a large selection of books on one side and DVDs and CDs on the other.

Tanya lived alone in the cottage which stood in a terraced row of four shepherd cottages, referred to from bygone days when the farm workers on the estate occupied them. Victoria heard the creak of the staircase and observed Tanya's dressing-gowned legs descending into the living room.

"Hi Vic, trouble at the mill?" asked Tanya as she stepped into the room, her hair wrapped in a pink towel. Tanya was used to Victoria's impromptu arrivals which were usually a result of an argument that had happened up at the big house.

"Oh, it's something and nothing. Only Jonathan whinging again. I needed to get out of there. I've stuck the kettle on." Victoria slumped onto the sofa.

"OK, I'll make it then, Milady," stated Tanya with an eyebrow raised, screwing her face up. "What do you want?"

"Oh, you're terrific. Coffee please." Tanya entered the kitchen and started preparing the drinks.

"He's such a boring arse," continued Victoria. Tanya leaned her head against the kitchen wall cupboard, away from Victoria's view. *Here we go again. The lady of the house is unhappy so I get the brunt of it.* She stirred the drinks.

"That's blokes for you," said Tanya. "Ignore him." She placed the drinks on the table and in an attempt to redirect the conversation, reached for the towel on her head. "Hey, what do you think of this?" With a dramatic flare, she bent forward, removed the towel and flicked her head and hair back, revealing a scarlet red mane. "Ta-daaaa!" Victoria made an audible gasp as her hands covered her mouth.

"What have you done?" Eyes wide open, Victoria began to laugh. "My god, Tan, you look different." Tanya registered the look on Victoria's face, trying to gauge her reaction.

"Different good? Different bad?"

"Well, I don't know."

"Thanks for your support. We've not all got long beautiful tresses, you know. I can't afford one hundred quid for a hairdresser."

"It's a shock, that's all."

"Good. I like to shock."

"Anyway, I've got a boring dinner party tonight, Tan. I can't stand it. Dad's trying to foist me off to that Fothergill boy." Tanya realised that her redirection had created little effect. Victoria was all about Victoria, with room for little else in between.

"Well, the meal will be good and I'm sure that he's not that bad. I'm nipping into town with Danny later on."

"Danny the groundsman?"

"Yes, why not?"

"Didn't think that he'd be your type. He's lush though. Lovely body. I could fancy him myself."

"Could you? Hands off, Lady Fanshaw, he falls well short of your social standing."

"Anything for a bit of fun." Tanya studied Victoria trying to work out why they were friends. Victoria was a massive flirt, never seemed to care about how she affected others and had no insight into her own behaviour. *Doesn't know how lucky she is.* They spent the rest of the afternoon together before making final arrangements to meet in the village pub the following evening.

***

The team all looked at the message on the screen.

"This is an image of the second note that has been delivered to David Fanshaw," said Sarah. "Delivered twenty years after she went missing. The first one was delivered during the initial enquiry."

"Envelope?" asked Ronnie.

"No. Not on either occasion."

"Fingerprints? DNA?" asked Jim.

"All checked on the initial note. Nothing came back. No marks. Printed note. They look similar."

"What about this one?"

"Not been checked yet, Jim. David has the note kept securely. I'll be speaking to someone to try and help with that."

"What do we know about Victoria then?" asked Tom. Rachel produced the file that she had received from David Fanshaw.

"All the documents that David has kept are in here. The police who completed the initial enquiry will have their documents and I'm sure that everything that they recorded will be detailed on their HOLMES system."

"Holmes?" asked Joe.

"It's a police system that records all actions taken, documents obtained, and enquiries completed during a major investigation to ensure nothing is missed," replied Rachel.

"And that failed to find her or the killer?"

"Correct."

"Then how are we going to do better?"

"We may not but David believes that we can. We can look at it all with a fresh set of eyes and see where it takes us. We'll never know unless we try." Rachel looked around the room trying to gauge everyone's reaction. "We all have to agree as a team though. We have to throw everything that we can think of at this." She looked to Matthew for support as Sarah intervened.

"I'm in, Rachel. We have nothing to lose. It will stretch us but as long as David Fanshaw's covering our wages then why not? If we solve a historical murder who knows what doors will open for us as a team."

"Is Fanshaw a suspect?" asked Tom.

"Everyone is of interest to us, Tom. Would Fanshaw resurrect an enquiry into the murder of his daughter if he did it? I doubt it, but we still need to be thorough. Check his alibi early and make sure that we're happy."

"Where do we start?" Rachel raised the file in her arms.

"Here. Let's work out what we have in here first. See if it points us in any obvious directions, and determine where our intelligence and investigative gaps are. Let's keep the time parameters of our enquiry tight to start with. The day that Victoria went missing, twenty-four hours after and the twenty-four hours before." Ronnie stood up and took the file.

"Jim and I will divide it out. Matt and Joe can work with Sarah and Tom and learn from their experience."

"Thanks." Matt walked over to Rachel as the others began talking.

"Nice one. It seems that everyone's in."

"It will be good for us and hopefully we can put an old man's mind to rest."

***

17th June 1997 – Preceding 12 hours

Victoria looked at her reflection in the mirror and wondered how boring the evening was going to get. Wearing a green leaf floral Dolce & Gabbana gown, diamond stud earrings and black slingbacks, she was dressed for dinner and dreading it. However, duty called and she would put in her best effort for her father. Victoria wandered over to her window, which was slightly ajar, to allow the thin trail of smoke from her cigarette, balanced on an ashtray, to sneak out into the fresh air. She crouched down, her head forwards, and took a drag, making sure not to drop any ash onto her dress, docked the cigarette and blew the smoke through the gap.

Now in her en-suite, Victoria vigorously brushed her teeth, sprayed a liberal amount of perfume and applied some lipstick.

"Come on then," she said to her reflection. "Best foot forwards." Victoria left her room and headed down to the lounge where cocktails would be served. A quiet murmuring could be heard in the hallway as Victoria halted by the door. She took a deep breath, fixed a smile on her face and walked in. Her father was talking with her brother. David turned as his daughter entered the room and smiled.

"You look ravishing, darling."

"Well, thank you, Daddy." Victoria swept past her brother and kissed her father on the cheek. She held him at arm's length. "You don't look too bad yourself."

"One must try," replied David, who wore a jacket made of Yorkshire tweed, with a dress shirt and a neatly fastened tie, with a pheasant embroidered thereon. "Fancy a cocktail? Our guests haven't arrived yet."

"I certainly do." Victoria headed towards the cocktail table where Fletcher waited expectantly. She had made no conversation with her brother who may as well have not been there.

"Archers, Madame?"

"Yes please, Fletcher. Thank you." Victoria took the drink and turned towards her brother, smiling. *Now I can tolerate you, you insidious little weasel.* Fletcher left the room and returned a few minutes later, opening the lounge door and announcing the arrival of the Fothergills.

"Lovely to see you, Charlie," Sir David walked forward, arm outstretched and shook hands with Charles Snr.

"Good to see you, David."

"Mary," Sir David kissed Mary on both cheeks, his kisses reciprocated by Mary pecking the air on either side of his cheek, reminiscent of a chicken. Sir David swept past Mary as he firmly grasped Charles Jnr's hand and pumped it vigorously. "And you, Charles. Wonderful of you to come."

"Delighted," replied Charles, spotting Victoria rolling her eyes as she sipped on a cocktail. Jonathan moved forward greeting each guest in turn.

"And Victoria is here," continued Sir David, turning towards her with arm outstretched, as if displaying her as a prize. Victoria was standing looking at the group. "Come and say hello," continued David, smiling but with his brow creased. Victoria dutifully placed down her glass and moved towards the group, frowning at her father and then forcing a smile as she said hello.

"Cocktails everyone? Please give Fletcher your order." Sir David rubbed his hands together, clearly loving the position of host. "Maybe you young ones…" he gestured to Charles and Victoria, "would like to take yours on the patio whilst we talk business." *Here we go,* thought Victoria, *forced to spend the evening with Charles.* She headed straight to Fletcher.

"Another please." She leant towards him speaking quietly. "A double if I'm going to survive this evening."

"Indeed, Madam." Fletcher's face didn't alter but she thought he would appreciate her dilemma. Victoria patiently waited for Charles to obtain his drink before they both walked out to the patio.

"It's a beautiful evening," said Charles in his attempt at conversation, "the grounds are looking stunning." Charles' plummy voice caused Victoria to raise an eyebrow.

"Aren't they absolutely beautiful," she replied in parody, which Charles seemed oblivious to.

"You know our parents would be happy for us to be together," he continued. Victoria reached into her clutch, taking out a packet of cigarettes.

"Can we walk this way, please?" she said, heading away from the lounge windows. Charles frowned but followed as if leashed.

"That's a bad habit, you know. You should stop." Victoria lit her cigarette, drawing deeply, and blew the smoke deliberately in his direction.

"Is that true?"

"Which? The smoking or our betrothal?" said Charles.

"Our betrothal is it? Calm down there."

"Would it be that bad? I have good prospects. I am already a junior at the bank and am sure to rise through the ranks. I have money and good breeding." Victoria struggled to comprehend how, in this day and age, such a young man (15 years her senior) could be so entrapped in values from the past. *Not a chance mate, but I'll make you work for it this evening and have my fun.*

"Indeed," she smiled sweetly at him, stubbing out her cigarette within a large ornamental pot, ensuring to push the butt end under the soil. "I seem to have finished my cocktail." Victoria handed Charles her empty glass, which he dutifully took and, linking in his arm, led him back towards the house.

Dinner went laboriously for Victoria. The endless talk about business, how the estate was doing, the successful career that Charles was building for himself, and what an eligible bachelor he was becoming. Her brother 'posturing' with the elders describing his acumen within the family business. Everyone's continuous hints towards Victoria and Charles that they would make a great match. If she saw her father wink across the table at her once more she'd scream. Luckily

Fletcher had kept her glass topped with wine, though she suspected that he'd watered down the white that she had been drinking with her meal.

With the evening coming to a close, the elders, plus Jonathan, had retired to the drawing room, once again leaving Victoria and Charles together alone. She kicked off her slingbacks and walked barefoot onto the neatly trimmed lawn. Charles followed her.

"What do you think then?" said Charles. Victoria turned towards him, squinting through a dusky alcohol haze.

"What do I think about what?" she slurred slightly.

"About us?"

"Is that a proposal?" Victoria swayed as she looked up at Charles. He took hold of her forearm to steady her. Victoria giggled. "Charles, I wouldn't marry you if you were the last man on earth," she giggled again and leant towards him as if telling a private joke, "You are the most boring fecker that I know." Charles' grip tightened and he pulled her closer to him, sneering at her.

"Listen you little drunken bitch. You'll be lucky to get a better offer." He took her face in his other hand and leaned forward, roughly kissing her lips. Victoria's body froze, stunned. She pulled away her voice rising,

"How dare —"

"Shut up," he laughed, "you'll get used to it." He let her arm go, turned and walked back towards the house where his parents had appeared on the patio.

"Time to go, my boy," called his father.

"Righty oh, we were saying our goodbyes." Charles' parents raised their arms in farewell to which Victoria automatically reciprocated, still stunned at what she had suffered. Quickly sobered, she watched the guests enter the house as she blindly scrambled in her purse for her cigarettes. She placed a cigarette in her mouth and tried to light it with her trembling hands.

Leaning against the trunk of a weeping willow within the lawned gardens, Danny had watched the whole incident from a distance. The gentle walk out onto the patio and lawns, the couple talking and the amorous kiss that ensued. Danny knew that Victoria was a flirt and he'd be blind if he hadn't noticed her stunning figure and natural beauty.

"Lucky bastard," he said aloud, as he walked away with a pruning knife and some stray branches of willow in his hands.

***

"We know that on Friday the 17th, Victoria was at home. We'll need to start documenting a timeline for this, Jim," said Rachel, looking towards Jim who was sitting behind a computer at a desk.

"Already on with it."

"Great. Accounts from the cook, the brother and Sir David confirm that. We know that she had a verbal disagreement with her brother Jonathan and that she went to see her friend in the village, who is —" Rachel checked her notes.

"Tanya," interjected Joe.

"That's her. Tanya. Thanks, Joe. Where did she go after Tanya's?"

"We don't know. No recorded sightings during the afternoon," said Jim.

"Intelligence gap," Rachel indicated to Matthew, who noted it down.

"We're going to keep bumping into this problem, Rach," said Tom, "we haven't got enough information to work with. We need all the information that the police hold. Statements, forensics, CCTV, the list is endless. Without that, we are going to struggle." Rachel looked at the team members, her hands gripping her notes revealing her exasperation.

"You're right, Tom. This is our starting point though. That's all we have until I can speak with Sir David and Jamal Kaur. Take a comfort break, everyone." Rachel walked slowly away towards the toilets as the team split in various directions. Matthew was sitting waiting at her desk on her return.

"You OK?"

"Yes, I'm fine. We'll get there." She smiled at him and walked towards the tea tray where Sarah had made hot drinks.

"Hang in there," said Sarah. "It's gonna take some time and a couple of minor miracles." Rachel laughed accepting a coffee. The team filtered back in.

"Right," she announced, "a bit of a change of direction." Faces looked at her attentively. "We have an unrestricted budget. What can we do to investigate this incident? The world's our oyster. What do we need to move this forward?"

"Access to the original case file and enquiries," stated Tom. Rachel wrote it down on the smart board.

"A bigger team," said Jim. Rachel continued writing their suggestions on the board.

"Someone to collate all our findings. Jim's talents are wasted behind the keyboard," said Ronnie.

"Unrestricted access to Evesham House and the village," said Sarah.

"The name of the murderer," said Ronnie, laughing at his joke. Everyone looked at him.

"We'll ignore that. Thanks for that one, Ron –," said Rachel. Ronnie remained stolid, unfazed by the comment.

"Unrestricted access," repeated Rachel. "How do we achieve that?" Joe had been listening in quiet contemplation.

"We need an informant," he said. Everyone looked at him. *Good lad,* thought Rachel.

"Go on, Joe. Elaborate," she said encouragingly.

"Well, someone knows the history around what happened. Not a family member. They are too emotionally tied up in it all. Otherwise, the note makes no sense. The note had to be hand-delivered. Maybe someone local. We need someone on our side in the village." Rachel smiled.

"If it was hand delivered there may be CCTV capturing the delivery. Have the estate got any?" asked Jim.

"How about a U/C?" asked Sarah.

"U/C?" asked Matthew.

"Undercover cop, slash person," she clarified. Rachel had continued writing on the board.

"Now we're getting somewhere," she said. "As most of us know, working a case is all hard slog, but it's the ideas that make the difference. The pivotal things that get us the information and evidence that we need. Now," she gestured to the board with her arm, "how are we going to make all of this happen?"

Chapter 5

18th June 1997

Victoria strolled down the village hill, relishing the warmth of the early evening. A swift rain shower had dampened the path but now, with the sun having reappeared, the smell of the warm tarmac and slight humidity surrounded her. The cleansed earth felt like a new beginning. She examined her forearm with a frown creasing her brow. Slight purple bruising was evident and also some tenderness where she had been fiercely gripped last night.

Anger welled in Victoria's body, only quelled with fierce determination. Now having got over the shock and disbelief that he had dared to touch her, Victoria knew that she would not even tolerate Charles' company again, nevermind agreeing to be his lifelong partner. Her father knew nothing of the incident and would be enraged if he did. Her brother wouldn't care. She suspected that privately he would believe that she deserved it. However, today Victoria did not wish to dwell on it and was looking forward to an evening in the pub with Tanya and the locals. Dressed in a shirt, jeans and trainers, her outfit was the antithesis of last night's regalia and she felt more comfortable for it being so.

As she approached a honeysuckle shrub, a hum filled the air, causing Victoria to veer slightly onto the road, in avoidance of the bees which worked voraciously collecting nectar and pollen. Hearing the deep rumble of an engine climbing the hill, Victoria placed on her Ray-Bans and, looking down the road, watched a tractor slowly ascending the hill. She bypassed the bush and returned to the path, peering through her lenses to see who was driving.

The tractor approached and Victoria recognised Danny as the driver. She raised her hand in greeting as the tractor slowed and pulled to a halt, its engine idling, then stopping. Victoria reached up to the door, opened it and looked up towards his tousled hair and tanned face. He was wearing a black vest and work trousers.

"Hiya. How's things?"

"Fine, thanks." He smiled at her, his teeth bright within his tanned complexion and slight stubble. Blue eyes looked straight at Victoria's, without the customary exploration of her body that she experienced with some men. *God, you are gorgeous*, she thought, admiring his broad shoulders and muscular physique.

"You coming to the pub tonight?"

"After I drive this up to the yard, grab a shower and a bite to eat, I'll be heading down."

"Great," replied Victoria, beaming up at him with her hand on the open door. He smiled at her. She didn't move. Danny had noted her eyes examining him.

"I can't go if you don't shut the door though." He moved, reaching for the ignition.

"Oh, yes. Sorry." Victoria replied, roused from her contemplation. "I'll see you there later." She closed the door and waved as he pulled away.

"What I'd like to do with you," said Victoria to herself as the tractor climbed the hill. She watched, waiting to see if there was a backward glance from Danny. The tractor drove from view. She had seen nothing. "You're not a kid, you silly woman. Get a grip of yourself." She bent and pulled up some grass reeds, braiding them as she walked down the hill.

In an adjacent field Jonathan had watched the interaction, having instructed Danny about fixing some fencing in one of the paddocks five minutes earlier. *Bloody flirting again you tart*, he thought. *You truly are a waste of space.* He started striding out, heading towards the yard where the tractor was heading. *Time to give Danny a reality check.*

***

Danny climbed down from the tractor, closed the door and locked it. He heard footsteps approaching from behind him and turned to see Jonathan Fanshaw.

"What the fuck do you think you are doing?" said Jonathan. Danny stood to his full height with a look of confusion on his face. "I told you that some of the paddocks needed fixing." Danny crossed his arms, standing his ground, and looked at his wrist.

"I've finished for the day, Mr Fanshaw. I'll do it first thing tomorrow." Fanshaw walked straight up to Danny, invading his personal space. Danny took a step backwards.

"And what if I told you that it needed doing now."

"Then I'd have to tell you that I'm sorry but I have plans." Danny realised that Jonathan was angry but remained confused as to why. He'd been fine five minutes ago.

"You have plans, do you? And what grand plans does a mere farmhand have?" Danny's arms dropped to his side. His body angled slightly.

"That's none —"

"Oh be quiet, it was a rhetorical question you fool. You do know what rhetorical means, don't you?" Danny was about to speak. "I don't want to hear what your bloody plans are," shouted Jonathan. He lowered his voice. "I do, however, wish to advise you that they will have nothing to do with my sister. She is off-limits. Of no interest to you. You will ignore any advances she may make to you. If I hear any rumours to the contrary then you will be sacked. Do I make myself clear?" Danny looked Jonathan in the eyes, his hands clenched by his sides. "I said, do I make myself clear?" Danny looked Fanshaw up and down.

"You're the boss."

"Fucking right I am. Don't you forget it." Fanshaw spun on his heel, turned his back and walked away. "Get the paddock done in the morning," he shouted. Danny made no reply and watched Fanshaw walk away.

"What a prick," he said quietly as he turned and walked towards one of the barns.

***

Jonathan Fanshaw stormed into the main house and through the entrance hall. Fletcher appeared from a corridor to the right.

"Can I help, Sir?"

"No. I will be in my study and do not wish to be disturbed." Jonathan stormed past Fletcher, entered the study, and slammed the door behind him. Fletcher's only reaction could be seen in briefly raised eyebrows as he walked to the front door and gently closed it. Fletcher had worked for many years with the family, was used to their outbursts and took them in his stride.

Now in his private study, Jonathan felt an air of calm descend. This was his room. A room that nobody entered without his consent, including his father. He walked to the sideboard where he poured himself a measure of malt whisky.

"What to do? What to do?" Jonathan took a seat in a leather recliner and contemplated his next move. The farmhand was simply an annoyance and would have little effect on the life which Victoria would lead. If needed, Jonathan would create circumstances where Danny's work wasn't up to scratch and he would arrange for him to be dismissed. Danny wasn't the problem.

He took a sip from his glass, enjoying the smooth burn as he swallowed. Victoria was the problem. She was a wild child, wilful, lazy, a pain in the arse, but unfortunately she was also the apple of their father's eye. In Jonathan's mind, she brought no value to the estate. He knew that Charles was the key. Charles was educated, had good social standing and liked Victoria. He also had the strength of character to deal with her. Last night's meal went well. It appeared that Victoria and Charles had purposely avoided the group gathering so that they could be together. Yes, Charles was the answer. Jonathan picked up his phone and made a call.

"Hi Charlie, it's Jonathan. How are you doing?"

"I'm fine. Just finished work for the day."

"How splendid. Do you fancy coming over?"

"Again? But I was only there last night."

"I'm sorry. Did you have plans?"

"Nothing I can't cancel."

"Great. Come on over then. I know Victoria would love to see you. She's down at the pub with her friends tonight. I thought we could join them. A more relaxed affair. No airs and graces. We can all have a few pints together."

"Sounds tempting."

"You can stay over. I'll have a room prepared."

"Well, if you're sure?"

"Strike whilst the iron's hot, my friend. We'll all be family soon. You can see Victoria in her natural environment."

"It's a deal. I'll head home, grab some things and I'll come over."

"Shall we say, here for about half seven?"

"Sure."

"See you then." Jonathan terminated the call looking pleased with himself. He walked to the chimney breast and pulled the call cord. Soon after, there was a knock at the door and Fletcher entered.

"Ah, Fletcher. Sorry about before. Can you make sure that one of the guest bedrooms is prepared? Charles Fothergill Jnr will be staying over tonight."

"Yes, Sir."

"That will be all," said Jonathan dismissively. Fletcher left, closing the door gently behind him. "If you won't be proactive yourself, you little bitch, then I'll force you." Jonathan raised his glass in the air and then swallowed its remaining contents.

***

Victoria watched a small red car climbing the hill towards her. The car looked familiar. Her mood dipped when she realised that it was Melthrop. The car slowed on its approach and she could see his beaming face. He raised his hand, slowed and stopped. Victoria halted.

"Good evening, Victoria. How are you?" Melthrop stopped the engine and looked up at her from the driver's seat. Victoria looked down at his balding pate, with its thin comb-over, noting that his eyes were focused on her breasts. She leant forward, resting her arms on the car door, giving the lecherous Melthrop a clear view of a golden pendant resting on her cleavage.

"Well, I'm fine thank you, Roger. How's Mrs Melthrop?" Melthrop blushed, dragging his eyes from Victoria's chest to her face.

"She is well, thank you. I haven't seen you at a service for some time."

"True. I haven't been there."

"We all benefit from the love and support of the Lord God in our lives."

"I currently get all the love and support that I need, Roger. I'm doing fine. I take it that God and Mrs Melthrop are looking after you?" Victoria smiled down at Melthrop, whose eyes again drifted to her bosom. She loved toying with this simple man, finding him easy to embarrass but wondered what Mrs Melthrop saw in him.

Melthrop coughed, feeling sweat gathering on his brow and the start of an erection in his pants. He knew that Victoria was a wanton spirit but felt it his duty, as it was with all his parishioners, to guide her soul. He also knew that she attracted him as a man but also challenged him as a devout Christian. The devil was casting his net today.

"All is well in the house of God," he stuttered. "Anyway, I have to go. I'm sure that you are busy." He started the engine and pulled away. "Cheerio," he shouted, waving his hand out the window. He looked in his rearview mirror to see Victoria laughing. *I'll need to speak to Sir David about her. She is a little flirt in need of some moral guidance,* thought Melthrop.

Melthrop drove up to the small church and parked outside its gates. He dabbed his brow and adjusted his trousers before climbing out of the car. The church door was open and he knew that Mrs Melthrop would be inside cleaning. He took in the majesty of the ancient stone building as his shoes crunched up the gravelled path. Pastor Melthrop entered the quiet cool embrace of the building and felt immediately calmed. The pews were empty, the dark oak benches facing to the front. Pews that in years gone by had been full but now on service days would be lucky to seat even ten people.

Sunlight permeated through the stained glass windows, casting fractured colours upon the large stone-flagged flooring. Within the apse, replacing a polished candlestick, Mrs Melthrop was standing dressed in her usual floral dress. He approached her silently. She turned at the last minute.

"Oh. It's only you, Roger. I thought I heard something."

"Surprise." He embraced her and kissed her, one hand drifting down to cup her bottom, his ardour unquenched. Mrs Melthrop pushed him back.

"Roger. What's got into you?" He laughed. "Here of all places. How could you?" Mrs Melthrop turned to a wooden cross hanging on one wall. "Sorry, Father." Roger reached forward again to have his hand slapped away. "Stop it. Now." His visage altered to that of a chastened child.

"It was only a bit of fun."

"Well, you should know better. Keep your hands to yourself. Especially here. Anyone could walk in. You're supposed to be a pillar of the community."

"Sorry, Dear."

"It's not me you should be sorry to. It's him." She nodded to the cross. Roger looked at his wife and stepped back.

"I'll make my apologies in the sacristy." He turned and walked away from her into his private room. Mrs Melthrop returned to her cleaning and began humming her favourite hymn.

***

Rachel waited in the cafe. The murmur of private conversations drifted around her. She smiled as the door opened and Jamal Kaur walked in. He smiled in return and walked over to her table.

"Hi, Rach."

"I've ordered coffee for us. Do you want anything to eat?" Jamal checked his watch and sat down at the table.

"Wish I had the time. You know how it is. Meetings upon meetings. You ever miss it?"

"Not at all. Best thing I did."

"No regrets?"

"Nope." They paused their conversation as the coffee was delivered by a waitress, who Rachel thanked.

"What about work? How's that going?"

"It's good. There's plenty of work out there and clients are prepared to pay good money for results." Jamal sipped his coffee.

"Good. Sorry to cut to the chase but what can I do for you?"

"David Fanshaw got in contact with me. I've taken on the cold case."

"I thought he would. You know that it's a non-runner? We've tried everything that we could. I passed your details on so that he could maybe get some closure from someone independent from the police. You know, someone with experience, who could tell him everything has been tried."

"Thanks for the referral. I do appreciate it. Which brings me to —"

"Go on."

"To give him that closure, I'd like to be able to review all the evidence. All the evidence that your teams gathered."

"But it's all held on the Holmes system."

"I know. That's the favour. Can you get me the access?" Jamal automatically started shaking his head. "Hear me out, please. You gave my details to Fanshaw and started this ball rolling. You want me to get him out of your hair. This could be us breaking new ground. You are breaking new ground. A cold case review, by a professional team, who are not utilising overstretched police resources."

"I can't give you access to the HOLMES system. You know that. It holds records of all the cases that we are running."

"How about just downloading the Fanshaw case to a drive? Any bits that you can. Anything will help." Jamal was now frowning. Rachel watched him thinking.

"I'd need to have an overview of your investigation."

"Agreed."

"Any breakthrough, I'd need to know."

"Yes."

"You'd need to sign a memorandum of understanding. Your team would need to sign non-disclosure documents. Even then I don't know if the Force will go for it."

"Convince them. Forgive me but, it's a dead cause. You got nowhere with it. Let me finally put it to bed. The Force has nothing to lose." Kaur's telephone rang. He answered.

"I'll ring you back in two." He terminated the call and looked at Rachel. "I need to go. Leave it with me. I'll do my best." Rachel smiled.

"That's good enough for me. Speak soon."

"I'll be in contact." Jamal stood up and left the cafe.

***

18th June 1997

The Red Lion's doors were open for business. The public house had been a constant in the village for as long as anyone could remember; mainly frequented by locals, it remained a focal point for the villagers. The pub sign swayed gently in the breeze. Wooden tables and benches provided seating outside the front of the pub. Attached to the beautiful stone building were bright petunia and lobelia filled hanging baskets. The tables were empty as Victoria approached but she expected that Tanya would be inside ordering their drinks. Sure enough, as she drew closer, Tanya walked out carrying three pints.

"Vic, grab one will you?" Victoria took one of the pints and set it down on a table. "Mark's come over to visit," said Tanya, explaining the three pints. Mark was Tanya's brother who worked as a trainee solicitor in Fenchurch. In Victoria's opinion, he was a good lad, certainly not eye candy, but good fun nonetheless.

"Great. Is he staying over?"

"We'll be getting too pissed for him to drive so, yes. He can squeeze into my spare room."

"Good. I've seen Danny. He'll be down soon."

"Brilliant. Am I looking OK?" asked Tanya.

"You look terrific as usual." Mark walked out of the pub to the table. At six feet four inches, he still seemed to tower above Tanya and Victoria. With dark hair carefully parted to the right, square spectacles and a crisp white shirt, he couldn't shake off the image of his job in Victoria's opinion.

"Hi, Victoria. How's things?"

"Same as ever. Avoiding work at all costs and living the life of a lady."

"Love life?"

"What's that? My dick of a brother is trying to foist me off on Charles Fothergill. That will not be happening." Unconsciously, Victoria rubbed her arm where the bruising was appearing. "I'm not ready to settle down yet. I need to get out more. By more, I mean away from here." She turned to Tanya. "How about Fenchurch next week? Out for tea then pubs and clubs?"

"Fuck the tea. Pubs and clubs all the way" replied Tanya.

"Oi, oi," interrupted Mark. "Incoming." Victoria and Tanya turned to see Danny walking towards them. Dressed in jeans and a plain T-shirt with damp hair pushed back, they both appreciated his lithe physique.

"Hey, Mark. Didn't know you were back," said Danny.

"Only for the night. Good to see you, mate." Mark drained his pint. "Same again? My round."

"Yes," replied Victoria and a thumbs up from Tanya, who was drinking. "Dan, pint of Taylor's?"

"Please."

"Grab a seat, Dan," said Tanya, patting the bench next to her. Victoria flashed Tanya a frown to which Tanya responded by sticking her tongue out. None of this went unnoticed by Danny.

"Busy day at work?" Tanya asked Danny.

"Always busy. Nice to get a night off. Back to it tomorrow."

"Not a late night then?"

"See how it goes. If I have to work with a hangover then so be it. It won't be the first time." Mark returned to the table, carrying a tray of drinks. Everyone grabbed their own.

"Nibbles?" asked Victoria.

"Couldn't carry everything. Back in two." Mark returned, holding the tray once again. It now contained eight shots of spirit, some crisps, peanuts and obligatory pork scratchings. Victoria leaned in towards Tanya.

"It's always the quiet ones," said Victoria.

"Who cares? As long as he's paying then I'm drinking. What we got, Mark?"

"No idea. Asked Alan to surprise us." Mark doled two shots to each person. "Bottoms up." He necked his first as everyone selected and joined suit. The second shot swiftly followed the first.

"Must have cost you a fortune?" said Victoria, whose foot had now found Danny's under the table.

"Not at all," replied Mark. "I put it all on your tab." Victoria looked at him astounded. Danny and Tanya burst out laughing.

"Cheeky bastard." She joined in the laughter. Dan had moved his foot away and was looking at Tanya over the top of his pint. She smiled at him.

"This is going to get messy," said Victoria as she placed the empty shot glasses back on the tray.

***

Richard Westbrook and Patrick Carmichael were sitting at the bar, in The Red Lion, talking about grass and sheep. On the face of it, they were an unlikely duo. Richard towered over Patrick and was at least ten years Patrick's junior. Where Richard was thick-set and large boned, Patrick was lithe and wiry. However, both had lived in the village for years and had formulated their friendship over a pint. It was not often that they couldn't be seen in The Red Lion on a Friday night, propping up the bar and setting the world to rights. Within the village, Richard was responsible for the upkeep of the church grounds, whilst Patrick, now retired, still dabbled in the care of the livestock around the estate. Both were employed by the estate. The door to the bar opened, and both men turned to see Mark leading his party.

"Here they come," said Richard

"Aye," replied Patrick. They turned back to the bar.

"They'll be pissed already."

"Suppose they will." Victoria and Tanya stumbled in giggling.

"Same again?" asked Danny, whose cheeks now had a flush to them.

"Indeed, young man," shouted Victoria. Danny approached the bar where the landlord was already preparing their drinks. Danny nodded his thanks and took hold of a pint.

"Dan," said Patrick, nodding a greeting.

"Patrick."

"Go steady there, son. She's well above your pay grade." Danny winked and smiled then carried the drinks to his group.

"He'll regret it," said Patrick to Richard.

"Maybe so, but she leads him on and he's only young."

"True, my friend. To be fair, she's a fine-looking lady." Richard turned to look at the group.

"She is that but she'll be in a right bloody state before the night's out. Another one, mate?"

"Don't mind if I do."

"Same again please, Alan," said Richard to the landlord.

An hour later, the effect of the alcohol was taking its toll on the group. The pub was now busy with locals holding both quiet and rowdy conversations. Music played in the background, coming the jukebox, and the clack of pool balls echoed across the room. Mark returned from the toilet once again.

"Once I break the seal I can't stop going," he said.

"It's your age," slurred Tanya, squinting towards the pool table. "Is that Jamie?" she asked, looking towards a young man who was playing.

"Jamie?" asked Victoria.

"He's a copper that I met a few weeks ago in Fenchurch. He was a nice guy. We've been texting."

"Texting him?"

"Yeah, he's a nice lad." The male looked over and smiled. Tanya stood up, slightly unsteady on her feet. "I'll say hello." Tanya walked over to Jamie.

Richard and Patrick had finished at the bar and walked towards the exit. Patrick nudged Richard and gestured to Victoria who had shimmied up next to Danny.

"This is all going to go pear-shaped," said Patrick.

"Let's go and leave them to it." They walked out into the evening air and parted company. As they walked away, two men approached the pub from a nearby lane. Richard squinted and recognised the figure of Jonathan Fanshaw. He didn't recognise the other man.

***

Danny watched Tanya, paying little attention to Mark who was extolling the virtues of monetary investment. Victoria noted Danny's look.

"She's a little devil, that one." She said, nodding towards Tanya. "You can do better than her."

"Meaning?" asked Danny. Mark continued talking, oblivious that no one was listening.

"She's been texting him for weeks. Apparently, he's a good one," continued Victoria, using her hands to indicate Tanya's speech. "Possibly off the market. Our Tanya, that is." Danny looked disappointed. "However, yours truly is free and available."

"For me? I thought you were only being a flirt." Victoria moved closer to Danny.

"Oh, I can be so much more than that." She leaned in to kiss him.

As if on cue the pub door flew open and Charles and Jonathan stumbled in. Charles immediately halted as he saw Victoria.

"Oh, excuse us," said Jonathan to the room. "We are a little bit tiddly." He closed the door gently, patted it and turned back to the room, giggling. "Is my sister here?" Victoria moved quickly away from Danny and towards Tanya and Jamie. Charles' eyes bored into Danny, who stood up. Victoria pushed Tanya to one side and embraced Jamie, choosing him as her protector. The pub exploded. Charles ran at Danny who braced himself as their bodies collided. Tanya grabbed Victoria's hair and pulled her head back.

"What the fuck do you think you are doing?!" shouted Tanya. Victoria's hands flew to her head as she screamed aloud, wrenched free and slapped Tanya across the face. They fell to the floor. Jamie stepped back, a smile on his face. He turned to the man next to him.

"Ten pounds on Tanya to win."

Danny pushed Charles back, not ready for the left jab that collided with his nose. His head snapped back as the jab was swiftly followed by an exuberant right hook which dropped him to the floor, immediately followed by Charles.

Charles jumped on top of Danny and wrapped his hands around his throat. Charles yelled.

"DO YOU WANT TO DIE."

Danny responded with both hands slapping either side of Charles' neck, colliding with the brachial plexus. Charles' eyes rolled back as he collapsed and Danny roared as he pushed Charles off and bounced to his feet. The women were rolling and screaming as Tanya landed a solid punch to Victoria's chin. Jonathan ran over to Charles, pushing Danny away.

"ENOUGH." An axe handle slammed down on the pool table top, its thwack splitting the air. It hit again. "GET OUT!" The landlord grabbed Danny, pushing him towards the door. "ALL OF YOU OUT." Charles looked up, still dazed.

"I'm taking him, Alan. Don't worry." Jonathan had sobered and looked around at the faces looking at him. The room had gone silent. "I'm sorry." The incensed face of Alan looked down at him,

"Out." A direct order that could not be misinterpreted. Jamie leaned down at the women who were now separate and breathless after the exertion.

"Come on ladies," he grinned, "you can continue your fight over me another time." He lifted up Victoria, as Tanya stood up.

"She's no fuckin competition for me," said Victoria, who leaned in and kissed Jamie.

"BITCH," screamed Tanya, moving forwards. Mark stepped in as a barrier. He wrapped Tanya in his arms and lifted her.

"Out," said Mark carrying her to the door and leaving. Tables and chairs lay strewn on the floor.

"LAST ORDERS," shouted Alan. "I've had enough of tonight." He straightened the furniture and went back behind the bar to serve the last die-hards. The vocal volume in the building was now louder as the customers discussed the event.

***

Outside, Mark had led Tanya away. She was holding her head and crying, clearly upset by the incident. Mark fired a disgusted look in Victoria's direction. Jonathan spoke to Charles quietly and walked back towards Victoria, who was standing between Danny and Jamie. He looked at them both and addressed Danny.

"You. I warned you before and I'm telling you now to fuck off." Danny tried replying. "Do not even try. You are my employee. Go." Danny walked away. Jonathan turned to Jamie.

"Who the fuck are you?" Jamie grinned back at Jonathan.

"Jamie."

"Well, Jamie. Unfortunately, this lady," he looked Victoria up and down with disgust, "happens to be my sister. She is off-limits to you so kindly leave. I am sorry if she has misled you but she is betrothed to my friend over there."

"He's a policeman," said Victoria.

"I don't care if he's WINSTON FUCKING CHURCHILL," yelled Jonathan. "Time for you to go." Jamie backed away with his hands up.

"I've only just met her, mate. She's all fucking yours." Jamie walked away towards a row of cars parked on the road. Jonathan addressed Victoria.

"Now, you are coming home with me. With us. Look at the state of you. You are an embarrassment."

"Fuck off, you prick. I'll go where I bloody like." Victoria turned, wobbled, gained her balance and tottered towards the lane. Jonathan watched her go and walked back to Charles.

***

Roger Melthrop looked across at his wife who was embroidering a cross on a sampler which she was completing for the church. Their sparse living room contained simple furniture and had little in the way of adornments. The television stood silently in one corner and was used for little more than catching up with the news. Mrs Melthrop (Audrey) was Roger's rock. Devout as anyone could be, she provided the religious support that Roger needed when his fears and doubts emerged.

Roger had entered the ministry at a young age and had progressed well. He felt that his partnership with Audrey had helped him immensely and he looked on her with fondness. Like a man would his sister. *Is this what life has come to?* thought Roger. *Evenings in silence with knitting Nancy completing yet another piece for the church. I am bloody bored.* Melthrop's mind wandered to his meeting with Victoria on the hill this afternoon. *I bet you don't get bored, Victoria*. He looked at Audrey. *I bet you do what you like*. Roger's mind pictured Victoria and her ample bosom. He couldn't remember the last time he'd ever seen Audrey's cleavage, never mind got anywhere near it. Roger felt unsettled. He stood up.

"I'm going out for a walk, dear."

"Are you sure, Roger? It's late," replied Audrey, who did not even raise her head from her work.

"I need to clear my head. I'll be fine."

"OK. Don't be too long."

***

Victoria had decided that she hated her brother. He was a conceited, self-important dickhead as far as she was concerned. Still influenced by alcohol, she knew that she wasn't being completely rational, and her spinning head was not helping either. She tripped, screamed and fell forward, ripping her shirt open as she did so.

"What a shit night," she exclaimed, as she pushed herself to her knees. Victoria looked up to see the moon high and bright, its patina silvering the skin on her chest and stomach. "Come on, girl." She stood up, gained her balance and pulled her mobile phone from her back pocket, flicking its torch on. To her left was an open field, and to the right a high blackthorn hedge. Ahead a dark tunnel created by overarching trees. A passage that the moon would fail to pierce. Emboldened by alcohol and comfortable within the village environs, Victoria walked forward, the minimal torch beam lighting her route. Victoria entered the tunnel mouth, immediately noticing a dampening of sound. Not silence. The countryside is never silent. Purely an alteration in noise.

She peered forward into the darkness. Her torchlight reflected back in two eyes that swiftly moved. A rustling in the undergrowth as a creature skittered away. She pulled her shirt around her with her free arm. Victoria could hear her heartbeat and realised her breathing had quickened. Her innate human response to darkness and the memory of imagined horror stories and films. She pushed on, knowing that the tunnel was short, and was rewarded by the nascent glow of light ahead. Pushing her hair from her eyes, Victoria felt the dampness of cooling sweat on her brow. Reaching the end of the canopy, Victoria stepped free from the oppressive atmosphere and stopped to take a breath.

"Get a grip," she said, looking back to the tunnel. Snap! She spun round. The sound of a branch breaking. Her heart hammered in her chest. Torch pointed outwards, she could see nothing beyond its beam. Victoria listened. Nothing untoward. She looked up at the waxing moon. *Bright enough,* she thought, switching her torch off. Her eyes adjusted to the ambient lighting. She saw the path as a dark line before her, its dried soils leading to a bench which she knew lay ahead. Victoria continued walking, continued listening, imagining footsteps, convinced she was being watched. She checked her watch and called out, "Is someone there?".

"Nearly eleven," said a familiar voice to her right. She turned. A figure stepped from the shadow of a tree. Victoria jumped back and screamed.

"What the hell are you doing?" *Slap*! A hand collided with her cheek. She grunted. Fell. Her head collided with a rock. She moaned in pain. Excruciating pain. Victoria looked up at the stars, at the moon. A familiar face loomed into view.

"You," she mumbled. Blood vessels ruptured. Her hand flew to her head. Victoria moaned, then felt nothing more.

Chapter 6

"I'll take you up to your room," said Sir David, as he led Rachel towards a central staircase. "I trust that the stairs won't cause you any trouble."

"Not at all, Sir David."

"David, please. No formalities required."

"David it is." Rachel smiled at David and they both slowly ascended the stairs.

"Most of the bedrooms are situated on the first floor. I have taken the liberty of placing you in a room near Victoria's old room."

"You've kept her room?"

"Yes, I couldn't bear not to keep it at first and then naturally, I haven't had the heart to change it. It's all as it was when she left us, though I have it cleaned once a week. We have plenty of other rooms for guests but they are few and far between these days." Sir David paused in thought. Rachel waited. He used the rail to steady himself, then continued climbing. "Please feel free to spend some time in there. It may help you get to know her."

"Thank you."

"Here we are," Sir David opened the guest bedroom door. "The Red Bedroom." Rachel entered into a room which was dominated by a large mahogany four-poster bed. Different shades of red had been used for both painted walls, bedding, cushions and throws. A window looked out onto the grounds and flowers had thoughtfully been placed in a vase on a small side table.

"Wow. I don't know if I dare touch anything."

"Don't be silly. Make yourself comfortable. I want you to feel at home. Let the house soak into your bones. Fall in love with it as I have." Sir David pointed to another door. "You have an en-suite in there. Anything else you need simply ask." Rachel opened the bathroom door and peeked in.

"Beautiful," she said.

"All the original fittings." Sir David was proud of his house. He handed her a key.

"For your bedroom. No one will enter it unless you request them to do so. All of your private papers and files will be secure, don't worry."

"Internet?"

"There is. The password is in the file next to your bed. Fletcher will look after all your needs. Come and go as you please."

"Thank you." Sir David checked his watch.

"Right, I have some work to do. I've arranged coffee in the lounge. We can finalise things there, then I'll leave you to it." Sir David left the room and headed towards the staircase. *A man used to being in charge,* thought Rachel. She followed him, closing the bedroom door behind her.

On entering the lounge, Rachel could smell the aroma of coffee emanating from the beautiful chinaware on the side table.

"Please, take a seat," said Sir David. "I'll pour." He continued talking as he prepared the drinks. Rachel chose to sit on the sofa. "Did you manage to get anywhere with Sergeant Kaur?"

"Yes. We have spoken. He'll be assisting me with the things I need as much as he can." Sir David walked over and passed Rachel her coffee. He settled himself in an armchair opposite her.

"Well, he bloody should be. Any problems with him then let me know."

"I'm not anticipating any. He's been more than helpful."

"Even so."

"I'll bear it in mind." Rachel took a sip of coffee, enjoying its roasted bitterness. "My initial thoughts that I'd like you to consider."

"Go on."

"I believe that the estate – you – own some private cottages in the village."

"I do. Most of them are rented out."

"Meaning that you have some houses free?"

"I believe that there are a couple free at the moment. They may need a little bit of work but they are habitable. Is my house not good enough for you?"

"Not for me, David. For one of my team." Sir David looked confused. "I'd like one of my team to move into the village whilst we conduct our investigation." She held up a hand, stalling David's next question. "As an undercover investigator. Another normal member of the public, but for me, they would be my eyes and ears on the ground."

"I could arrange that."

"It's important that only you and I know about it though, David. You can't tell anyone. Not Fletcher, your son, your closest friend. Not anyone. It would be our secret. I need someone to get into the community. Hear what their thoughts are. Work out who is who. Who's a suspect and who isn't."

"I understand. I'll arrange it. Anything else."

"Can you employ a new gardener and handyman for the estate?"

"Not for the estate, no. Too obvious and they'd have to go through a full interview process. The man who looks after the village greens, paths, hall and such like has moved away though. He's been meaning to for a while and we haven't found a replacement yet. Would that vacancy assist you?"

"Perfect. We'll take it," Rachel smiled.

"You've got a grip of this haven't you?" said Sir David. "I knew it."

"Let's see where it takes us, David, but yes, I'm laying some solid foundations."

"Terrific." Sir David checked his watch and stood up. "I'm sorry but I need to go. Can you let yourself out?"

"Yes." Rachel stood up. "I'll move in some of my belongings later this week."

"Good. We'll talk then." Sir David turned and placed his coffee cup down. He left the room with a spritely step. Rachel looked around, taking in all the grandeur.

"Now, all the hard work starts," she said, as she walked towards the lounge door.

***

Emily parked her car and walked towards the small cut-through which would take her to Hanson's Park. Though confident that she had not been followed, she halted by the snicket entrance and scanned her surroundings to make sure. The roads were quiet and no one was on foot in the vicinity. A couple of cars and a van were parked on the residential street and had been there for some time. She had waited in her car, to ensure that they were empty, before getting out. Emily assumed that one of the vehicles would have one of her handlers secreted within the back, monitoring her movements towards the meeting location. Emily was now well versed in the tradecraft skills, utilised at every meeting, which were used to ensure the safety of all. She entered the small path and headed to the park.

Hanson's Park was situated behind a residential housing estate and comprised a grass-running track, a hard basketball court and a children's play area. Dressed in joggers and a T-shirt, Emily headed to the track and began walking around. A couple of people were already punishing their bodies with morning exercise. Emily held the outside of the track thereby giving them the benefit of an unobstructed inside lane.

Everything looked ready to her and sure enough, on glancing to her right, she spotted Trimble strolling towards the track with a dog on a lead. He headed towards a bench, settled upon it and took a tennis ball out of his pocket. Emily continued walking the circuit as she again checked the environment. Now with Trimble to her left, she saw that he was throwing the ball for the dog who was retrieving it. The tread of footsteps grew louder behind her as one of the runners approached. The runner moved to lane five and Emily continued as the runner approached.

"All clear, Heather," said a woman's voice as the runner passed Emily. Emily watched as the lycra-clad female pulled ahead. Trimble remained in place as Emily cornered a bend when, as if suddenly recognising her, he stood up and waved to her. She waved back and walked from the track towards him.

"I didn't recognise you at first. You caught the fitness bug?"

"I sure have," replied Emily. Codewords were exchanged, and it was safe to meet.

"Walk with me," said Trimble. The dog returned with the ball and he put it back on its lead. "How was last night?"

"Same old. We all drank too much but had a laugh."

"Everyone behave themselves?"

"Yes."

"Good. That's how leaving parties should be."

"Leaving parties? Who's leaving?" Trimble stopped and looked at Emily.

"That would be you. We need to transfer you to another station."

"But —"

"No buts. Keep walking." Trimble continued on his route. Emily followed. "I know that it's not ideal but we have an important job for you."

"I'm settled here, though."

"I know you are and it's great that you've fitted in. You know the job though. We have an agreement."

"You and that fucking agreement." Trimble spun round and looked at Emily.

"Would you prefer the alternative? That fucking agreement and me is what has kept you in this job." *For how long*, thought Emily.

"Where are you sending me?"

"On shift in Fenchurch."

"Why there? What do I say to my shift?"

"We'll cover all that. I've got a meeting room booked. The car's around the corner."

"What's the job?"

"I need you to get to know someone. An officer who works at Fenchurch."

***

Jamie rolled over in bed on hearing the bedroom door opening and turned to face his wife.

"Morning, darling. Cup of tea?" Tanya was wearing a long T-shirt and carrying two mugs. He sat up in bed and accepted one of the mugs as Tanya sat down carefully beside him.

"Thanks, love. Hangover?"

"Surprisingly not. You?"

"I feel a bit rough but not too bad. Open the curtains will ya?" asked Jamie, taking Tanya's tea from her hands. Tanya dutifully stood back up and opened the curtains to a beautiful day outside. The sun beamed down on their view of the Yorkshire Wolds and a slight breeze gently nudged the branches of the rowan tree in their garden. Tanya climbed into bed.

"A rare day off together," said Tanya. "What shall we do today?"

"What do you fancy?" Jamie took a slurp from his cup. "Beautiful," he said aloud.

"What about a trip into the city? We could grab a bite to eat, and do some shopping. Catch the train, if you don't fancy driving." Jamie's phone pinged. He lifted it from the bedside table and saw that a text message arrived. He read it and frowned.

"Please don't say that it's bloody work. They never leave you alone."

"Now, now, sweetheart. Don't be like that," said Jamie climbing out of bed, "it's not work but I do need to make a quick call." He walked out of the bedroom, pulling the door closed behind him.

"Remember that we have plans," shouted Tanya, at the closed door. She placed her cup down, climbed out of bed, and walked over to the full length mirror. Tanya stretched, pulled her shirt tight, and checked her side profile.

"Good for your age, Tan." Tanya took gym classes, looked slim, and was still happy with the boob job that Jamie had paid for a couple of years ago. With no children to run her ragged, Tanya led a relaxed life encompassing self care, meals out and holidays. Jamie earned the money for them and Tanya was happy with that. She stripped off her shirt, tossed it on the bed and walked into the ensuite to shower. She was looking forward to a day of shopping.

Five minutes later she walked back into the room wrapped in a towel. Jamie was already fully dressed and putting his Rolex watch on.

"Not showering?" she asked, releasing her blonde locks from her turbaned head.

"I already grabbed one in the main bathroom. Get a shifty on. Plans have changed."

"What do you mean changed? Why the rush?" Tanya brushed her hair through.

"I'm gonna take you across to Barnston this morning. Take a look at the sea. It'll clear our heads."

"Barnston? I'm not bloody shopping there. It's a shit-hole." Jamie looked at Tanya as if she was a naughty child. "I mean, the shops are a bit naff aren't they?" Jamie walked over and placed his arms around Tanya.

"How about we nip over there this morning? We'll drop in at home on the way back, grab our overnight bags and we'll have a night out in Fenchurch tonight. Stay over, come back tomorrow."

"Where will we stay?" asked Tanya, warming up to the idea.

"I'll book us into the Hilton. We can have dinner, tour around the pubs and clubs if you want. What do you think?"

"It's a deal," squealed Tanya. Jamie pulled gently at the top of her towel.

"Get changed quick then. We're setting off in ten."

"I'll do my makeup in the car." Jamie walked out of the room taking his phone from his back pocket.

"I'll get the car ready." Jamie went downstairs as he made a telephone call. "Don't worry, I'll be there within the hour," he said to the person on the other end.

***

Jamie and Tanya were standing in a glass elevator, descending into the small shopping centre.

"Look," said Jamie. 'They've got a Debenhams in here. You can take a look around there. Next is over there, Laura Ashley Topshop. What more do ya need?"

"You haven't got a bloody clue, have you?" The lift doors opened on the ground floor and they stepped out into the hubbub of noise from other shoppers. Jamie checked his watch, leaned in, pecked Tanya on the cheek and slipped some banknotes into her hand.

"There's two hundred. Spoil yourself. Take a look around. I need to nip to see someone. I'll be back soon." Without waiting for a reply, Jamie walked away and left the centre by the main doors. Tanya looked at his back as he departed, checked the cash and put it in her bag.

"Why should I expect anything different," she said to herself.

***

Jamie strode up the busy precinct, passing shops and navigating through pedestrians, none of which barred his way. He looked to be a man on a mission and people naturally parted to let him by. Turning right at the top of town, he headed past the police station where a marked car had illuminated its blue lights and shot off to a job. Jamie checked his phone, confirmed the address and headed towards the rows of town centre housing that he could see ahead of him. It didn't take him long to reach the houses.

He stopped, checked behind himself, then turned into a side street where he halted again and waited. Jamie watched cars pass by on the main road and a couple of pedestrians wandered passed. Jamie wasn't known here but he was not a fool and didn't take chances. Although confident he was not being followed, he now took a circuitous route heading towards his end destination.

Five minutes later, Jamie was looking up a street which contained neat terraced and semi-detached houses. Cars were parked on one side of the street and a couple of kids were kicking a football towards the far end of the road. The house he was looking for was on the left. Outside it stood a teenage boy. Jamie approached him.

"I've been asked to visit." The boy looked surprised but recognising the given code words indicated that Jamie should follow him. They both walked to the front door of the house. The boy entered first, followed by Jamie.

The strong sweet smell of cannabis assaulted Jamie's senses. He smiled. *Quality grow*, thought Jamie. He passed the electric cupboard, noticing that the supply had been bypassed.

"Where is he?" the boy pointed towards the kitchen, then bolted upstairs out of sight. Jamie kicked the front door shut behind him and closed the electric cupboard door. *Slack,* he thought, walking through the small hallway and opening the kitchen door. The aroma of food being cooked smelled delicious.

Standing at the cooker was a tall Asian male who was flipping food in a pan. He turned and looked at Jamie as he entered, smiled, and removed the pan from the heat. The kitchen was dominated by a large table with two benches on either side. Window blinds lowered, the room was illuminated only by the orange tinged glow of dim lighting. Now that the sizzling had stopped, the hum of a fridge penetrated the air.

"I've been sent to sort an issue out," said Jamie, lifting a carving knife from a work surface.

"You are Jamie?"

"Yes."

"You are too late."

"How come?"

"We resolved the issue ourselves. Now we have a different issue. Come with me." The male beckoned Jamie further into the room. He followed, unconsciously grasping the knife tightly. *This doesn't feel right,* thought Jamie, *What the hell is going on?* The Asian male stopped by a door at the back of the kitchen and pointed. "He's in there. You won't need that." The male gently took the knife from Jamie's hand. Jamie noted that the he was wearing blue disposable gloves. He pushed on the door and entered what he discovered was a downstairs bathroom. The smell hit him first, making him gag. He coughed.

"Fucking hell, man. Do you ever clean this place?" Jamie covered his nose and mouth, "I'm not working for bloody Dinorod." He froze. A clothed leg hung limply over the bath side, poking out from under a drawn shower curtain. Jamie reached forward and pulled back the curtain. He screamed and jumped back. Lying in the bath was a male, covered in blood, his face pulped beyond recognition, his arms broken. Jamie backed out of the room and slammed the door. He turned to the chef. "What have you done?"

"Sorted the problem," replied the man. "Now, he's your problem."

"Is he fuck. You've brought me to a bloody murder scene. I can't believe it. I can't be here." Jamie pushed the man aside. "I need to leave. I need to get out." He felt panic rise. "What if the house is being watched? I can't be here. Have been here. Is there a back door?"

"But the body. You need to sort?" replied the chef. "That's what they said."

"Not a bloody chance. He's your bloody problem. I've never been here. You have never seen me." He fronted the chef, face to face. "Back door?" The chef nodded to the right. Jamie turned, entered a small corridor, covered his hand with his sleeve and reached for the door handle. He opened the back door and peeked out. All was clear. He listened intently. Nothing. Sweat drenched his back and armpits. He looked back at the chef who was watching him.

"You've never seen me." Jamie stepped out into the backyard and walked to a back gate which was locked. He vaulted the waist-high wall into the rear small alleyway, landing in a small pile of dog excrement. He didn't even notice as he made his escape through some alleys to an adjacent road. Back in the kitchen, the chef made a phone call.

"He has been, and gone." He listened intently. "I have a knife that he was holding. He wore no gloves. He entered through the front and left out the back." The chef listened again. "Yes, I will. Are the cleaners on the way?" He paused. "Good, the body is already starting to smell."

***

Jamie entered a neighbouring street from the rear alley, rapidly breathing and heavily sweating. He was panicking. His head and body were in flight mode.

He turned towards the town and walked swiftly away from the area. He tried not to run. Ahead he could see the red bricks of the police station, a location in which he should feel comfortable and familiar, but not today.

He turned left and cut down a street which ran parallel to the main road. He checked his phone. No calls or texts from Tanya. Jamie pulled out his burner phone. Nothing on there either. *What the fuck are they up to?* He thought. *Why did they send me there?* He paused, and wiped his brow, unsure of what to do next. Breathing deeply, Jamie tried to calm his mind and body. His burner phone rang. Hands shaking, he answered. A female spoke to him.

"You didn't complete your job."

"MY JOB! That's not my fucking job. What the hell do you think you are doing?" An old lady walked past, frowning at Jamie. He raised a hand in apology, turned away and lowered his voice. "He's bloody killed someone. Do you know that? I should have bloody arrested him."

"And yet you haven't, Jamie."

"No, because that would put me up to my neck in it. I can't be involved in that."

"But now you are involved, Jamie."

"Fuck you." Jamie threw the handset on the ground, stamped on it, jumped on it, and then ground it into the tarmac. Like a man possessed he knelt, searched through the smashed handset and peeled the SIM card from the broken remnants. Looking left he saw a bin, picked up the phone carcass and threw it in. The SIM card he pocketed as he walked quickly away, heading towards the shopping arcade and back to Tanya.

***

Tanya was standing looking at her reflection in a mirror, trying to decide whether to buy the jeans or the miniskirt, both of which she was holding. She saw Jamie appear behind her and watched him close in on her.

"What do you think, lovey?"

"We need to leave." Tanya turned, noting Jamie's damp hairline and flushed face.

"You OK, love? You don't look good."

"Now," he repeated. "Where's menswear?"

"Up the escalator." Jamie took both of Tanya's items and guided her by her elbow towards the escalator.

"I need some things." Tanya looked at him, unsure what to say. He smiled at her. "Nothing's wrong." He held up the jeans and skirt. "I'll buy you both." Tanya smiled. They alighted at the top of the ramp. Jamie let go of Tanya and walked to the men's department. He scanned a rail and grabbed a T-shirt in his size, then did the same with a pair of jeans. Tanya followed meekly behind, confusion on her face. "Shoes," said Jamie to himself. He walked around and spotted the shoe department. "Brogues, loafers, boots, slippers," again to himself. Jamie selected some slip-ons and headed for the tills. He grabbed a cap from a mannequin as he passed it. "Come on, Tan," he said, "we're paying and going." Jamie approached an empty till where a female assistant was waiting.

"These, please."

"That's great, sir." Jamie scanned the floor nervously.

"Would you like your hangers?"

"No."

"Can I interest you in any of our reduced products?" The lady gestured to the products which were displayed on the cashier desk.

"No, love. Thank you but I'm in a rush," Jamie turned to Tanya, "my partner will pay." Jamie handed Tanya his wallet. "Are there any toilets nearby?"

"Straight out the main doors, across the first floor. They are clearly signed."

"Thank you, pet. I'll take that carrier bag and," Jamie reached over the counter and grabbed an empty bag, "I'll see you at the car," Jamie said to Tanya. He walked away from the desk.

Jamie shoved the new clothes in the carrier as he left the shop. He stopped, saw the toilet signs and headed there. Entering the men's, his nose was assaulted by the odours of human waste with the pervading scent of citrus in the background. The urinals were all in use. Luckily there was a free cubicle. He entered, shutting the door behind him and securing it with a flimsy lock which had seen better days. He looked in the toilet, almost choking at the state of a bowl, which an inconsiderate customer had failed to clean after their use. He slammed the seat down and started to strip.

***

Tanya leant against the car, Debenhams bag in hand, smoking a cigarette. She watched a man exit a stairwell and walk towards her. He wore jeans, a fetching two tone T-shirt with a pocket and a red baseball cap. The man carried a bag. Tanya started to laugh as Jamie approached her.

"What the hell do you look like?"

"In the car." Tanya stubbed out her cigarette. Jamie was not in the mood. She walked towards the passenger side as Jamie climbed in, throwing his bag in the boot. Tanya opened her door and climbed in also.

"What is going on?" she asked. Jamie started the car as Tanya was closing the door and headed towards the exit.

"Things that you don't need to know about." Jamie was now focused. "Sometimes it's better not to know. Now let's get home."

"We still staying in Fenchurch tonight?"

"Hell yeah. After today I need a drink." Jamie paid at the barrier, descended a slope and headed away from Barnston. *I'll need to burn these clothes when I get home*, he thought.

***

Back at the house where the cannabis grew and a dead body lay in the bath, a laundry firm had arrived outside. Dressed in overalls and wheeling a large laundry basket, they entered the house. The chef directed them towards the ground floor bathroom where two of the men began disposing of the body. The chef then showed a third male the areas that Jamie had touched with his hands. Firstly, the knife was seized and secured by this man, and then he carefully lifted fingerprints from the handles and surfaces which Jamie had touched. Evidence secured, this male texted his criminal counterparts informing them that his work was complete and that a replacement worker could now be sent to assist with attending to the cannabis.

***

Ron pulled the solid wood door closed behind him as he stepped out onto the front garden path leading to 4, Nooks View, Evesham.

"That'll do fine," he said, reaching into his pocket for his cigarettes. Lighting one, he drew deeply, then coughed as the smoke hit the back of his throat. He looked at the cigarette, as if to blame it, then held it between his lips as he searched for his car keys. Ronnie turned and looked up at the house, which was the end terrace in a set of four old shepherd cottages. Its old stone walls were solid and had been built to last. To the side of the house was a small alley which led to a rear yard, a long garden and a small wooded area which backed onto the garden. The front garden was small. The other houses in the row were similarly constructed and the row was book-ended by privately owned houses. "Very quaint."

Ronnie noticed a net curtain move in a window two doors down. He smiled and turned away, walking to his old battered vehicle. "Time to fetch some home comforts." Ronnie climbed in the driver's seat which creaked in protest as he tucked himself behind the wheel. Though partly furnished, Ronnie wanted to make the place feel more like home and had decided that he'd grab a couple of things from his flat. He started the engine, slipped the gears with a crunch and headed down the small road with a small plume of smoke coughing from the car's exhaust pipe.

Ronnie headed steadily out towards the main road with an estate wall to his right and open fields to his left. Driver's window down, he heard a car approaching the blind corner ahead. He slowed and tucked to the left of the road as a silver Golf GTI came whipping around the corner.

"Bloody idiot," said Ronnie, as the car screamed past him, heading down the hill. He watched it disappear in his rearview mirror.

***

"Bloody idiot," said Jamie, as he headed toward the bottom village. "He was in the middle of the bloody road, the old fart." Tanya looked across at him, her hand holding tightly to the passenger grab handle. Jamie had hardly spoken on the journey home, his mind clearly on other things. He had driven at ridiculous speeds. Tanya hadn't dared to say anything but knew that he should slow down in the village.

"Maybe he didn't hear you coming, love. Shall we slow down a bit? You know what they're like here and they do know that you're a cop." Jamie eased his foot from the accelerator. The vehicle slowed to a reasonable speed and slowed again as they approached a T-junction.

"Sorry, love. I got a bit carried away. We're here now though." He smiled at her as the car approached their house. "Quick change, throw some stuff in a case and we're off." He stopped the car outside of the house.

"You want me to drive to Fenchurch?"

"No way. I mean, no it's fine. You relax. I'll slow it down." They climbed out of the car and entered the house. "I'll ditch this stuff and get changed." Jamie disappeared upstairs and returned five minutes later carrying the clothes that he had worn and that they had just bought in Barnston.

"Kettle's boiling, love. I'll nip and grab our stuff. You make us coffee."

"Will do," yelled Jamie as Tanya ran up the stairs. Jamie walked to the back door and went out to the bottom of the garden where an incinerator bin was situated. He threw his clothes and shoes in, grabbed a nearby can of fuel and poured some in. Producing matches from his pocket he struck a light and threw it on the clothing. With a whoosh the clothing caught fire. Jamie stepped back as an initial cloud of smoke bellowed out, unaware that upstairs Tanya was watching from their bedroom window.

Chapter 7

"Down here on the left, mate," said Ronnie to Matt. Matt slowly descended the road, settling outside the address which Ronnie indicated.

"Nice little spot."

"It'll do me."

The vehicle halted and Ronnie climbed out of the passenger side. The team had rented a transit van to move some of Ronnie's things to his new abode in the village. Matt slipped a cap on and climbed out. The day was warm and the sound of grass being cut could be heard.

"Your garden needs sorting," said Matthew.

"Yes. Joe will be here tomorrow to start on it." Ronnie walked to the front door, opened it and turned to Matthew.

"Come on in and I'll show you where I want things," said Ronnie aloud, maintaining his role as the client. Matt followed him into the house. The small front room had a sofa and inbuilt bookshelves. A small open fire grate was the main means of heating the room. The walls were painted a pale cream.

"Cosy," said Matt, removing his hat. "At least it's summer and you won't be hunched over that little fire."

"There's night storage heaters too."

"Throwback to the sixties, Ron. You'll fit in fine." Matthew laughed as he walked towards an archway. "What's through here?"

"Kitchen and bathroom."

"Bathroom?"

"It's an old house. Downstairs bathroom."

"You'll be telling me that your toilet is outside next."

"Used to be but they've modernised and brought it in." Matthew opened a small cupboard which revealed the electric mains for the house. He closed it quickly.

"Best not to look too closely at that, mate. Don't think the wiring will meet modern standards."

"As long as it all works, it will do me," said Ronnie. "That's why I've been selected for this role. Someone like you wouldn't survive here without all of your home comforts."

"That's true. I probably wouldn't. Let's get your stuff in shall we?" The van didn't take long to unload with the few possessions that Ronnie had brought with him. The front room now contained Ronnie's comfortable chair, all his bedding, a decent TV and several cardboard boxes.

"Plans?" asked Matt.

"Spend the afternoon unpacking and then wander around the top village. May as well get my face known and start to get to know the locals."

"I'll head off. Remember, check in with me once a week for a full debrief."

"Yes."

"A couple of texts a day to let me know that you are still alive and kicking."

"Yep."

"Contact me at any time if you need me, or if anything significant turns up."

"Will do," said Ronnie, ushering Matt towards the door. "All memorised. I'll be fine. Now bugger off so I can get settled in." Ronnie opened the front door for Matthew. Matt turned and was handed some cash by Ronnie.

"Thanks for your time," said Ronnie.

"No problem. Hope you like it here." Matt walked back to the van, climbed in and drove away. Ronnie stepped out into his front garden and lit up a cigarette. *What a beautiful spot,* he thought. The sound of the lawn mower could still be heard. A couple of cars were still parked on the roadside and also within driveways. People were probably at home enjoying the summer sun.

Ronnie turned and closed his front door, then stepped out onto the street. He wandered down to a corner where he stopped, taking in the view of the rolling Wolds. In the distance, he could see a tractor working across a field and above, a kite circling the sky, making the most of the thermals. He bent down, stubbed his cigarette out on the ground, palmed the fag end and turned to head back home. Looking left, he saw a middle aged lady in her front garden, checking over her blooming flowers. He raised a hand in greeting and received a timid wave in response. He smiled and headed home.

"Still got it, son. Still got it," said Ron.

***

Audrey Melthrop was standing within the church grounds, attending to some flowers at a graveside. She stood up and looked down the road and spotted a portly, bearded male walking towards the shepherd's cottages. The man seemed to be in no rush and wasn't a person who she recognised as a local. Gravel crunched behind her. She turned to see Roger approaching.

"Hello, dear. Working hard?"

"Keeping things tidy. Looks like there's a new man in the village." She pointed surreptitiously towards the cottages. Roger peered, seeing the man stop before one of the cottages.

"He may be a new tenant."

"Well get down there and find out," said Audrey. "He could be a new recruit to our flock."

"I was going to head down to see old Alfred in the bottom village."

"That's great. You can call on the new man on the way and then continue down to Alfred's. It will do you good. Run along." Roger scowled at Audrey but dutifully headed to the church gates and left the curtilage of the graveyard. Audrey watched him as he went, with a self-satisfied smug look on her face, as Roger headed out on his mission.

Ronnie entered his garden, turning as he heard footsteps approaching. *The vicar is quick off the mark*, he thought. Roger Melthrop beelined towards him with a big grin fixed upon his face.

"Good morning, sir," bellowed Roger as the distance closed. Ronnie smiled.

"Your honour." Ronnie dipped his head in a nodded greeting. Melthrop giggled at Ronnie's mistake.

"No, my good man. Simply the local pastor, or Roger if you prefer. No need to stand in ceremony. Welcome to the neighbourhood." Melthrop reached out, took Ronnie's hand, and shook it vigorously. "And you are, my friend?"

"Not your friend. Simply Ronnie Cuthbertson." Melthrop's handshake halted and he frowned. *Come on, son. You'll get there.* Ronnie watched the penny drop as the smile returned to Melthrop's face.

"Ah ha, I see what you did there. Very good, Ronnie. Very good. That's if I may call you Ronnie?"

"You may. Good to meet you, Roger."

"Have you only arrived today?"

"Yes. Unloaded my gear into the house. Preparing to get settled in."

"Have you travelled far?"

"Not too far." There was a pregnant pause as Melthrop waited for Ronnie to elaborate. "Nice to get a change of scenery though. The village looks beautiful."

"Oh it is, it is. Friendly people. Salt of the earth. I'm sure you'll be happy here. There's a small shop in the bottom village, a pub, a village hall, and the church up the hill from you."

"And the big house."

"Evesham Hall. Lovely spot and a lovely owner. Terrific café."

"One owner?"

"Well, the family are the custodians only. Sir David is a personal friend. Regular attendee at the church. Can I expect to see you attending services?"

"Oh, I love a good sing-along."

"Terrific. We have a small choir, you know. It would be a good way for you to meet people." Melthrop stepped back, looking Ronnie up and down. "What are you? A baritone or a bass? You don't happen to be a tenor, do you? We are so in need of tenors." Roger checked his watch.

"No idea to be honest. Love a bit of Sinatra though."

"I suppose that's a start." Roger checked his watch again. "Sorry, but I need to be going. I've got a planned meeting with old Alfred in the bottom village. He's not doing too well at the moment."

"Don't let me hold you up."

"Thank you. I must dash." Melthrop scooted away. "I'll see you at the next choir practice. Lovely to have you on board," yelled Melthrop as he disappeared around a corner from view.

"Bloody choir practice. What the hell have I got into?" mumbled Ronnie, as he walked around the side of his house to check out the back garden.

***

Matt entered the office where the team were working hard to put some investigative structure around the enquiry. He walked across to the kettle, flicking it on.

"That's Ronnie deployed. He seems happy."

"Good," said Rachel. "Let's get these up on the board if you can, Tom." Rachel handed Tom a handful of images. "You happy with your access, Jim?"

"Yes. They've got me logged onto the HOLMES system for this enquiry only. DI Kaur has restricted the files, statements, and policy logs to our team only. He's not included Joe though, as you may expect."

"One step too far, allowing one of the crims into their systems," said Joe.

"Ex-criminals," clarified Matt. "Their loss, mate."

"True," said Rachel. Matthew poured hot water into the team teapot. "Anyway, Joe, you have more important work to do."

"Brew's up," said Matt. The team stopped and migrated towards the teapot. Tom finished with the board he had been working on and joined them. "Grab your own, but let me through first," said Matthew, edging through his colleagues. He handed a mug of tea to Rachel.

"Cheers, love." She sipped on the drink. "Right, everyone. Scrum down." They moved to their lounging area and settled down. "Where to start?"

"Ronnie," piped up Matthew.

"OK."

"Deployed him this morning. He's going to get settled in this afternoon and show his face in the village later. We dumped his car in the visitor car park at the hall so he'll collect it later this afternoon. The house seems fine. Daily contact with him and weekly debrief. All's good."

"Great. Jim, your access to HOLMES is sorted. Can we get the team logged onto the system also?"

"And Joe?"

"No, I'll have that fight another day. Don't worry, Joe, you're not missing out on anything. Anything the team gets to read you can too. You simply won't have your own profile on HOLMES."

"No problem," said Joe.

"Matt, where are we at with Joe's deployment?"

"His van's downstairs in the garage. Used gardening tools and equipment are all packed within."

"I've made sure I know how to work the strimmer, mower, chainsaw," said Joe.

"Good stuff."

"He's deploying tomorrow. It'll be the first honest day's work he's done in his life." Matthew laughed.

"From the man who's been sitting on his arse reading books for most of his," said Joe.

"Touché," replied Matt.

"Now, now boys. We're not in the playground," said Rachel. "Are you happy with everything, Joe?"

"Yes, Rach. Looking forward to it."

"Right, Tom. Take us through the board." Tom stood up, mug in hand, and moved to the board.

"I've been working with Jim and Sarah, as per Rach's instructions, to narrow down the investigation parameters. For the record, when doing this we have ignored – well, not ignored – but put to one side, the lead investigator's views. His views on who were persons of interest, the suspects, and who he thought were witnesses only. We are starting with a clean sheet. Our central point to work outwards from is the pub. The hub of the community. Specifically, the last place where Victoria was seen alive. On the board are all the persons who were present in the pub on the night of her death. We know there was a fight and that tensions were high. Any of these people could be our murderer."

"Thanks, Tom." Rachel walked up to the board and looked at the images. She turned to the team. "We start with profiling them. As they were twenty years ago and where they are now. We rule them out as possible offenders or keep them in as persons of interest. Ronnie and Joe are our guys on the inside. They'll infiltrate the community, work as our eyes and ears, and get into the places we can't. This is our starting point." Rachel gestured to the board. "How can we narrow down this group, Tom?"

"We know that Victoria met up with her friends that night." Tom moved Victoria's photo to one side of the board. In that group, we have her friend Tanya Holt, Tanya's brother Mark Holt, and Danny Pape. Danny was a farmhand on the estate. He may still be one." Each image was placed in a horizontal line below Victoria's photo. "On the face of it, they all seemed to be having a good time until we had the appearance of Jonathan Fanshaw, his mate Charles Fothergill Jnr, and a lad called Jamie." Tom moved their images across the board as he spoke.

"Jamie?" asked Rachel.

"Jamie Hyatt. That is Jamie Hyatt, who was a serving police officer at the time." That caught everyone's attention. Rachel remained calm.

"Rank and role?"

"A police constable in uniform then. No idea at the moment."

"Stationed?"

"Fenchurch back then. Don't know now."

"That's got to be a positive, right?" asked Matt.

"Don't be so sure," said Joe. "A copper who was there on the night of her disappearance and still we have no idea what happened?"

"Joe's right," said Rachel, "Let's treat him with caution. Everyone up there is a potential offender until we say that they aren't. Anyone else, Tom?"

"A few in the pub," he indicated to the other photos on the board, "regulars, a couple of visitors, and the landlord."

"OK. We start with the people that you've placed underneath Victoria's image. Matt and I will take Jamie. We'll need to tread carefully with him. Tom, Sarah and Jim, split the others between you. Whoever takes Jonathan, you can task me with anything you need. I'm sure I'll bump into him. Joe, you take a good look over Danny's account of the night and also his history before tomorrow. You're likely to meet him first."

"Will do."

"Let's get cracking." The team broke up and headed to their desks to get started. Matt turned to Rachel.

"Where do we start?"

"You can start by taking a look at Jamie's statement. I'm going to ring Jamal and ask him why he didn't tell me that there was a serving cop present in the pub on the night of her disappearance. Doesn't seem right, does it?"

***

Fenchurch was busy this morning. All the routes into the city had been heaving with the rush hour traffic as everyone tried to get in to work on time. Emily had been amongst the commuters, gaining first-hand experience in the frustration of city life. She hoped that her stint working in the city would not be too prolonged. The job had provided her with bed and breakfast accommodation until they could sort out something more permanent for her. Emily was now sitting on a bench, coffee in hand, watching the world pass her by on the river that cut through the city. Her new home was a large detached house set back from the river and was only a ten-minute walk from the local nick.

Although Emily had visited the city a few times, it was primarily on a shift night out when they'd hit the pubs and caught the last train home. She stood up and started walking along the riverside, towards the city centre.

"Watch yourself," called a male. Emily jumped in shock, spilling coffee on her hand, and turned to see a cyclist heading towards her.

"Shit. That's hot," she exclaimed. Emily moved aside as she transferred her cup and wiped her hand on her jeans.

"Cycle path," yelled the man as he cycled past, pointing to the ground. The tarmac was demarcated with pedestrians to one side and bicycles to the other.

"Sorry," called Emily. The man raised a hand in acknowledgement as he continued on his way. Stepping back onto the footway, Emily positioned herself in the correct lane and continued strolling along. As she neared the city, the bustle of busy traffic permeated the air.

Fenchurch, though named a city due to its architecture, was relatively small but was a popular commuter location and tourist destination. Emily took a path up from the riverbank and headed in towards the centre. She wasn't due to start on shift until tomorrow and a day orienting herself to her new surroundings could only help her. A free day with no work, no friends, no real agenda and best of all no Trimble. She walked past the Hilton Hotel entrance and took a left towards the cathedral.

***

The foyer of the Hilton was quiet as Jamie and Tanya gently walked through and exited via the front doors.

"Your car is ready, sir," said a member of staff gesturing towards Jamie's vehicle.

"Thanks, mate." Jamie carried the couple's cases and bags to his car and threw them in the boot. "Come on, Tan," he called. Jamie climbed into the driver's seat and watched Tanya slowly walk to the passenger side before lowering herself in.

"My head is fuckin' banging," she moaned.

"Too many cocktails, love. You should have stuck on the lager with me."

"Have we got any painkillers?" Tanya opened the glove compartment to search. She pulled out some sunglasses and put them on. Jamie revved the engine. "Not so loud, please," begged Tanya.

"Last drive, love. Got to give it a thrash."

"Where we going?"

"Out to the BMW garage. I've arranged for a trade-in. I fancy something new." Jamie set off.

"I need to lie back," Tanya reclined the chair. "Grab me some painkillers en route will you."

"Course I will. Great night though, wasn't it?" He received a moan in reply as he pulled into the traffic and headed to the car dealership.

***

Emily continued on her route, wending her way through a multitude of pedestrians who were enjoying the delights of the old buildings and streets. She passed a square where a street performer was sitting upon a tall unicycle juggling daggers. The people who were around him were fixated on his daring deeds. The juxtaposition of willing him to stay upright and unhurt yet anticipating the thrill of a mistake, a fall, a slip.

Emily wasn't enjoying the atmosphere. She wasn't used to the crowds and knew that getting through the public swarm when required to do so as a police officer would be a challenge. She tucked herself into a quieter side street and nipped through to the main precinct, which was pedestrianised and open-planned. A water fountain dominated the main square, its walls being used as a seating area by people who consumed takeaway lunches and coffees.

Adjacent to the fountain was one of the city's law firms with large oak doors open to its customers. Emily's attention was drawn to a tall man who ran out of the building and observed him begin to look around desperately. He appeared to see what he needed, running over to an elderly couple whom he spoke with. Emily moved on hoping that her new beat area would be on the outskirts of the town.

***

Mark opened the internal door and swiftly moved through the reception and out through the front doors. Dressed in a three-piece suit, white shirt and dark tie, he held a man's wallet in his hand. Mark remained slim and though he had averted the onslaught of middle-aged spread, he had not been so lucky with his hair. Now balding, with a thin wisp of hair combed over, and thickening spectacle lenses, his face had aged. He looked around, spotted Mr and Mrs Bottomly, and walked swiftly over to them.

"Mr Bottomly. Your wallet." Mr Bottomly turned on hearing his name. "You dropped it on leaving, sir." Bottomly patted his breast pocket and was surprised it was empty.

"Thank you, young man. I hadn't realised. Would lose my head if it wasn't screwed on." Mark handed the wallet over.

"What does he want?" said Mrs Bottomly, squinting up at Mark.

"Nothing, dear. He's returning my wallet. Nothing for you to worry about." He turned to Mark. "Thank you again."

"All part of the service," said Mark. He turned and walked away from the couple, heading back towards the offices. Walking before him, two smartly-dressed ladies were talking animatedly. The lady on the right, a brunette, laughed out loud. Victoria's image sprung into his mind. Mark stopped. *I haven't thought about you for years.* Mark shocked himself and looked down at his hand where a gold band now surrounded his finger. *If only things had turned out differently.* He preferred not to think of that night and the terrors which it uncovered.

***

DI Kaur was sitting behind his desk, wading through the red tape that was, today, performance reviews. His mobile phone rang. He answered.

"Jamal, how are you doing?"

"Fine, Rachel. You? How's the investigation going?"

"Slow start. You know how it goes."

"Certainly do. How can I help you?"

"You never warned me about Hyatt."

"Hyatt?"

"Jamie Hyatt. The copper that was featured in your initial enquiry. He was present in the pub. You could have let me know."

"Honestly, Rach, I forgot. It's been a while since I reviewed the case. Sorry, my error."

"Apology accepted. Where's he now?"

"Hyatt? No idea. Let me take a look. I'll put you on hands-free." Kaur placed his mobile phone down on the desk and started typing on his keyboard. "You still there?"

"Yes, I can hear you."

"OK. Jamie Hyatt," Kaur spoke as he typed. "There he is. Looks like he's working on shift at Fenchurch. Uniformed PC."

"Anything on his record?"

"Not on this system. He's not a name that I've heard much about."

"OK. We'll need to speak to him at some point but I'll let you know when."

"Do that." Kaur checked his watch. "Got to go, mate. Another meeting."

"Enjoy. I don't bloody miss them. Speak soon." The call was terminated. Kaur closed down his screen and headed out of his office.

***

John Trimble was sitting at his desk, going over Emily Dutton's last meeting notes, when an alert popped up on his computer screen. He tapped his keyboard, entered his email, and opened the message.

"Interesting," he said aloud. "Bob, can you come in here?" he called. Bob's head popped around the corner.

"What's up, Gov?"

"Have you had any dealings with Jamal Kaur?"

"Not for a while. He's a DI now, over in the Eastern area I think."

"Certainly is. He's also had a look at Hyatt's personal record."

"Has he now? You want me to ask him?"

"Not yet. Something that we'll need to monitor though. Maybe have a sniff around and see what Kaur's workload is at the moment. I may need to speak with him. Let's work out what his interest is in Hyatt if we can."

"Will do. You want a coffee?"

"That would be great." Bob left the office and Trimble continued working.

***

A tractor, pulling a green canopied beaters wagon, headed down the hill as five four-by-four vehicles turned into the top village at Evesham. The cars stopped in a row before by an entrance to a field.

"Thanks so much for inviting me, Jonathan. I haven't been on a shoot for ages."

"That's OK, Charlie. Do you think that you'll be able to hit anything?"

"Doubt it, to be honest, but maybe Lady Luck will be on my side."

"How are Melissa and the children?"

"All fine. Away at our château in the South of France. Lucky buggers."

"Gives you a break, though."

"Yes it does, but who is going to look after me? To be fair, when she's here, Melissa does a good job managing most of my needs, boring though she is. Not sure that I would cope without her."

"She certainly is a bit dull, if you don't mind me saying."

"Not at all, old chap. Efficient though and I can always nip into the city for any decent entertainment, if you know what I mean."

"Not sure I do, or want to." Both males laughed. The convoy moved slowly forwards and entered the field, heading down to the vale where their designated shooting pegs awaited them. The track was pitted with bumps and craters which were marginally absorbed by the vehicle's suspension.

"We have a visitor coming to stay at the house for a while," said Jonathan, as the car hit a particularly nasty hole. Charlie lifted out of his seat, ducking his head to avoid a collision with the roof.

"Steady, old boy. What was that? A visitor?"

"Yes. A lady called Rachel Barnes."

"And who is Rachel Barnes? Never heard of her."

"Ex-cop turned investigator." Charlie looked at Jonathan in shock.

"Of what?"

"Cold cases. She has been employed to re-investigate Victoria's disappearance."

"You're bloody joking?"

"I'm not."

"Who has employed her?"

"My father."

"For fuck's sake. Can he not let it go? No one wants the past dragging up again. She's gone. Nothing's going to bring her back."

"Well, it's happening, so brace yourself. No doubt she'll want to speak to you."

"That's all I need. Bloody woman. Melissa needn't know. Good job that she's away." Charles nervously chewed his nails. "I could do without this." He stared into the distance as the vehicle came to a stop.

"Here we are." Jonathan set the hand brake and climbed out of the vehicle. "Your peg is over there." He pointed to a white post stuck into the ground. "Take out your frustration on the peasants. I mean the pheasants. Although, either will do." Jonathan laughed. Charlie gave no response. "Anyway, good luck." Jonathan walked off towards his peg, shotgun in hand. Charlie opened his door, turned in his seat and knocked his foot against a box of cartridges on the floor. The cartridges spilt out onto the grass.

"Shit!" He climbed out and scrabbled on the ground, retrieving the ammunition, then stood up, grabbed his shotgun and slammed the car door. Charles Fothergill stomped off with a grim look of determination on his face.

***

"What you doing it like that for you bloody idiot? How many times have I shown you before? Twist the bloody wire the other bloody way," said Pat.

"Get away, old man. It matters neither. Long as the thing's pegged," replied Richard. Richard was in the backfield behind his garden, fixing some fencing that had become loose. Pat had called around for a morning coffee and could not help but offer his advice.

"It'll come loose I tell you," said Pat, handing Richard a mug of coffee.

"It'll be fine. Cheers." He took the mug and sipped it, grimacing as he did so.

"Is it OK?"

"Well, it's warm and wet. Could do with some coffee in it though."

"Cheeky fucker." Pat looked in the distance where the convoy of cars was descending a field. "'ere they come. More money than sense."

"Aye," replied Richard, "but whilst they're playing at being cowboys they're not bugging me."

"True, lad, true. Here come the beaters." Patrick pointed to a row of people holding flags as they waited to the right of a small wooded area. The convoy of cars disappeared into the vale.

"Beaters will move forward soon to flush them out." Richard turned and frowned at Pat.

"You're not talking to a bloomin' idiot, you know. I have helped with the hunt on many occasions. I don't need it spelling —"

"There they go. Into the trees" Pat continued, oblivious to Richard's comments. "Pheasants will be flushed soon."

"Poor little innocents," said Richard. "God didn't give them life for us to snatch it away."

"What was that?" Pat muttered as he concentrated in the distance. He didn't wait for a reply. "There they go." The men watched pheasants take flight from the trees and the sound of discharging shotguns could soon be heard in the distance.

***

Danny Pape moved through the trees with Meg, his springer spaniel, holding to his heel. He felt rough this morning, following a bender last night. He removed a hip flask from his back pocket and took a swig of neat whisky. Replacing the cap, then thinking better of it, he unscrewed it and took another gulp. Anything to help stop the shakes. His stomach was cramping and nearly purged itself of the cheap alcohol. He swallowed and managed to hold it down. The row of beaters to his right moved forward and started calling and waving their flags.

"Get on, Meg," said Danny. Meg moved swiftly through the underbrush. The years had not been kind to Danny. The young strapping lad that he once was had faded from memory. Now skinny, with thinning hair and a face aged beyond its years, Danny resembled the slave to alcohol that he was. He managed to make money where he could, mainly working on adjoining farms, but had never recovered from losing his job on the estate all those years ago.

The neighbouring farms took him on when he was needed for work, of which there was plenty. However, Danny had gained a reputation for being unreliable and a man to call in only if there wasn't anyone else available. Luckily for Danny, trained farm hands were often few and far between, so he had been able to stay afloat through his earned skills and sympathy from the farmers who knew him from his youth.

He raised one hand and held it as still as he could. A faint tremor remained but had calmed through the morning. Through the trees, he could see Fanshaw's silver Land Rover parked and watched Fanshaw walk away from it. He would recognise the build and look of him anywhere. Though dressed in the same country clothing as all the other shooters, Danny recognised him. The arrogant prick who was the orchestrator of Danny's demise. Danny halted and lifted his beating stick to his shoulder, mimicking a rifle. He aimed at Fanshaw, sighted, and squeezed the trigger, making the sound of a round discharge as he did so.

"Should have been you." Danny lowered the stick and looked to the right where a young beater was looking at him in shock. He laughed then continued walking forwards, calling out to Meg.

Chapter 8

Joe pulled into the top village in a little white box van. He parked up and stepped out, lighting up a roll-up cigarette as he did so. The grass hadn't been cut for about four weeks and it required some serious attention. He walked along the road towards the church, noting that the church grounds and graveyard were well maintained. He could hear the church organ being played as someone practised.

"Terribly quaint," said Joe. Turning back to his vehicle, he checked out a couple of residents' gardens as he passed them, noting that they were well cared for. Climbing back in the car, he drove around the horseshoe and parked outside the house he knew to be Ronnie's. After setting the handbrake, Joe climbed out and made a show of checking the kerbside grasses as he walked past Ronnie's and down towards an open field entrance. Vehicle tyre tracks led into the field and he could hear the sound of shotgun fire bouncing through the air. Joe turned around and then, heading back towards his car, spotted Ronnie stepping out of his front door. Ronnie walked to his front gate and leaned his elbows upon it. He looked Joe up and down.

"Can I help you, mate?" asked Ronnie.

"No, I'm fine. I'm the new gardener for the village. I was taking a look at the work I need to do."

"Gardener, eh?"

"Yeah, I'm Joe."

"Nice to meet you, Joe. Ronnie."

"And you, Ronnie. I'll get out of your way." Joe moved to the driver's side of his van and opened the door. Ronnie opened his gate and stepped onto the pavement.

"You do any private garden work?" asked Ronnie.

"Yup. You mean this one?"

"Moved in this week. It's a bit of a state. Could do with a hand to get on top of it."

"Let me crack on with the verges first. I'll be around tomorrow, too. I'll call round then and give you a quote?"

"Sounds good to me." Joe climbed into his vehicle and lowered the driver's window."

"Off out for some exercise?" asked Joe.

"Think I'm in need of some." Ronnie sucked his belly in.

"Can't disagree with you there." Joe laughed. Ronnie leaned on the car door frame.

"Cheeky bastard," he muttered. Joe winked at Ronnie and grinned.

"I'll see you tomorrow." He started the engine and Ronnie stepped back as the car pulled away.

Ronnie disappeared inside and returned shortly after, wearing a jacket and a flat cap. He locked the front door and walked from his house, heading round the horseshoe to the road which would lead him to the road which descended to the lower part of the village. He needed to familiarise himself with Evesham, especially whilst there was still light. Now descending the hill, he observed a couple of cars ascending the road. The drivers gave him friendly waves as they passed. He reciprocated with a wave in reply, turning and noting the cars' makes and models as they drove by. He knew that he wouldn't remember all the registrations but was confident that he would start to recognise the regular cars in the village the more that he was out and about. Ronnie looked back up the hill, not relishing the thought of the steep climb home after a couple of pints.

After a steady ten-minute walk and a wander around the bottom roads and cul-de-sacs, Ronnie located the village shop and entered. A bell tinkled as he did so. The shop was empty of people. He looked around and smiled at the familiarity of his younger days. The shop was well stocked with shelves full of produce of all types. A row of sweet jars stood on shelving behind a long wooden counter.

"With you in a minute," called a weary gentleman's voice.

"No rush," replied Ronnie.

On the counter was a selection of the daily papers, some of which had customers' names handwritten on the top corner, clearly awaiting collection or possibly delivery. A large glass-door fridge held red, green and silver-topped milk in bottles. Ronnie wandered around the small area. Wine, beer, bread, bags containing fresh veg. Everything you may need. He opened a small cupboard and found light bulbs, packs of playing cards, candles, needles and threads. He laughed to himself. A man coughed behind him.

"Can I help you?" Ronnie turned and looked at a thin elderly male with grey wispy hair who was standing behind the counter. The man peered over the top of his glasses at Ronnie.

"Sorry, I was only having a nosy."

"That's fine. There's stuff all over the place. All for sale. If you can't find it in here then you proba

bly don't need it." Ronnie walked back to the counter.

"A ten pence mix then, please." Ronnie chuckled. The man smiled.

"If only. Them were the days."

"Damn well they were. What can you get for ten pence now?"

"Absolutely nothing, I'm afraid. Visiting the village?"

"Recently moved into the top village. The old shepherds' cottages."

"Nice solid builds up there. You'll be fine. I'm Alfred by the way."

"Ronnie." The men shook hands. "I haven't been in a spot like this for years. Takes me back."

"No need to change. If it ain't broke, don't fix it."

"How long you been here?"

"Forever. Took it over when my mother died. Never felt the need to leave." Ronnie's eyes drifted towards the back of the counter.

"Take it you sell cigs?" Alfred turned and pulled open a drawer.

"Not allowed to display them now. What do you want? I've got B and H, L and B and Regals."

"Twenty Regals please." Alfred pulled a pack from the drawer and placed it on the counter. "You'll be needing a lighter."

"Nope."

"Can never have too many lighters." Alfred placed a lighter on top of the cigarettes. Ronnie handed him a twenty pound note which was placed in Alfred's trouser pocket. He pushed his spectacles up his nose and, retrieving a stubby pencil and small pad from his shirt pocket, wrote down the price before retrieving Ronnie's change from a small tin under the counter. Ronnie checked his watch.

"Reckon I'm off for a pint. Check out the pub."

"Don't mind if I do," said Alfred, reaching up to a hook and retrieving his coat. He stepped to the right of the counter where he lifted a hatch and stepped through.

"You closing up?" Ronnie smiled.

"No, I'll leave it open. If anyone wants owt they'll get it and leave the money behind the counter." Ronnie looked confused.

"Honest people round here, Ronald. Well, mainly. Let's go. Mine's a double brandy." Ronnie allowed himself to be ushered to the door and stepped out into the shop's curtilage. *Result*, thought Ronnie. *What a village shopkeeper doesn't know about a village isn't worth knowing.* The men set off to the Red Lion, chatting as they walked.

***

"After you, Sir."

"Thank you, Ron." Alfred entered the pub followed by Ronnie. Both removed their coats and hung them up on a coat stand situated near the door. Ronnie inhaled the ale-infused air and smiled.

"Double brandy was it?" asked Ronnie.

"That'll do for a chaser, then I'll have a pint of Black Sheep"

"Think I'll join you."

"Evening, gents," said a young lady as she started pulling a pint. "Early one."

"I'm introducing Ronnie here to the pub, Amy. He's started renting in the top village." Two men propped up the left side of the bar. "Pat, Richard. How you doing?"

"Good, ta," replied Pat. Richard supped from his pint as he looked over. He gave a slight nod in greeting.

"There's your pints. I'll get your chasers," said Amy.

"Thanks, love," said Ronnie, selecting a glass. "I'll grab us a table, Alfred."

"Tall one in the corner would be grand, Ron. The high stool is better for my knees."

"Tall table it is." Amy placed their shots on the bar. "On tab?" she asked Alfred.

"I've got these," said Ronnie. He returned to the bar and handed over thirty pounds. "Keep the change. If there is any." Ronnie collected the shots and Alfred carried the pints over. They raised the brandies in cheers, and swallowed them. Alfred coughed.

"Hits the back of your throat," he wheezed. Ronnie felt the burn as the alcohol descended to his stomach.

"Nice warmer though," said Ronnie. Richard leaned to Pat at the bar and said something, causing Pat to laugh. "Locals, I assume." Ronnie nodded towards the bar.

"Oh yes. You'll find them here every night. Been here all their lives. Not in the pub mind, in the village," Alfred clarified.

"Lovely little spot." Ronnie took a sip of beer. "Good ale." He looked around the room, which looked like it hadn't changed in years. Pictures adorned the walls, and antique items, books and paraphernalia crowded the surfaces. "Some of this stuff is even before our time," said Ronnie. Alfred chuckled. Ronnie looked to the wall at his left shoulder where a formal photograph depicted a family.

"Who's this then?"

"Well that's the Fanshaws," said Alfred. "The owners of the estate and many of the houses in the village. Sir David, the older man, will no doubt own yours." Ronnie looked closer at the photograph.

"Don't recognise him. Young lady is a looker though."

"Oh yes. That's poor Victoria. Sir David's daughter. She's no longer with us."

"Moved away?"

"No one knows. Disappeared one night. Never to be seen again. Presumed dead."

"You're kidding me?" Alfred warmed to his subject as he sipped his pint.

"Not a subject to kid about, Ron. Last seen outside here. Took the path to the big house. Then, gone. Just like that." A chair at the bar scraped and Ronnie turned to look. Pat was standing up.

"That's me, Amy," said Pat to the barmaid. "Busy day tomorrow."

"Me too," said Richard, standing and following Pat.

"OK, lads. See you tomorrow." Both men walked towards Alfred and Ronnie.

"Shop open, Alf?" asked Pat.

"Yes, yes."

"Could do with some fags if you are free?" Pat's hand moved to Alfred's shoulder and he squeezed it.

"Help yourself. You know where to leave the money." Ronnie sensed tension in the air.

"You go on, Alfred. I'll step out and have a cig. I'll still be here when you return." Ronnie stood, grabbed his coat and stepped out of the pub. He was shortly followed by the men.

"Gents," said Ronnie. He nodded to Pat and Richard.

"Back in a minute, Ronnie," said Alfred as he walked in the direction of his shop.

"I'll be here," reassured Ronnie. He watched the trio walk away then turned to look at the lane which Victoria had last taken all those years ago. *It's a start, Ronnie.* He suspected that Alfred may not be so chatty about Victoria on his return. After all, he was a newcomer to the village and many villagers were suspicious of newbies. *No rush. It's a good start.*

***

Joe wandered back to his van, placed the strimmer down and removed his helmet visor and ear defenders. He looked back and was happy with his work. There was something about strimming that he enjoyed. The noise was a pain, but he found the sweep of the machine as it scythed and trimmed long grasses, nettles and weeds fulfilling. Once he'd run over all the grass with a mower and cleared the debris up it would look good and be a job well done. Not as exciting as playing detective but supported his self-worth. He opened the back doors of the van, propped himself on the boot and poured himself a coffee from a flask.

Whilst working, he'd noted a couple standing by the main doors of the church in deep conversation. The man towered over the woman who looked older. He had kept glancing over at Joe and, now that Joe had stopped, was walking over towards him. *What you got to say, mate?* Joe started rolling a cigarette. The man walked up to the car and looked down at Joe. Joe looked up as he continued rolling.

"Now, then," said Joe.

"Who are you, then?" Joe lit his fag, drawing deeply. He smiled and blew the smoke to the side, away from the man. Joe stood up and looked up to the male.

"I'm the new gardener, mate. Started today."

"Are you? No one told me."

"Should they have?"

"Would have been nice. I do the church, you see."

"Do you?" Joe didn't know what the man was talking about.

"Yes, I do the church. It's mine." Joe looked confused. "I look after the grass in and around the church. It's all mine." Joe's brow smoothed as he grasped the man's meaning. "Are you a bit daft? The church is all mine," clarified the male.

"Right. I've got you. You can have it. I'm only here for the roadsides and the greens."

"Good. That's settled then. What's your name?"

"Joe. Yours?"

"Richard." Richard raised his arm, offering Joe a handshake. Joe automatically reciprocated as his hand was engulfed in Richard's grizzly paw. Richard shook once, dropped Joe's hand, turned, and walked away.

"What a strange, giant of a man." He drew on his cigarette as he watched Richard return to the church grounds and speak to the woman at the church door. After a few seconds, the woman raised a hand and waved. Joe waved back and watched as both people disappeared into the church. "You'll fit right in here, Ronnie. Keep you all in one place. Safer for the rest of the world."

***

Emily walked into the front office at Fenchurch Station, ready to start her first day on shift. Carrying a kit bag over her shoulder, she approached the front desk and showed her warrant card to the receptionist.

"Can you buzz me in, please? First day. I don't know the door code number."

"No problem. Once you are through the door, straight down the corridor, first right, first left and you'll find the sergeant's office."

"Cheers." She walked to the interior door, heard the buzz, then pushed it and entered the inner sanctum of the station. Ahead in the corridor two men in suits were standing talking. She approached. The men continued talking and were blocking her way.

"Excuse me." One of the men looked her up and down, then stepped to one side, allowing her through. Emily could feel their eyes boring into her back as she continued. A fresh new face for them to check out, form their opinions on and discuss with their mates in the CID. "Nothing to see here, gents. You can carry on," Emily was used to the misogyny of the police service which was begrudgingly being dragged into the twenty-first century. She followed the directions given and arrived at the sergeant's office where the door was partially closed. Emily knocked and waited.

"Come in." She entered. A uniformed sergeant was sitting behind a desk computer. Bespectacled with an unruly fringe of hair, his face was flushed. He turned as Emily entered.

"Bloody things," he said, gesturing to the computer. "They are a bloody pain in the arse. What do you want?"

"First day on shift, Sarge. I'm reporting for duty."

"On my shift?"

"I believe so. If you are Sergeant Wilson?"

"See what I mean. This bloody job. No one's told me anything. Not even the decency to send me a bloody e-mail on this thing." He slapped the computer keyboard. "Yes, I am."

"I can go to the parade room if you tell me where to go."

"I'll show you." Wilson stood up and held out his hand. Emily shook his hand. "Sorry, you know what it's like. I'm Tom."

"Emily Dutton."

"Good to have you on board, Emily. How long you got in?"

"Six years."

"Thank goodness. An experienced cop. You are more than welcome. This way. Come and meet the team." Sergeant Wilson walked towards the door. His office phone rang. Wilson looked from the phone, to Emily, and back to the phone.

"I'll find my way," said Emily. "You get your call." Wilson smiled and lifted the receiver, which he covered with his hand. "I'll be two minutes. Right and then first right. Ask for John Longshaw." She smiled, turned and left the office.

Emily walked up to the door of the briefing room. She could hear the chatter of her colleagues, enjoying a few minutes before they were thrown into the chaos of the day. She took a deep breath, steeled herself and walked into the room. The door closed behind her. A group of faces turned to see who had entered and the chatter stopped as they realised that Emily was an unknown person. The police officer's suspicion of determining friend or foe came naturally to them all.

"Nowt to worry about," said Emily. "Emily Dutton. Six years. Starting on shift today. I don't think you were expecting me, but I'm glad to be here. I've been told to ask for John Longshaw." Emily scanned the room. *Hyatt's not here*. An officer raised his arm.

"I'm, John." Emily walked over to where he was sitting at a desk. She dumped her bag on the floor.

"Looks like you've got the short straw, mate. Babysitting the newbie."

"Maybe you can teach him a thing or two," said a curly-haired young constable.

"You should be so lucky, Longy," interjected another officer. Some of the cops laughed. Curly-hair rolled her eyes.

"Ignore them, Emily," said Longy. "Good to meet you."

"You too, John. I'm sure I can handle it."

"I'm Jess," said the curly-haired female, walking up to Emily. "Good to have another woman with us. You can help me keep them in order."

The door to the room burst open, its handle clipping the wall. A tall, broad-shouldered male walked in. Emily immediately recognised Hyatt from the photos which Trimble had shown her.

"Don't panic, everyone. I have arrived. No need to stand."

"Dickhead," muttered Jess. Hyatt surveyed the room, his eyes resting upon Emily.

"And who have we got here?" asked Hyatt, smiling at Emily. "We got ourselves a newbie? Stick the kettle on, love." Hyatt laughed at his humour, as did a couple of the team. The rest ignored him, except for Jess who looked at him in shock, then looked to Emily to gauge her reaction.

"Don't mind if you do, mate. I'm sure we'd all be grateful. Oh, and do you mind closing the door? There's a rank smell drifted in from the gent's toilets." The room was silent. Jamie looked at Emily in confusion, trying to work out if she was joking. Emily smiled. Jamie laughed and reached his hand out.

"Touchè. I'm Jamie. Good to meet you."

"Emily. Likewise."

"Budge up, Longy, and make some room." Jamie forced a space between Emily and Longy and propped himself against the desk. Emily's senses were overpowered by Jamie's exuberant use of aftershave as it enveloped her. Jamie leaned in towards Emily. "I'll keep you right, Em. How long you got in?"

Sergeant Wilson came into the room looking slightly flustered as he counted how many officers he had.

"Cheers, Jamie," whispered Emily.

"Right," said Wilson. "Great start to the day. They've got a major incident running over at Barnston. I've taken a call and we've been asked to supply some staff." A groan sounded from the team. "Alright, calm it. Not ideal but some of the early shift is going to stay on and support us in town. Could be a long shift at Barnston. Volunteers?"

"What's the job?" asked Jess.

"Volunteers first. Then I'll tell you." Emily looked around the room, seeing the reticent faces. *May as well try and make some friends*, she thought.
"I'll go, Sarge. I haven't got a workload yet so it makes sense."

"You worked Barnston before?"

"A couple of times."

"Cheers, Emily. That's a good help. That's two of you then. You and Longy, who you are crewing with today."

"No problem," replied John.

"One more then." Jess and Jamie raised their hands. Wilson looked shocked at Jamie. "You feeling OK, Jamie?"

"Awfully funny, Sarge. We'll flip a coin. What's the job?"

"They've found a decent-sized grow in town and over on the north side a dog walker has found a human foot and hand."

"You are joking?" said Jess. Jamie's complexion paled. "Do they think it's a murder?"

"Well, I doubt that somebody has lost them," said one of the officers.

"I'll go," said Jamie. *I need to go*, he thought. *SOCO will be sweeping the house. They'll find my prints.* "Anyway, Jess, you've got a couple of people answering bail at five, if I remember right?"

"Bollocks, I'd forgotten. All yours then, Jamie. Free tomorrow if we're still needed though, Sarge. I've not been involved in a murder yet." The officers laughed. "You know what I mean." Jess joined in.

"Emily, Longy and Jamie it is then. Grab your kit. There are some keys." Wilson threw Longy a set of car keys. "I'll let them know that you are on your way." The officers stood up. Emily grabbed her bag and followed Longy and

Jamie out of the room. Both men grabbed their kit bags from the locker room as Emily waited in the corridor. Longy appeared first.

"This way, Emily. Cars are out in the rear yard." They headed out to the back where Jamie joined them. Longy pressed the keyfob and the hazard lights illuminated on a marked police vehicle. They headed towards it.

"You wanna drive?" Longy asked Jamie.

"Nah, I'll give it a miss." Longy was surprised.

"Must be rubbing off on him already, Emily. You?"

"No, mate. You've got the keys. I'll drive us back later," replied Emily. The three threw their kit bags in the boot. Jamie quickly jumped in the back seat.

"Front it is then," said Emily climbing in the passenger seat. Longy climbed in the driver's and looked in the rearview mirror with worry at Jamie in the back seat.

"You ok, mate?" Jamie was reading something on his phone. Longy started the vehicle and repeated, "Jamie. You OK?" Jamie looked up.

"What? Oh, yeah. I'm fine. Letting Tan know that I'll be late." Longy pulled out of the parking space.

"Must have swallowed a chivalry pill," he muttered.

"What was that?" asked Emily.

"Nowt to worry about," said Longy. "Anyway, what brings you to Fenchurch?" Emily started recounting her memorised cover story as the three set off towards Barnston.

***

Rachel closed the boot of her car and extended the pulling arm on her travel suitcase. She walked carefully forward, case in one hand, stick in the other, as she negotiated the gravel drive heading to Evesham Hall. The large oak door to the house opened and a middle-aged man wearing a dark suit, shirt and tie walked briskly out of the house towards her.

"Let me help if I may, Inspector." Fletcher gently took the case from Rachel for which she was grateful. He led the way to the house. "We've been expecting you." He gestured to the door encouraging Rachel to enter first. She did so and he followed, closing the door behind him.

"Thank you, Mr Fletcher."

"Fletcher is fine, Inspector."

"Not any more. No longer in the Force. Rachel is fine." Fletcher looked uncomfortable.

"Can we settle on Detective, ma'am? It seems more respectful."

"Yes, Detective is fine Fletcher."

"Thank you, Detective." Fletcher bowed his head. Both nervously laughed. "If I may, I shall take your case up to your room. I'll leave it outside, naturally. Firstly, let me take you to the lounge. The gentlemen are coming in from the shoot. I've prepared you a cup of tea, or you can have something stronger if you like?"

"Tea is fine, thank you. Is Sir David around?"

"Not in the house, ma'am but somewhere in the grounds. He likes to have a potter round."

"Not shooting today?"

"No. He rarely does these days. Young Mr Fanshaw is out with the shoot though." They entered the warm lounge where Fletcher poured Rachel a cup of tea. He turned to her with an expectant look on his face.

"A drop of milk, thank you." Rachel looked across the grounds and observed a convoy of four-by-fours heading towards the house.

"Is that them?" Fletcher handed her a cup and saucer.

"Yes, indeed. They'll have travelled up from the hunting lodge where the beaters will be organising the game." Fletcher checked his watch. "Excuse me, but I must be getting on. Make yourself comfortable." Fletcher left the room as Rachel watched the vehicles approach.

At the head of the convoy, a muddied dark Land Rover approached the house, coming to a stop facing the building. The other vehicles copied its manoeuvre until they were all lined in a neat row.

Middle-aged men with white hair, and various degrees of paunch, climbed out of their vehicles. The men all wore muted green and brown jackets, with matching trousers or breeks. The masculine nide all migrated towards the lead Land Rover, where the driver started handing out stirrup cups, and the sport of the day was discussed. The men being indifferent to the lives they had taken.

Rachel sipped and watched as hands were shaken and the two men from the Land Rover walked towards the house. She heard the front door open and close and two male voices talking and laughing as they approached the lounge.

"Boots off, Charlie, or Fletcher will kill me." Rachel waited and turned as the door opened. Jonathan Fanshaw entered. A man was standing behind him in the doorway.

"Sorry," said Jonathan, "I wasn't expecting anyone. You are?"

"Rachel Barnes, a guest of Sir David."

"Detective Inspector Barnes?"

"Rachel, please." Jonathan turned to Charlie.

"As I was saying, Charlie. Detective Barnes." Charlie looked flustered. He pulled on the one boot that he had removed and stood up straight.

"Sorry, Jonathan. I forgot. I have an appointment. I'd better head out or I'll be late. Apologies detective. Maybe another time."

"Are you sure? You never said," said Jonathan.

"Slipped my mind. Perfectly sure, Yes. Apologies. I'll show myself out." Charlie walked towards the lounge door.

"Nonsense, old boy. Let me," Jonathan followed in Charlie's wake. Rachel watched, her interest piqued as she finished her cup of tea. She placed her cup and saucer on the sideboard and heard cushioned footsteps return towards her. Jonathan entered the room, walked over to the sideboard and poured himself a whisky.

"One for you, detective?"

"Thank you, but too early in the day for me, Mr. Fanshaw."

"Jonathan, please."

"Please, call me Rachel. Good to meet you."

"Don't be too hasty, Rachel. You may hate me." He laughed. "Am I a suspect?"

"Should you be?"

"For the murder of my sister? Don't be so ridiculous."

"And you believe that it was a murder?"

"Ah ha, you're one of them?"

"One of them?"

"Everything's a question. A probe." Jonathan sipped his drink. "Never a straight answer, Maitre Barnes." Rachel smiled and poured herself another tea.

"I suppose that's my job. To question, to explore the possibilities. I'm not a monster, though. I'm here to try to help." Jonathan studied Rachel. The air in the room was thick with tension.

"True. Perhaps you are." The tension eased. "Apologies but even after all these years her disappearance," he raised his glass, "still makes me angry." *Angry*, thought Rachel.

"And you miss her?" There was a pause as Jonathan thought about his answer.

"I suppose I do. Don't get me wrong. We had our ups and downs, as all siblings do, but she was still my flesh and blood." Jonathan finished his drink. "I'd better go and secure the guns. I wouldn't want to get in trouble with the police now would I?" Rachel smiled. Jonathan moved to the lounge door and was halted by Rachel's voice.

"If I may ask? The name of the gentleman who came in with you?"

"Charles Fothergill. Splendid gentleman."

"Good to put a face to a name."

"You know him?"

"Only from the file. I'll need to speak with him."

"I'm sure he'll oblige but he's a busy person."

"As we all are."

"Unquestionably. Please excuse me." Jonathan left the room, closing the door behind him. Rachel took her phone from her pocket and sent a message to Jim to pull together Fothergill's profile and email it to her. She looked out the window where Jonathan had now returned to his vehicle with Fletcher in tow. Jonathan removed two shotguns from the rear of the vehicle and handed them to Fletcher.

***

"Drop us here, mate," said Jamie.

"You sure you don't want to cover the crime scene cordon?" said Longy.

"No, thanks. All yours. Em and I are happy with the grow."

"But the sergeant crewed Emily with me."

"Wilson won't care." Jamie climbed out of the vehicle and opened the passenger door. "Come on, Em." Emily gave Longy an apologetic look and climbed out of the car. "See you in a few hours, John," said Emily.

The officers walked towards the terraced house, a house which Jamie knew well. A uniformed police officer guarded the gate. Jamie approached the officer.

"We've arrived from Fenchurch. Who's in charge?"

"Sergeant's inside with her team." The officer thumbed backwards, towards the front door, and transmitted on his radio. "Two from Fenchurch entering."

"Cheers," said Jamie as he stepped into the garden and walked to the front of the building. He halted at the door and stepped to one side. Emily thought he looked unsure of himself.

"You OK?"

"Yeah. I'm fine. Ladies first." Emily pulled some blue gloves from a pouch on her police belt and put them on. She turned the front door handle and walked in. Jamie followed behind with one hand in his pocket. The other he brushed against the door handle as he passed. Jamie was nervous. This was a step into the unknown for him. Return to a crime scene where he should have never been in the first place. The pungent sweet smell of cannabis dominated the air. He could hear the tread of the officer's feet upstairs as they examined and dismantled the grow. A head popped out of the front room.

"Can you pop in here, mate? Detained is in here and I'm dying for a piss." Jamie looked at Emily.

"Either of you. Doesn't matter which."

"I've got him," said Jamie.

"Exhibits officer is back in the kitchen. May need a hand." The officer said to Emily. She headed to the back of the house. "In here then —" said the officer.

"Jamie."

"Jamie. I'm Dave." They entered the room where one man was sitting on an armchair. "Don't know his name, won't speak to us and pretends that he can't understand us. He's all yours. I'll be back in two." Dave scuttled from the room. Jamie looked down at the chef to whom he had spoken last time he was here. The chef smiled at him. Jamie leaned over his face until he was mere inches away.

"Don't say a fuckin' word. You keep your gob shut. Got it." The man smiled. Jamie grabbed his throat and pushed him back in the chair. "You have never fuckin' seen me." He roughly pushed the man's head to the side and stepped back. Jamie got out a cigarette and lit it. He heard footsteps in the hall. "Not a bloody word." The door opened. Another officer entered.

"I'll take him, mate. Transport to the nick." The officer frowned at Jamie's cigarette.

"Thought he may want one?" The officer wasn't convinced.

"I'd put that out, mate. The skipper won't be happy." Jamie docked it in an ashtray on the coffee table, leaving the stub end in the ashtray.

"Over to you." Jamie left the room and headed towards the kitchen where an exhibits officer was being assisted by Emily. Hands in pockets Jamie walked towards the bathroom, halting at the kitchen sink and resting his ungloved hand there. "What's in the back?"

"Bathroom, I think," said Emily, holding up some toothbrushes which had been handed to her in an exhibit bag. Jamie continued through to the back and stepped into the bathroom.

"Could do with a clean," he said to a scene of crime officer (SOCO) who was examining the mirror. The officer turned, looked at Jamie, and knocked a half-empty bottle of green shower gel from the bath side. Jamie stepped in and picked up the bottle.

"Where's your gloves?" asked the SOCO, looking at Jamie's hands. "For fuck's sake. It's a bloody crime scene. Get some gloves on." Jamie stood transfixed. The SOCO followed Jamie's eyes to the spot where the shower gel had been standing. The area now had a clear red ring of congealed fluid where the bottle had been. The SOCO reached for a swab, quickly took a sample and placed it in a tube. "Looks like blood," she said aloud. She turned to Jamie. "Get the search coordinator in here please." Jamie turned and walked into the kitchen. His head was spinning. *Shit. They're gonna find more. They're bound to now. What should I do?*

"You OK, Jamie?" asked Emily, resting a hand on his shoulder.

"They've found some blood."

"Blood?"

"Yeah, they want to see the skipper." His hand went to his brow. Emily noticed that he wasn't wearing gloves.

"I'll get her." She walked away. The exhibits officer was focussing on logging exhibits. Jamie moved to the cooker. Grabbed a pot handle, released. Picked up a spoon, released. He heard footsteps in the hallway. Jamie reached to his belt for some gloves and pulled them out. The sergeant entered the kitchen, noticed his hands.

"Get those bloody gloves on. What are you playing at?" She walked straight past him, not waiting for a reply, and entered the bathroom. Emily approached Jamie who was now calm and collected.

"Could be nothing," said Emily.

"Maybe," replied Jamie. Emily noted the time. *Ten minutes in the house with no gloves on. Probably nothing but I've been instructed to report everything back.*

Chapter 9

Joe parked near the church, climbed out of his vehicle and was immediately buffeted by a chilly wind. Grey clouds dominated the sky with an oppressiveness that thickened the air. Rain was on its way. Looking left, he spotted the woman he had previously seen at the church. She stood looking towards a gravestone, then squatted down and tended to some flowers. The woman stood back up, rested a hand on the headstone, and walked back to the church doorway, where she was met by a man wearing a dog collar.

"Poor woman," said Joe, turning away so as not to intrude on her moment of grief and reflection. Joe walked further down the road and headed towards Ronnie's new house. He entered the garden and gave a rap on the front door. He waited, rolled a cigarette, tucked it behind his ear and fastened his coat. He knocked on the door again and heard a muffled response from the house.

"Come on, man. I haven't got all day," he mumbled. The lock rattled from within and the door opened. Ronnie stood before him wearing loose grey jogging bottoms and an off-white vest. Looking tired and with his hair dishevelled, Ronnie belched.

"Oh. It's you." He turned and walked into the room. "Come on in. Make yourself comfortable."

"Nice to see you too, mate. Working hard, I see." Ronnie raised a hand, beckoning Joe to follow him into the kitchen. He disappeared through a door. "It's nearly two o'clock, grandad. You only just got up?"

"No, young man. I was having a snooze."

"A snooze? I thought you were supposed to be working."

"Calm yourself. I am. I haven't got it easy like you, you know, with your steady nine to five hours. Drift in, titillate some flowers and bugger off home. I'm on it twenty-four hours a day. I grab a chance to power nap when I can. It's all part of the character."

"Part of the character," mimicked Joe. He sniggered. "You're not Tom 'bloody' Cruise. What character are you playing? A layabout?"

"Cheeky, sod." Ronnie laughed. "Cup of tea?"

"Yes please, mate. As long as you can manage that?"

"I'm sure it's within my capabilities." He flicked the kettle on, straightened his hair and turned to Joe.

"How's it going?"

"I'm OK. Had a beer with the village shop owner last night. He's gonna be a well of knowledge."

"Nice one."

"Neighbours haven't poked their heads out yet but they will. A nice village, on the face of it."

"With a dark secret."

"Who knows what happened? I think I'll get something out of Alf from the shop. I'm seeing him later for a game of chess."

"Chess? Never put you down as a player."

"Used to play a lot. Game of Kings. And Queens, of course."

"Well, you learn something new every day."

"That you do, young man. You'll never guess where I'm off tomorrow night."

"Go on."

"Choir practice." Joe started laughing.

"You are having a laugh?"

"Not at all. Invited by the vicar himself. You see. Working hard. Infiltration into the community from different angles. Not anyone could do it." Ronnie reached for a packet of cigarettes from the kitchen table.

"I met a guy from the church yesterday. A bloody giant. Said his name was Richard. He looks after the grass around the church. Didn't want me treading on his turf," said Joe.

"Was he OK with you?"

"Once he knew that I wasn't nicking his job, he was. Strange bloke."

"That's villagers you see. Don't like outsiders."

"You seem to be doing OK."

"Yeah, but I've got that talent you see. I can fit in anywhere. That's why I have been hand-picked by Rach for this job." Joe rolled his eyes. "Fag?" asked Ronnie, holding out his packet of cigarettes.

"Sure," said Joe, taking a cigarette and placing it in his mouth.

"Outside," said Ronnie. "Let's take a look at the garden and I can tell you what I want to do with it. We haven't got all day to stand around chin wagging." Ronnie winked at Joe, turned, and smirked as he walked to and out of the back door, with Joe following.

***

Charles arrived at his lovely detached house on the outskirts of Fenchurch. Pulling swiftly onto his driveway, he parked and climbed out whilst fumbling for his house keys. The keys dropped to the ground and, turning, he inadvertently kicked them under his car.

"Fucking hell." Charles got onto his knees and looked underneath the car, spotting the keys nestled against one of the front tyres. He stood back up and noticed his elderly neighbour was watching him from his front garden.

"Lost something, Charles?"

"Dropped my keys. Spotted them though, thank you." Charles forced a grin though inside his anger seethed. *Bugger off and leave me alone.*

"Can I help? Maybe my stick will reach them." The man held up a wooden walking stick. Charles strutted around the car to the tyre in question. He bent down, retrieving the keys.

"No need. All in hand. Thank you." Charles turned, walked to his house and entered. The neighbour looked perplexed at Charles' abruptness, shook his head and wandered back to his house.

Charles closed the door, took a deep breath and walked into the hallway. He stopped and looked back. "Bollocks." Forgetting that he still had his outdoor footwear on, he now looked at a trail of muddy boot marks on the carpet. He kicked his boots off and considered cleaning up the mess. Melissa would have known how to sort it straight away. *What would Melissa do?* Charles walked into the kitchen and opened a cupboard where cleaning products were stored. He pulled a couple out and looked back at the prints. *Leave them to dry,* he thought.

Leaving everything in place he ran upstairs, walked into the ensuite and stripped out of his hunting clothing. Returning to the bedroom, Charles opened his wardrobe where his trousers and shirts hung, neatly pressed. He selected some chinos and a dress shirt and swiftly dressed. Whilst doing so, he kept glancing at his briefcase, which was placed on the end of his bed. He had left it there this morning. He walked across to it, decoded the lock and tentatively opened the case.

Within lay the envelope. Within that the note. Not the first note that he had received but it was the first that he had received at home. He couldn't bear to look. Charles closed the case gently, pressed the clasps and spun the lock. He couldn't look at it. Wouldn't look at it. It needed to go into the safe place with the other two. Returning to the ensuite he splashed his face with water, looked at himself in the mirror and smiled.

"Come on, Charles. You've got this." He collected the case and headed to his car.

Thirty minutes later Charles walked through the centre of Fenchurch, checking his watch. He would make it to the bank before closing. His steps quickened as he approached the doors and climbed the steps.

Inside the bank it was quiet. One teller was working, he smiled and walked through to the security door where he punched in the keypad code. Charles entered, approached his secretary's door and knocked, before popping his head around.

"Afternoon, Cynthia. Only dropping something in my office." Cynthia was startled.

"On your day off, Charles? You are a workaholic."

"I was in town anyway. I'll only be two minutes." Charles walked through his secretary's office towards his own.

"I've taken a call for you. It can wait though. Nothing to bother you about today." *Clearly, you want to*, thought Charles. He waited expectantly. "I've made an appointment for you tomorrow afternoon." Cynthia checked her notes. "A Detective Barnes wishes to see you." Charles froze. Cynthia noticed his reaction. "Is that OK? I haven't done wrong, have I?" Charles controlled himself and smiled.

"No, you haven't but I thought that I had a full diary tomorrow."

"You had a gap at two. She said that it wouldn't take long." Charles took a breath.

"Have I got a gap later in the week or even next week?" Cynthia checked his diary.

"Monday is looking OK."

"Great. Monday will do. It can't be that important or they'd be knocking down the door." Charles laughed. Cynthia smiled. Charles entered his office, closing the door behind him. He was sweating, his pulse throbbing. He placed his case on his desk and took out his mobile to ring Jonathan. Stopped himself. He then opened his desk drawer and removed half a bottle of malt. Charles looked at it, put it back, then stood up and started pacing. "Think, Charles, think." He returned to his briefcase, opened it and removed the note.

***

The loud resonant tones of the church organ reverberated amongst the rafters, bouncing from roof to wall, ricocheting from the stone floor as Audrey struck the keys and pedals with purpose. She took her practice seriously, eyes closed in rapture, imagining the pews to be full, as she threw her heart into the praise of God, her only important critic. Audrey didn't hear the small wooden portal open, or her brother enter, slowly closing the door behind him. Richard looked around, noted that the church was empty and walked up behind her. He reached towards her, the music stopped with a groan.

"What do you want?" Audrey's eyes, reflected in the organist mirror, pierced Richard.

"He's down visiting that new bloke?"

"Who?"

"The new gardener."

"And why did you need to interrupt my practice to tell me that?"

"Well, I was passing his house and thought I'd come up here for a cuppa." Audrey frowned at Richard.

"The new gardener's movements within the village are of no interest to me. Honestly, I wish that you would stop worrying. He has nothing to do with the church. Your job is safe. Now, stop fretting." Richard looked suitably chastised. "Now you have interrupted my practice, my private time with Our Lord. I suggest that you reflect upon that instead," Audrey nodded towards the altar, "and I will put the kettle on." Audrey stood up and headed towards the small kitchen as Richard dutifully genuflected to the altar before taking a pew.

***

Ronnie stood up from the toilet, pulled his trousers up and tucked his shirt in. He belched, rubbing his chest as he did so. The remains of curry cooked two days ago was proving not to be the wisest of decisions. Still, a gentle walk down to Alfred's and a couple of drams of whisky over a friendly game of chess would settle things down. He splashed some water over his face and pushed back his hair with damp hands.

"Boy you are getting old," he said to his reflection. He raised his chin, looking at his beard, then covered it with his hands and imagined himself clean-shaven. "May take a few years off." Ronnie picked up his electric toothbrush, pressed on and when it didn't vibrate, realised that he had forgotten to charge it. He brushed his teeth anyway and laid the item back down on the shelf above the sink, where no doubt it would remain, uncharged for some time. "OK Kasparov, let's go show him." He went downstairs and headed out of the house.

Margaret Epstow was standing in her front garden pruning her roses as she watched the new gentleman walk towards her. Smartly dressed and sporting a fedora, she felt that he cut a dashing figure, with a strong confident walk and an air of assuredness about him. She straightened her apron and removed a gardening glove so she could tidy her greying hair. The man stepped from the road onto the pavement and walked past her.

"Good afternoon," she squeaked, in an uncharacteristic show of bravery.

"Hello there," boomed Ronnie, tipping his hat. "Enjoying the garden?"

"Yes, but there's so many jobs to do when you're on your own."

"You are telling me," said Ronnie. "I'm getting a lad in to tackle mine. I've moved into one of the shepherd's cottages."

"Yes, it's been vacant for a while."

"Ronnie Cuthbertson."

"Mrs Epstow."

"And Mr Epstow?"

"He passed away many years ago."

"Oh, I'm sorry. Thoughtless of me."

"Not at all. He's long gone."

"And a young lady like you has stayed single?" Margaret blushed.

"Hardly young, Mr Cuthbertson."

"We all are in here," said Ronnie, pointing to his head, "please call me Ronnie."

"We are, Ronnie." Ronnie waited.

"Oh, sorry. I'm Margaret." They both smiled.

"Lovely to meet you, Margaret."

"And you, Ronnie."

"I must go. I'm off to beat Alfred, in the bottom village, at chess."

"The Game of Kings." Ronnie looked surprised.

"A lady of culture. Do you play?"

"Not since university. Please, don't let me delay you."

"Lovely to talk," said Ronnie, walking away. He halted and turned. "Maybe a cup of tea? Sometime, when you're free?"

"That would be lovely." Ronnie continued to walk with a spring now in his step. Margaret smiled at his back. *What a nice gentleman,* she thought.

***

Thirty minutes later Ronnie was sitting in Alfred's kitchen at the table. The room was warmed by an oil-fired Aga upon which Alfred was drying his vests. Above the Aga, a Sheila's Maid was festooned with socks, pants and a pair of long johns. The kitchen work surfaces were clear and the sink was empty. Ronnie had noted Alfred's tidiness on entering the room. A tidiness which reflected the man himself and would undoubtedly feature in his gameplay.

A bottle of malt and two glasses were waiting on the kitchen table, beside which the battleground was set. The black and white of opposing armies facing each other. Alfred poured them both a measure, as the men faced each other across the chequered field of play. He pushed a glass towards Ronnie who accepted it graciously, tipping it in salute, before taking a sip. The smoky liquid caressed his taste buds as it passed through his mouth and oesophagus, gently igniting his competitive edge as it descended. He looked across at Alfred, whose gaze was firmly fixed upon the board.

Ronnie raised a hand to the board and opened by moving king's pawn forward two places. Alfred's eyes flicked towards Ronnie's face, which remained impassive. A wry smile came upon Alfred's face as he moved his hand, and without looking at the board, moved his piece. Ronnie looked down, and moved his next. Alfred reciprocated. Ronnie moved again and Alfred responded.

"Morra Gambit accepted," said Alfred as he moved. "You can play?"

"A little bit, my friend. A little bit." Ronnie rubbed his hands together and took Alfred's black pawn.

"Game on," said Alfred. An hour later both men looked down at the depleted board.

"I enjoyed that. Another whisky before the pub?" asked Alfred.

"I'll have the whisky but maybe refrain from the pub for tonight." Alfred poured. "I don't want to be getting home too late at night. Not after you told me about that young lady going missing."

"That was years ago. There's no need to worry now."

"Even so. Missing is missing. It's not every day that you move to a village where the landowner's daughter has mysteriously disappeared."

"True, but she was a good-looking young lady, not an elderly gent like yourself."

"I'm not worth the effort?" Ronnie looked affronted. Alfred chuckled.

"Probably not, I'm afraid."

"Could have been an accident. Hit by a car and someone panicked?"

"Can't have been. She took the lane up to the big house. No cars there."

"Maybe she got lost on the way. Fell down a hill, in a hole?"

"Nope." Alfred was looking flushed with the whisky taking effect.

"Sorry, I didn't realise that I was in the presence of Hercule Poirot."

"You joke, Ronnie, but I see a lot of things. Hear a lot of things. I'm part of the furniture around here." Alfred raised an eyebrow as he looked at Ronnie.

"And I will be if I don't make a move," replied Ronnie, checking his watch. "A mystery for tomorrow, mate."

"You take care on your way home."

"You are taking the piss now." Ronnie slipped on his coat.

"Not at all. The killer has never been found. I could be wrong. Maybe they will strike once more." Ronnie laughed.

"Bugger off. I'll be careful though. Maybe see you tomorrow?"

"I'll be here." Alfred moved to stand.

"I'll let myself out. You keep warm." Ronnie opened the back door, halted and turned. "I'll give the mystery some thought but if you don't see me tomorrow, then you'll know what's happened." Ronnie left the house and stepped out into the dark. He lit a cigarette and walked away from the house, happy with himself. *A good night's work*, he thought. He had lost the game but had touched upon Victoria's death. He felt if he played Alfred slowly, something of use would be revealed.

***

Danny opened the back door to his house and walked into the kitchen. He kicked his shoes off, removed his coat, and dumped it on top of them. The kitchen was a mess. The sink spewed unwashed dishes and work surfaces were littered with ready-meal boxes and beer cans. Danny didn't even appear to notice the smell emanating from a bulging black bin bag which loomed in a corner. He opened the fridge, took out a large bottle of cheap cider, selected the best of the unclean glasses and walked into his living room.

In stark contrast, this room was tidier. An armchair faced the television and next to it a side table where a couple of empty bottles of Bud stood next to the TV remote control. Danny lifted the empty bottles, replacing them with cider and glass and, returning to the kitchen, tossed them towards the bin. The liner gobbled them gratefully with a clanking churn as they collided with other empties. Picking up the remote control, Danny flicked the TV on as he collected his week's worth of ignored mail from the carpet by the front door.

The TV screen displayed a PlayStation log on screen. Danny slumped into the chair, dropping the mail in his lap, as he used the PlayStation remote to select a game. Passing Assassin's Creed, Hitman and Grand Theft Auto, he selected Call of Duty and waited for the game to load. Danny reached for the cider and poured a glass with a shaking hand, took a large gulp and examined his post. He discarded each to the floor as he checked the red typed envelopes.

"Council tax, electricity, water, TV licence. You can all fuck off." He took another drink, emptying the glass as he looked at a blank envelope left on his lap. He poured another glass and placed his PlayStation headphones on, then opened the envelope. Inside was a single note. Danny read it.

"What the fuck." He twisted, looking to the front door, and spun to face the kitchen. He read the message again, then checked the back of the paper. It was blank. Danny stood swiftly, moved to his front window, parted the blind and peered out. The street outside was clear. "No, no, no!" He turned, snatched up the blank envelope, stuffed the note back in, crumpled it and threw it towards the empty fire grate. Danny's legs were shaking, he crouched, cowering and cornered. *Not again. I can't go through this again.*

***

"Do we have to do this now?" asked Emily.

"How'd your first day go?" said Mick, her handler, on the other end of the phone.

"It was long. I'm tired, I need a hot bath and a glass of wine. Can we do this in the morning?" She received no response except silence. Emily strained to hear something, anything.

"Did you make contact with the subject?" Mick was not going to wait.

"Yes, I did."

"Good, good. Was he OK with you?"

"Cocky at first but settled down. He thinks a lot of himself."

"And his colleagues?"

"Mixed reviews, I would guess. I only saw them for a short time when we briefed on. Went across with him to Barnston."

"How was he at the murder scene?"

"Murder scene? Cannabis grow. Unless you know differently."

"Trust me. It's more than simply a grow. How was he?"

"Volunteered to go. Seemed happy to be doing something different."

"Did he now?"

"Yes. Sent a lad called Longy to patrol one crime scene and took me into the grow."

"Longy?"

"John Longshaw." There was silence. Emily waited as Mick took notes.

"Longy OK with that?"

"He accepted it but I was supposed to be shadowing him all day. Jamie took over."

"And in the grow?"

"We both went in. Jamie looked after a prisoner and I worked with the exhibits officer."

"Was Hyatt left alone?"

"Only whilst one of the cops went for a piss."

"Where was he left alone?

"In the front room with the prisoner."

"OK. So you are with the exhibits. What did Hyatt do?"

"As I said, he was with the prisoner. Then, shortly afterwards, he came into the kitchen where I was and then he checked out the bathroom where SOCO was. That's when they found some traces of blood."

"Who found them?"

"I dunno. SOCO or Jamie. I'm not sure who spotted it."

"Hyatt's reaction?"

"Seemed a bit shocked. I checked that he was OK though."

"Anything else?"

"He wasn't wearing protective gloves?" Emily walked up her stairs to the landing and entered her bedroom.

"When?"

"He only put them on when he was told to. I'm guessing that he wore no gloves from entering the house up until then." Again there was silence on the other end. "Then they locked the bathroom and kitchen down and called for another SOCO. We were used to bag the cannabis plants. Cut them at the stalk and seize them, leaving the rest of the grow intact." Emily walked into her bathroom and started the bath running. Her caller took the hint.

"OK, I can tell that you're tired. We'll need a full debrief by the end of the week."

"After this set of shifts?"

"Yes, that'll be fine. Keep in with him."

"Will do."

"And, Heather — nice one. A great start." Emily went back downstairs as she terminated the call, loathing herself for the role which she was fulfilling. She tossed her phone on the sofa, walked into the kitchen and grabbed a beer from the fridge.

"Will I ever get away from this?"

***

"That's fine. Thank you for letting me know. I'll see you on Monday." Rachel ended the call. She was sitting in her vehicle outside of the team's office. Charles Fothergill's secretary had changed the appointment, which she had advised now clashed with his other appointments. Accidental or deliberate, Rachel would never know. She climbed out and headed into the office.

"How are we all doing?" Rachel asked as she entered the room.

"Good," replied Sarah, "You?"

"Fair to middling. I've brought you all some treats from Evesham." She placed some white paper bags containing cakes and pastries by the kettle.

"Cheers," said Tom, "I'll put the kettle on." He lifted the kettle, found it sufficiently full, replaced it and switched it on. "How's life at the big house?"

"Different," replied Rachel. "It's a beautiful place. Busy during the day and quiet at night time. The modern world encroaches when it's open to visitors and the staff. The cafe is a busy little spot. At night there's nothing. An empty house with only Sir David, Jonathan, and Fletcher to look after them. The cook leaves after dinner. You could be on your own all evening and not see a soul should you choose to."

"Sounds like a right bundle of fun," said Sarah.

"Purely a different way of life," said Rachel. "The house needs a family."

"What about Jonathan?"

"A conundrum. Wealthy, successful and due to inherit the estate. You'd think he'd be a catch. Not sure what his story is. That's why I'm here. Catch up on where we are. Where's Matt?"

"Here," called Matt, walking from the direction of the toilets. "You OK?"

"Yes. You?"

"How do you bloody do this? I am up to my eyes reading statement after statement. Reading them again. Cross-referencing them. It's driving me insane." Matthew mimicked pulling his hair out. Rachel laughed.

"It's a crucial part of an investigation. We don't get the advantage of being there and seeing what happened. We have to rely on their accounts from the night. We need to be thorough."

"I know, but bloody hell. It's a ball-acher."

"Have a cake," said Rachel gesturing to the white packets. "It'll make you feel better." Matthew looked into the packets. Rachel turned to Jim who was studiously working on a computer.

"Jim. Got anything for me?"

"I've sent you Charles Fothergill's updated profile."

"Anything of note?"

"He was expected to marry into the family. Approved by Sir David but not so much by Victoria. He was at the pub on the night of her disappearance. He started the fight. Now married with two kids and doing well for himself."

"A suspect?"

"As much as anyone is. A jilted lover or fiancee, whatever you wish to call it. Fighting for the woman he loves. Probably drunk at the time. He knew she was heading home. He'd have known the route she took."

"He's cancelled a meeting that I was due to have with him tomorrow."

"Has he now? Why?"

"I'm not sure. His secretary says he's now busy. Convenient, eh?"

"Yes."

"It's reset for Monday. I'll take a look at his profile with you this afternoon. Prepare some questions together, if that's OK?"

"Fine by me."

"I'll sit in with you," said Matthew. "It'll give me a break from statements and I can observe how the detective mind works." Tom handed Matt and Rachel mugs of coffee.

"First, let's review where we are with the others. Guys, can we all gather in." The team took seats on sofas. Rachel perched on the arm of a chair. "Who's gonna start us off?" Matt raised his hand.

"Ronnie seems to have settled in well. He's out regularly in the village, getting his face known."

"Contacts?"

"He's got friendly with the local shop owner, Alf. Seems to think that he is going to be a good source of intelligence. Ronnie's taking it slowly with him, but thinks it will pay dividends."

"Good," said Rachel.

"He's also been chatting to a couple of the neighbours. He's getting the impression that most people have lived there for years. He's regularly in the pub and he's in with the vicar."

"The vicar?" said Tom.

"Yes. Met him on day one. Pastor Melthrop is trying to recruit him into the church choir and Ronnie has shown that he is keen."

"The sacrifices that some people make," said Sarah.

"Ronnie or the vicar?" asked Tom.

"Both," said Sarah. "Ronnie as a chorister? I don't know who will suffer the most." Tom laughed.

"Well, he's getting in there and that's what we need," said Rachel. "Thanks, Matt. Next."

"Mark and Tanya Holt," said Tom. "Brother and sister. Profiles are complete on both. Research has identified him as living in Fenchurch, married and practising as a solicitor. He's doing OK for himself."

"And Tanya?"

"You mean Tanya Hyatt." Tom paused for dramatic effect. "Yes, now married to Jamie Hyatt, our serving police officer. Both are living in a lovely cottage in the bottom village. No kids. She doesn't appear to be working. They've got a nice spot on only a copper's wage."

"Maybe they've had some inherited money?" stated Matt.

"Not that we can find," said Jim.

"An interesting couple, though," said Tom. "On paper, it doesn't add up. A bit more digging to do there, I think. When can we talk to her?"

"I'm looking at starting some interviews soon. We'll come on to that," said Rachel. "How's Joe doing?" she asked Matthew.

"Slow going there. He's had no sightings of Danny yet. Had a slight run-in with a bloke called Richard. Richard looks after the church grounds and thought that Danny may have been treading on his toes. He's smoothed that out. Richard seems friendly with a woman at the church."

"That will be Audrey Melthrop. The vicar's wife," said Jim. He tapped on the keyboard. "Her brother is called Richard."

"Built like a brick shit house."

"Sounds like him."

"Joe's going to nip to the pub for a pint when he finishes on Friday. See if Danny's there."

"Good shout," said Rachel. "Which leaves me with Jonathan, Charles Fothergill and Jamie. Fothergill I'll speak to on Monday." Rachel looked thoughtful. "What do you think about a couple of days at the house, Matt?"

"For you?"

"Both of us. Let's see if we can get some time with Jonathan. Work out what he's all about."

"Sounds good," said Matt.

"And Tanya?" asked Tom.

"Let's get a plan together for midweek when I plan to see her brother. I'd like to orchestrate you speaking with her as I'm speaking to Jamie. I want to check in with Kaur before we do that though."

"What about some technical?" said Jim.

"What are you thinking?"

"Something in their house. Maybe a listening device? Tracker on their car? Anything to help us develop the intelligence picture."

"Have we got the authority to do that?" asked Matt.

"We don't need it. We're not in the police. No longer subject to their rules."

"He's right," said Tom, "we need to tread carefully though. Remember Kaur's got oversight of the investigation."

"I'd prefer to get a bit more on them before we go ahead. Let's see what we get from Mark Holt's interview and if Kaur has any new intel for us. Prep some kit ready though, Jim. I understand what you are saying." Tom gave Jim a wink.

"Will do."

"Thanks, everyone. Let's keep going. This has the feel of a proper investigation." Rachel smiled and stood up. "Jim, twenty minutes then we'll go over the profile." Jim gave her a thumbs up. She turned to Matt. "Let's talk about the upcoming weekend." Rachel walked towards her desk, followed by Matt.

"Enjoying yourself?"

"Loving it. This is what we should be doing."

Chapter 10

Kaur stared at the computer as he tried to make sense of the analyst's report, which detailed the latest crime trends within the division. Supported by graphs and pie charts, he ploughed his way through it, resisting the urge to go directly to the last page, which would give him the analyst's recommendations for action. The desk phone rang, and with relief, Kaur lifted the handset.

"DI Kaur," he said.

"Jamal, John Trimble. Have you got a few minutes?" Kaur leaned back in his seat, frowning. He recognised the name though he had never met the man.

"Have I any choice?"

"No. Fancy a coffee? I'm buying."

"Sure. When and where?"

"Now would be great. Mrs Bakehouse's, down from the nick."

"Five minutes OK?"

"Sure. What do you want?"

"Americano, please. We've not met. How will I know you?"

"I know you, Jamal. See you soon." The phone line went dead. Kaur replaced the receiver and pushed back his chair. *What the hell does he want?* Standing up he reached for his coat and shrugged it on. Confident that he had done nothing wrong personally, he still felt the internal trepidation of being summoned by Complaints and Discipline. He left his office, descended the back stairs and slipped out of the nick without encountering anyone.

A few minutes later he opened the door to the cafe. His senses were assaulted by the smell of fresh coffee and baked pastries. He looked around and saw a man smiling at him from one of the tables in a far corner. The man beckoned Kaur over, indicating to the coffee waiting for him. Kaur approached the table. Trimble stood up and reached out with his right hand.

"Jamal, good to meet you." Kaur took Trimble's hand and they shook. They both settled down.

"No problem, John."

"Nice coffee in here," said Trimble.

"What can I do for you?"

"Straight to the point. I like that." Kaur waited. Trimble looked at Kaur, assessing him.

"I'd like to take you into my confidence. Can I do that, Jamal?"

"Do I have anything to worry about?"

"No, no," Trimble laughed. "If you did then this would be a totally different type of conversation. I can assure you that you have nothing to worry about. None of your team have anything to worry about." Trimble had already made his decision before meeting Kaur. "Tell me what you know about Jamie Hyatt."

"Jamie Hyatt?"

"Yes. You checked him out the other day on the intelligence system. Why?"

"He was a witness in an old murder investigation. It's being investigated by an outside team as a cold case."

"By ex-DI Rachel Barnes?"

"Yes. You obviously know."

"I know a lot of things, Jamal. I believe that you have oversight. How's it going?"

"It's in the early stages. What's your interest?"

"Hyatt is my interest. How did you find him back then?"

"I don't recall him much. A young copper who seemed a bit cocky. Arrogant. Not unlike a lot of cops."

"Has Rachel spoken with him yet?"

"Not that she's made me aware."

"Can you find out, please?"

"Yes."

"I think that we can help each other here. I have a file in my car which I'd like you to look at. Strictly between my department and you. Hyatt is more than he appears."

"Corrupt?"

"Undoubtedly. We are in the process of gathering the evidence to prove it. The, shall we say, unique means by which the cold case is being investigated may help us. In return, we may be able to help the investigation." An elderly couple walked into the café. Trimble watched them select a table to sit at. "Rachel was a good officer. But for now, I'd like to keep this purely between us. I don't want Rachel or her team to know we are having this conversation. Is that clear?"

"I trust her, if that helps."

"Her trust is not in question. We'll need to speak with her but all of her team will not need to know."

"Understood." Trimble smiled then stood up.

"Drink up then. The car's around the corner." He waited for Kaur and they both left the café.

***

"I feel important being driven around by our lead investigator," said Matt. Rachel pulled her vehicle to the front of Evesham House and came to a stop. "I could get used to it." He stepped out of the car and walked around to the driver's side, where he opened the door for Rachel. She climbed out.

"Thank you."

"I'll get our cases from the boot." Rachel leant back into the vehicle and retrieved her walking stick. Her leg ached slightly this morning and she had grown used to the reassurance the stick offered her. The boot closed and Matt's head appeared with a big grin.

"Having fun?"

"Oh yes. This is more me. Out in the field at the sharp end. Right-hand man to Miss Marple."

"She didn't have a sidekick."

"And look what she achieved. You'll achieve so much more."

"I'm sure I will," she laughed. Both turned as the front door to the house opened and Fletcher stepped out. He walked down the entryway steps and smiled.

"Detective," he said, nodding towards Rachel.

"Fletcher." She turned towards Matt. "Matt, this is Fletcher, the man who keeps the house running and looks after the family's needs." Matt placed a case down, stepped forward and extended his hand to the butler.

"Good afternoon, Fletcher. Matt, Rachel's partner." Fletcher declined to shake his hand but stepped forward retrieving the case that Matt had placed down.

"Very good, sir. Can I take your other case?" Fletcher extended his hand, waiting for Matt to pass it over.

"Yes, indeed." He handed the case over and turned to look at Rachel with a bemused look on his face. Rachel smiled back.

"I'll take your cases up to your room, Detective. Tea is available in the lounge."

"Thank you, Fletcher. I'll show Matt the way." Fletcher led the way into the house, moving to one side to allow Rachel and Matt into the large open hallway first. Matt turned to close the door.

"I'll get that, sir," said Fletcher who quickly placed the cases down and stepped towards the entrance.

"Come on, Matt. Let Fletcher do his job." Rachel took Matt's hand and they headed into the lounge.

"He's keen isn't he," said Matt, looking around the room and walking up to the large windows which picture framed the grounds.

"Efficient," clarified Rachel. "He believes that things should be done in a certain way. This is his domain and he's proud of it. Shall I pour?" Rachel poured tea into delicate china cups.

"Still," said Matt, "time has moved on. We're not in the nineteen-twenties now." Rachel handed Matt his teacup.

"I think it's quaint. There's no harm in it. Fletcher is happy in his role and the family feel that they are well cared for."

"How the privileged live, eh."

"How indeed," said Jonathan, rising from a high-backed Chesterfield chair. Matt jumped. The chair back had been facing them from across the room and he had not realised that it was occupied. Jonathan briskly folded the paper that he had been reading and walked around to a coffee table where he placed it down. "One of yours, Rachel?" he asked.

"Matt, please meet Jonathan Fanshaw." Matt looked flustered. Rachel's face showed amusement.

"I didn't mean to offend. It was purely an observation. You know, each to their own and all that."

"Mmm." Jonathan looked Matt up and down and was unimpressed. "Well, I hope that you will enjoy the privileges extended to you, by my house, during your stay."

"I will. Thank you for having me." Rachel contained a laugh.

"We'd like to ask you a few questions about Victoria, Jonathan," said Rachel, "Will you be at dinner tonight?"

"I'm afraid I'm away tonight. I'll be back tomorrow."

"Tomorrow it is then."

"How about a walk around the grounds? Meet here at ten?"

"That would be great." Jonathan checked his wristwatch.

"Right, must be off. I need to ask Fletcher to prepare the horse and carriage or I'll be late for my appointment." Jonathan looked at Matt, with one eyebrow raised, as if challenging him to comment. Matt did not remark. "Good evening to you both." He turned and walked out of the room.

"Well that's you put firmly in your place," said Rachel, laughing.

"Why didn't you tell me he was in the room?"

"I didn't see him either. It could have been worse."

"Worse — The man thinks that I'm a complete buffoon."

"Maybe he has a point. How have I managed to miss that about you?"

"You cheeky —"

"I'm joking, I'm joking. He'll be fine. He doesn't know you. Let him think that about you. Use it to your advantage. His guard may be down with you if he doesn't see you as a threat." Matt nodded as he looked out of the window in contemplation. "This will be an interesting weekend," said Rachel.

***

A white box van pulled up outside the Red Lion and parked. Joe stepped out of the driver's side of the vehicle and, having closed the door, entered the pub. A young lady was standing behind the bar, putting some glasses away. She looked up as he entered and smiled.

"Hi there. What can I get you?"

"Pint of Black sheep, please, love." It was still early and the pub was empty, apart from one man who was sitting at the bar. Before him an empty shot glass and a nearly empty pint. The man looked over at Joe. *Danny*, thought Joe. "Alright," said Joe.

"Now then. I'll have another when you're ready, Sharon,"

"Alright, Dan." She placed Joe's pint in front of him and he handed her a tenner. Joe took a sip.

"That hits the spot," said Joe aloud.

"Finished work?" asked Danny. Joe noted a slight slur in his speech and also that Danny looked like crap.

"Yeah. That's me for the week. You?"

"Day off."

"Nice."

"What do you do then?"

"Gardener. Just keep on top of things around the village." Sharon placed a shot and a pint before Danny. Danny necked the shot.

"Early for them, mate," said Joe, nodding towards the empty glass.

"Never too early," said Danny laughing. "Used to farm this village, you know."

"Did you?"

"Yeah. Fuckers sacked me."

"That's tough." Joe took his tobacco from his pocket and rolled a cigarette.

"Still working though. Next farm over. They're alright, they are."

"What's wrong with this lot?"

"Mr Johnny Fanshaw. That's what."

"Is he a bit of a tosser?"

"Bloody right he is." Danny took a pack of cigarettes out of his pocket and placed one in his mouth. Joe lifted his pint and headed to the door. "Hang on. I'll have a smoke too." Danny stood, grabbed his pint, spilling as he did so, and followed Joe out. "You're alright you are," said Danny to Joe, as he walked out of the pub. Sharon watched the men exit and wiped a cloth over the bar top.

Outside it was chilly and starting to get dark. Joe lit his cigarette and offered up his flame for Danny to light his own. Danny leant forward and drew deeply as the flame caught the tobacco.

"Cheers, mate." Danny coughed as the combination of cold air and smoke hit his lungs.

"The Fanshaws own a lot around here?" asked Joe.

"All the land, all the rental houses. The pub is even owned by them and leased out."

"That big house will swallow up all their money though. Asset rich, cash poor, if you know what I mean."

"Maybe so, but they're still living a more comfortable life than me."

"And me."

"Gardening eh?"

"Yeah. Pays the bills I suppose. Farming for you?"

"Farm hand, not owner. Pay's crap but I love the outdoors. Given up on the bills. Stuff them. They can wait." Danny docked his fag and necked the rest of his pint. "Another?" he asked. Joe looked at his pint which was still half full.

"Nah, I'm driving."

"I'll quickly nip and get another."

"I'll still be here." Danny disappeared into the pub as Joe strolled across the car parking area to a lane end. Darkness was descending, with the greyness of dusk fading on the fields. The lane was dark. Lights flickered outside the pub and the car park was illuminated by exterior building lights. Joe turned as Danny walked out of the doorway with another pint in his hand. He wandered back over to him.

"Where's that lane lead to then?"

"The big house."

"Handy for the pub. Long walk?"

"Ten minutes." Danny held out a cigarette for Joe, which he received gratefully.

"Who was it? Johnny Fanshaw? He's not your favourite then."

"He's a prick. Sacked me for nothing. His sister fancied me and he didn't approve. Years ago now, like."

"And yet you still hold a grudge. Don't let me ever get on the wrong side of you." Joe laughed. Danny smiled.

"My life's never been the same since."

"Where's she now?"

"Missing? Dead? Fuck knows. Last seen walking up that lane twenty years ago. Not been seen since." Joe could see the emotion in Danny's eyes. "What a bloody mess." He gulped his pint and wiped the back of his mouth with his hand.

"How you getting home?" asked Joe.

"No bloody idea." Joe finished his pint and placed his glass down on an outside bench.

"Come on. I'll give you a lift. I need to get going anyway." Joe walked to his van and opened his door. Danny finished his pint and walked to the car.

"Smoking's fine. Jump in." Both males climbed into the car and Joe started the engine. "Where to?"

"Up the hill. I live about three miles away." Joe set off. Danny reached into his jacket and retrieved a hip flask which he offered to Joe.

"No thanks. You, my friend, are going to be absolutely shit-faced," said Joe.

"Used to it, mate. Only thing that keeps me going. Cheers." Danny raised the flask and took a sip.

Fifteen minutes later Joe and Danny were sitting in Joe's van outside of Danny's house. Danny had told Joe the full story of the night of Victoria's disappearance on their journey, expounding on his hatred of the Fanshaws, the police, and nearly everyone else who was present in the pub that night. All to blame, in Danny's opinion, for his downfall.

"An anonymous letter?"

"Yes. After all these years another letter. Someone is messing with me, Joe. Some bastard who wants to stick the boot in when I am down." Danny's speech was even more slurred. "Some sick bastard." He tipped the flask to his mouth and realised that it was empty. "Shit." Concentrating fully, he screwed the cap back on and handed the flask back to Joe. "You want one for the road?"

"No, mate. I need to get going." Danny popped his door open. "You gonna be OK getting in?"

"Yup. No problemo. You're a good 'un, Joe. Not like the rest of them." Danny climbed out of the car and searched his pockets. He pulled out his house key and fob, fumbled it and, as it dropped, caught it. Danny laughed and leant into the car. "Still got it, mate. Still got it. See ya." He walked towards his house, illuminated by the vehicle headlights. Joe undid his seatbelt and leant across the passenger seat, grabbed the passenger door handle and pulled the door to.

He watched Danny slip as he reached his front door and then steady himself with its handle. Danny raised his right arm, back still to Joe, and indicated that he was fine.

"Poor bastard," said Joe. Danny managed to get his key in the lock and entered his house without a backward glance at Joe. "What a state." Joe pulled the vehicle away and headed out to the main road. *What do I do with all this?* He knew that Matt and Rachel would be busy at Evesham, as would Ronnie. *Jim*, he thought. He dialled Jim's number.

"Hi, Joe. You OK?"

"I'm good, mate. You busy?"

"Never too busy for you. What do you need?"

"Grab a pen. I've been speaking with Danny. Take some notes for me. Rachel will need to know this."

***

Matthew opened the bedroom door, stepped out onto the landing, and nearly jumped out of his skin.

"Good morning, sir. I trust that you slept well." Fletcher was standing at the head of the sweeping staircase looking towards Matthew. Matt's hands flew to his chest.

"Good god, man, you scared the life out of me." Fletcher regarded him with one eyebrow raised.

"Apologies, sir. I happened to be passing."

"Do you get any sleep? You always seem to be working."

"I do, sir. If you could kindly let Miss Barnes know that breakfast is served then I'll be out of your way." Fletcher nodded his head and silently descended the staircase. Matt entered his room where Rachel was brushing her hair.

"He's everywhere. I caught Fletcher at the top of the staircase."

"In his own house? Disgraceful."

"He could have been standing there for hours. Waiting for us. I'm not sure that I like him."

"Don't be so ridiculous. He's simply doing his job. That's all."

"Well, I'm keeping my eye on him."

"Top suspect, Hercule?"

"Have you not read any Agatha Christie? He's the butler. The butler always does it." They both laughed as Rachel stood up, turned around and cuddled Matt.

"I love you, but — we have a fair way to go until you win your detective badge."

"I get a badge? Brilliant." Matt held Rachel at arm's length. "I was a Warlord Secret Agent, you know. Still have the badge and the secret code book." He stepped away from Rachel looking thoughtful. "Maybe I should dig them out." She laughed.

"Idiot."

"I know, but I'm your idiot."

"Yes you are. Did Fletcher want anything?"

"To tell us that breakfast is served."

"Now you tell me. I'm starving." Rachel grabbed her jacket and swept out of the room. "This way, Matthew. Stop lingering." Matt followed her out onto the landing, closing the bedroom door behind him.

Rachel led Matthew to the dining room where two places had been set for them. The beautifully polished table could seat at least twelve people and was complimented by a sideboard on which silver terrines held the breakfast selection.

"You've been served in this manner every day?"

"Yes, love. It's amazing how quickly you become accustomed to it."

"Well don't get too comfortable. You won't be getting this treatment when you get back home."

"Why ever not? Do you not think I'm worth it?"

"Now, I didn't say that. You are, but this isn't us. We're more than this ostentatious nonsense." Matt was heaping eggs and bacon onto his plate as he spoke.

"You don't seem to hate it all that much." Rachel took her place at the table with a small plate of toast and scrambled eggs. The door to the room opened.

"When in Rome," said Matt. Jonathan walked into the room.

"Indeed, Matthew. Nice to see you both up and about." Jonathan was dressed in muted colours and held a dog lead in his hand. "I take it that you had a comfortable night. Big appetite, Matthew?" Jonathan nodded to Matt's full plate.

"Well, I wouldn't want to see it go to waste." Jonathan ignored Matthew's reply.

"I'm sure. A walk in say, twenty minutes, Rachel?" asked Jonathan.

"Yes, we'll be ready."

"I've had the Gator parked at the far end of the park for our return. It's downhill most of the way there. Didn't want to tire you too much, if you know what I mean." His eyes flicked towards Rachel's walking stick which was balanced on the arm of her chair.

"That's considerate of you. Thank you."

"Splendid. I'll go and check on Walter and meet you at the side of the house." Jonathan departed, closing the door gently behind him.

"Who the hell is Walter?" asked Matt.

"Family dog. A beautiful Springer. You'll love him." Matt took a large mouthful of bacon and sausage. "You'll need a walk after stuffing all that in." She looked at him, frowning. "Have you been putting weight on?" Matt looked astounded and nearly choked on his food.

At ten o'clock they walked to the side of the house where Jonathan was waiting. Walter bounded up to Matt, tail wagging as Matt crouched down and petted him.

"Bang on time," said Jonathan. "If there is one thing that the police are good at, it is being on time."

"I hope that is one thing on an extensive list," said Rachel.

"That is certainly debatable, detective. Let's head this way." Jonathan and Rachel turned towards a wooded area which would lead them towards the walled garden. He whistled and Walter abandoned Matt and ran to Jonathan where he walked to heel. Matt ran after Rachel and did likewise.

"You have him well trained," said Rachel.

"And you likewise," responded Jonathan, looking directly forward with a smirk on his face. "Now, where shall we start?"

"How's Sir David doing?"

"Well, thank you. I think that energised would be the appropriate term. He's putting a lot of faith in you, Rachel. He believes that you will solve this riddle." Rachel noted his use of the word, Matt seemed oblivious.

"And you?"

"Honestly? I have my doubts. It all happened such a long time ago. Some things are better left unsolved." The group emerged from the small copse of trees and Jonathan walked to a red wooden door set within an aged brick wall. He held it open for Rachel and Matthew and they entered the walled garden. "Walter, come." The dog pulled his nose out from an animal burrow and dashed through the opening, his tail wagging furiously. Jonathan followed and gestured right with his arm to a path which headed through the gardens.

To either side neat lawns were bordered by loam beds. Differing browns signified the hibernation of plants for the winter, framed by evergreen box-hedging to add colour. In one corner the chirp of birds sounded as they pecked on the nuts and seeds within a feeding station. Ahead on the path, natural willow rods arched over the pathway, framing a carp pond and folly, centred on a crossroads.

"We'll head to the centre, then left up to the greenhouses." Rachel fell into step with Jonathan, foregoing the need for her walking stick upon the level pathway.

"Did you like Victoria?" she asked.

"She was my sister."

"Is that a prerequisite to like someone?" Jonathan pondered her question. Rachel remained silent.

"As a child, yes. We were inseparable. We spent hours in this garden playing. We were knights of the realm battling evil and slaying monsters. Or super spies finding clues, thwarting villains and saving the world." Jonathan smiled in recollection, his features softening into the visage of him as a younger man.

"And as an adult?" Jonathan's face changed, and the hardness returned.

"Frankly, she was a pain in the arse. Self-centred, spoiled in the extreme, and lazy. She had my father wrapped around her little finger. She abhorred me, I think. Resented that I would inherit all of this." He gestured to the gardens with his arms.

"Would you not inherit equally?"

"Not at all. The eldest man, i.e. me, would inherit. Victoria would have received a handsome amount of cash and still be able to come and go as she pleased. She would have had an easy life. A life of luxury for doing nothing. All the work would fall on me, the upkeep and development of the estate. Holding onto our little piece of England." They reached the centre folly. "Left here."

"And what did Victoria want?"

"To be left alone to do as she pleased. To party, to drink, to flirt and to hell with the consequences."

"And you didn't like that?" Jonathan stopped and looked Rachel in the face.

"No, I didn't. It's not the real world. There are always consequences." They continued walking up towards a large wooden-framed greenhouse. The door was open and they walked into its relative warmth. Walter stayed outside and explored a compost heap.

"I've read your statement, provided the day after Victoria went missing. About your argument with her, your attendance at the pub with Charles, the fight." Jonathan stood silently. Matt watched Walter digging in the heap.

"No one has written down what you thought happened. Did nobody ask?"

"I didn't know. I was in a mess. Father was in a mess. The press was relentless. Accusations were flying around everywhere."

"And what about during the case review?"

"They covered the facts. They didn't want my opinion. They treated me like a suspect." Rachel laid a hand on Jonathan's arm to calm him. Matt observed the interaction.

"They don't always get it right. I'm sorry, but they don't, but I'm asking. What do you think happened?" Jonathan smiled, his shoulders relaxed, he looked at Matt and then back to Rachel, who could see the relief in his face. Someone had bothered to ask.

"I think that bastard Danny killed her. I don't know how, but it was him."

"Why Danny?"

"Look at the state of him now. He's a piss-head. Has been since she went missing. Disappeared off the farm straight away. He fancied her, you know. No doubt she was leading him on but that gave him no right. You need to look at him." Matt stared at Jonathan, frozen in position. Rachel stepped in front of Matt, blocking his view and, more importantly, his reaction to Jonathan's statement. *Close your mouth, Matt*, thought Rachel.

"Take me through what you know about Danny, Jonathan." She produced a digital recorder from her pocket. "Do you mind?"

"Not at all." The group spent the next hour recording information as they slowly made their way through the estate to the awaiting Gator.

"Keys are in the ignition," said Jonathan to Matt. "She's fully electric so it'll be a steady drive back to the house." Matt and Rachel were sitting in the front of the vehicle.

"You're not coming back with us?" asked Matt.

"No thanks. I need some time alone."

"Fair enough." Matt turned the key and heard the quiet hum as the battery engaged. Rachel placed the recording device in her pocket.

"Thanks for spending that time with us," she said.

"Anything to help." She smiled.

"Before we go. What do you think about the letters?"

"Letters?"

"The anonymous ones that Sir David has received. The one that reopened the investigation."

"I don't know. Someone clearly knows something or simply wants it resolved."

"Or wants to upset Sir David?"

"Possibly, but what would they have to gain? He's respected around here. I don't know of anyone who dislikes him."

"That's good to know. Have you received any letters?"

"Not at all."

"We'll head off," said Rachel, "leave you with your thoughts." Matt pulled quietly away. Rachel looked back to see Jonathan staring across at the herd of deer, with Walter sitting loyally by his side. She was pulled back to the present by Matt.

"That was bloody brilliant," he said, with a big smile on his face. "Absolutely, bloody brilliant. We have a suspect." Matt was tense with excitement, leaning forwards in the vehicle, as he powered up the hill at ten miles per hour.

"It's given us something to think about."

"Think about? Let's get him in. Grill him. Do a Rachel on him." Rachel laughed.

"Patience, love. We take our time with this. It needs to be right. It's only Jonathan's opinion. It doesn't mean that he is right. He's biased, remember. He doesn't like Danny." Matthew's telephone rang. He checked the screen and answered.

"Hi, Jim." Matthew slowed as Jim spoke. "She's next to me now." He stopped the Gator. "You're kidding." He looked at Rachel. "Let us get to our room. We'll ring you back." Matt terminated the call.

"What is it?" asked Rachel.

"Joe reported in, late last night. He spent the evening with Danny."

"And?"

"Danny's been receiving anonymous letters too. The same message as Sir David's."

***

"That was a lovely cup of tea." Ronnie was sitting in Margaret's kitchen. She took his mug and rinsed it at the sink. "The rain is holding off out there. Shall we head out?"

"Yes. Let's get going." Ronnie stood up and lifted his coat from the back of his chair. He pulled it on then, reaching in his pocket, produced a flat cap hat and put it on. Margaret dried her hands, neatly folding the tea towel, which she then placed upon the Aga to dry. Ronnie picked up Margaret's coat and held it open for her to slide her arms in. She smiled.

"Why, thank you." They headed out of the house and out to the street. Ronnie placed his hands in his coat pockets and held out an elbow for Margaret to take.

"We need the support at our age," said Ronnie. Margaret linked in and they set off. "You'll have seen a lot of change in the village over the years," said Ronnie.

"Not as much as you'd think. The modern world is still held in abeyance here. There's been no new houses built here for years. The land is still farmed by the same family and the Fanshaws control what happens on their estate." They turned at the end of the road and headed down the hill towards the bottom village.

"What do you think of thcm?"

"They seem OK. I don't have much to do with them. The house and café seem to do well and they employ local people there, so that's good."

"Alfred mentioned the death of Sir David's daughter to me."

"Victoria. That was a shocking time. She was a beautiful young lady, you know. Wild at heart, impetuous and strong-willed. I heard that Sir David took it hard."

"Not surprising."

"Not at all." Ronnie could see the pub in the foreground.

"Now, Alfred also told me that there's a walk from the pub that leads towards the big house."

"Yes. It loops back towards the top village. It takes about forty minutes."

"You OK with that?"

"That would be grand." The couple descended the hill and approached the car parking area of the pub. Margaret indicated to the right where a kissing gate led towards the lane in question. They approached the gate where Ronnie pushed it open, allowing Margaret to step through first. He followed afterwards and they entered the thin muddy track.

Margaret took the lead through the narrow passage which then opened up. To their left was an open field, and to the right a high blackthorn hedge. Ahead a dark tunnel created by overarching trees. A passage in which daylight struggled to penetrate. The couple entered the mouth. Ronnie immediately noticed a dampening of sound. Not silence but nature muted by the overarching greenery.

"Peaceful," said Ronnie, his voice sounding loud within the green walls.

"I haven't been up here in years," said Margaret. The path had widened to allow them to walk side by side.

"I don't think I'd attempt to come up here at night, though."

"Why would you even want to?" They looked ahead where the trees opened up and their route lightened. "There used to be a bench further ahead which gave a good view of the hall." She looked at Ronnie, noting a blue tinge to his complexion. He was also breathing heavily. "Are you OK?" He smiled and straightened his posture.

"I'm fine. I think I need more exercise. It's about time that I got rid of some of this." Ronnie patted his stomach. "Walking is the answer."

"Well, we can rest at the bench, enjoy the view and then stride on from there."

"Suits me."

They emerged from dimness and continued up the slight incline. Ronnie felt better as the hedges thinned and, looking ahead, spotted something bright red to the right of the path.

"What's that?" he asked, pointing to the right.

"I'm not sure." Margaret squinted and they both kept their eyes focussed on it as they approached.

"Flowers," said Ronnie.

"Chrysanthemums," said Margaret, "they look newly planted. The soil looks fresh around their base." Ronnie looked around at the drab browns and muted greens of the surrounding undergrowth with a look of confusion on his face.

"They're the only bit of colour around here."

"They do look out of place, but they must be here for a reason. We should push on. We can almost see the bench."

"Let me have a quick smoke." Ronnie drew a packet from his pocket.

"OK. I'll see if the bench is still there. I'll be back in two." Margaret walked ahead. Ronnie turned to look at the flowers which were set forwards from a sparse area of hedgeline. A large oak guarded the site.

"Who planted this then?" Ronnie said aloud, as he lit his cigarette. He took his mobile phone from his pocket and, using the camera, took some photos of the area. "Interesting." He followed Margaret and, cresting a small rise, looked across at open fields to his right. A broad tractor track skirted the fields and in the distance, Ronnie could see a person walking towards the village road. He saw dark movement out of the corner of his eye and looking, recognised the form of a dog running towards its owner. Ronnie could see no one else around. He quickly took a photo of the person, though the distance was likely too far to achieve clarity.

"It's still there," said Margaret as she appeared from around a bend in the path. "Come on, you can rest up there." Ronnie docked his fag and placed the stub end back in his pack. He smiled at Margaret as she approached, her cheeks flushed with colour. She returned his smile. *What a fine woman*, thought Ronnie. They continued on their walk.

Ronnie and Margaret were coming to the end of their small hike through the countryside. The hall had looked resplendent and they were now approaching the village church. Within the graveyard stood a woman wearing dark clothing. She faced a gravestone and looked to be in quiet contemplation. With arms held behind her back, she held a dog lead, though Ronnie could see no dog in the vicinity. The lady crouched down at the gravestone and Ronnie saw a splash of red as she did so.

"Come on," whispered Margaret, "Let's not disturb her." They walked quietly beyond the cemetery and descended the road towards Margaret's house. "You ready for a cuppa?"

"Could kill for one but quick cig first." They stopped outside Maragaret's house. "I'll put the kettle on." Margaret walked down beside the house and disappeared from view. Ronnie lit the stub of the cigarette that he had docked earlier. He could see the woman in the graveyard stand back up. She rested a hand on the gravestone and walked towards the church from his view. *Maybe nothing*, thought Ronnie, knowing that he would have to go and check out the gravestone later. He finished his cigarette and went to join Margaret.

An hour later Ronnie left Margaret's and headed towards his own home. He'd enjoyed his walk with Margaret followed by a cup of tea and a slice of homemade cake. Having lived on his own for so long it was refreshing to have some company. However, he was here to do a job and knew that any personal interest should come second. *Would you understand, Margaret?* He pushed the thought away as he neared his house. He opened the gate and was about to enter the garden when he changed his mind. The woman in the graveyard was still nagging him. Dusk was approaching but he would have enough light to have a quick look.

Ronnie walked to the church, quietly opened the church gate and entered the graveyard. He oriented himself and was drawn forward to the grave in question. Placed upon the plinth of the headstone lay a bright red single chrysanthemum. He leaned forward and read the inscription on the headstone, "Reginald Chiswick, February 10th to June 5th". Ronnie took out his phone and took a picture, the camera flash illuminating as he did so. He turned and looked around. The area was well tended, the grass neat and trimmed short at each headstone. A couple of gravestones held small sprays of flowers, none of which were chrysanthemums. He left via the gate, closing it carefully behind him.

Navigating a small path he walked onto the road when he heard a car engine start. He turned and was illuminated by bright car headlights, on full beam. Shielding his eyes he turned and walked down the hill and headed for home. The car did not follow, though he could still hear the hum of its engine as he walked towards his front door.

Chapter 11

Jamie was standing admiring his new BMW 1 series which he had parked proudly outside of his house. Tanya, still wearing pyjamas and a dressing gown, walked from the front door carrying two mugs of coffee.

"Pleased with yourself?"

"Yep. She's a beauty."

"It's only a car." Tanya handed him his coffee, took his lit cigarette from his hand, drew in deeply and handed it back.

"Only a car. She's more than a car. She's a statement. A flying machine. Looks good, beautiful to drive, and fast as fuck."

"Sounds like me."

"Well, you're a close second." Jamie nudged Tanya with his hip, causing her to spill her coffee.

"Oi! You stupid idiot."

"Only joking, only joking." Tanya wiped her hand on her dressing gown. "I'm gonna take her for a spin this afternoon. We have a couple of mates coming around this evening. Said I'd pick them up. We could go to the pub." Tanya looked at Jamie in annoyance.

"You could have warned me." He put an arm around her shoulder and pulled her in for a hug. "Who's coming?"

"It'll be fine. Ross and one of the new girls on shift, Emily."

"They together?"

"Nah. Both were free tonight, was all."

"They staying over?"

"No idea. Either that or a taxi back. Their choice. Make up the spare room bed, will you? Ross can doss in the living room. He won't care."

"He'll be too pissed to care, you mean."

"Won't we all."

"Right, I'd better get moving. Lots to do." Tanya walked back towards the house. "There's a quiz night at the pub tonight."

"Bloody hell."

"Don't be so miserable. It'll be a laugh. You've got your car to keep you happy."

"Britney, you mean."

"Britney?" Jamie stroked the bonnet of the vehicle.

"That's what I've called her. Britney." Tanya turned and entered the house. Closing the door she poked her head back around before shutting it.

"You are a sad man. Enjoy your time with Britennee. I'll be in the house if you want me." Jamie chuckled as she closed the door. Jamie's phone vibrated in his pocket. He pulled it out and, looking at the screen, saw that he had received a text from a number that he didn't recognise. He opened the text, which read 'Check your email'.

"What the fuck?" Jamie quickly opened his email app and saw that he had received mail from an unknown source. He opened the attachment and looked at his screen. "Shit!" Displayed before him were two images. The first image showed him entering the curtilage of the house in Barnston, now locked down as a murder scene. The second showed him exiting a few minutes later. The images were timed and dated. Both evidence that he had visited the house before the police in Barnston even became aware of it.

Jamie pressed his home button and shoved the phone in his pocket. He looked around frantically. *Are they watching me? How have they got my phone number and email?* He backed towards his house as he watched the street, reached behind him for the door handle and entered, closing the door cautiously. Jamie sensed panic building. He breathed deeply. Panic subdued to anger. "No fucking way. I'm not being treated like this." He straightened his shoulders and stood tall. Tanya popped her head out of the kitchen.

"You OK, love? Can you grab me the hoover from upstairs?"

"Fine, darling. On my way." Jamie ran up the stairs, his brain already planning what he needed to do. He grabbed the hoover from the main bedroom and placed it on the landing. Returning to the room he opened up the inbuilt wardrobe and reached for a small safe box from the top shelf. Moving to the side table, he pulled out the drawer, reached underneath it and withdrew a key that had been secreted there. Using it to open the safe he opened the lid. Within lay his insurance policies that he had been collecting since he joined the police. "Two can play at this game," said Jamie, determination etched upon his face.

***

Matt and Rachel walked out of the café at Evesham House.

"By, they certainly know how to bake a cake in there," said Matt as they strolled towards the visitor car park. The couple had enjoyed tea and cakes but now felt that they needed to get away from the village for a few hours. It would be easy to get suckered into their luxurious environment but Rachel knew that she needed to maintain objectiveness. They climbed into the vehicle.

"Where to?" asked Matt.

"Anywhere. Somewhere private. We need some space to think. You choose."

"How about ours? We can check things are all OK. Grab a coffee. Come back here later. I know, I'll take you out for dinner. A change of scenery."

"Sounds great."

"Let's sleep at ours tonight. We can come back here tomorrow. It feels intense in the house. We can relax at home. Give me two minutes." Matt climbed out of the car and went to Evesham House's reception. He returned after a couple of minutes. "All sorted. Fletcher is now expecting us for lunch tomorrow. I've told him soup and sandwiches will be fine." Matt started the car, manoeuvred from the car park, and headed away from the village.

Rachel turned on the radio, which Matt took as a sign that she wanted some private time to think. He knew that she would share her thoughts when she was ready. The day was bright and clear so he could enjoy the drive across to Barnston. Rachel's telephone rang. She checked the screen and turned it to face Matt. He glanced across and saw that Jamal Kaur was ringing. He nodded and turned down the radio. Rachel answered the call.

"Jamal, how are you doing?"

"I'm good, thanks. I could do with seeing you today."

"Is it urgent? I'm heading to Barnston."

"Barnston's good for me. I can kill two birds with one stone. I can be across there this afternoon."

"Fine. I'll be at home. Give me a bell when you land in town and I'll get the kettle on. I'll text you my address."

"Will do. It'll be round about two. See you then." The call was terminated.

"What's he after?" asked Matt.

"He wants to meet up this afternoon. Must be important."

"No rest for the wicked."

"It seems not." The vehicle approached a dual carriageway and Matt gradually accelerated.

"We'd best get back then."

***

"That's him pulling up outside now," said Rachel, opening the front door. Matt flicked the kettle on and spooned coffee into three mugs.

"Afternoon," Rachel called out the door. A car door shut and footsteps could be heard.

"Hiya."

"Come in." Rachel stepped back allowing Jamal to enter. He wore jeans and a T-shirt with a corduroy jacket over. "This is Matt."

"Hi. Good to meet you." Jamal reached out and the men shook hands.

"Coffee?" asked Matt.

"Please, with a drop of milk." Matt made the drinks.

"Grab a seat," said Matt. Rachel and Jamal selected a seat at the kitchen table. Matt placed their coffees down and joined them.

"To what do we owe this pleasure?" asked Rachel. Jamal's eyes flicked to Matt and back to Rachel. "You can speak in front of Matt. He's on the team." Jamal looked chagrined.

"Sorry. All new territory for me."

"That's OK. My team's secure."

"Even so, I've been asked to speak with you only, Rachel." Matt sipped from his mug and stayed silent, watching Rachel for her reaction.

"Well, we're both here," said Rachel. "You can tell us both or we'll just enjoy a coffee and a chat. Your call, or do you need to ask your superior?" Jamal frowned and was ruffled. He looked at Matt and then back to Rachel. His frown disappeared and his mind was made up.

"Right. To be kept between you and Matt only at this stage. Is that OK? I'm sticking my neck out here."

"Yep, that's fine. What you got?"

"I've had a visit from complaints and discipline. What they've got is an undercover officer." Matt joined them at the table with a grin on his face. Rachel gave him a stern look and he lost the smile.

"And the relevance to my enquiry?"

"She's being deployed into Evesham tonight." Matt's eyes went wide.

"To aid my enquiry?"

"Not directly no, but who knows what she might hear. She may get something that can help you if we can task her correctly."

"Who's her target?" Rachel raised a hand, halting Jamal's reply. "Wait. It's Hyatt, isn't it?" Jamal nodded his head. "Corrupt cop?"

"Oh yes. Up to his neck in it. They want to nail some evidence."

"And the UC?"

"Young PC. New on his shift. They've deployed her there to get to know him. She's already made some inroads. He's invited her to a pub quiz tonight. This could work well for all of us if we play it right."

"Apart from Hyatt?"

"Oh, yes. Not for Hyatt." Jamal reached inside his jacket and produced a file. "I'll explain what we've got and where we want to take this."

"We're all ears," replied Rachel.

Two hours later Rachel closed the front door as Jamal walked back to his car. Matt remained sitting at the kitchen table, nursing a fresh cup of coffee.

"Well, I wasn't expecting any of that," he said.

"Me neither. It's good though. Complicates things a little, but it's good."

"Should we keep it from the team?" asked Matt.

"No. We tell them everything."

"Even with strict instructions not to?"

"Yes. We're not the cops. They can have their rules and their paranoia about security leaks within their ranks, but that's not how our team works. We trust each other and we are honest with each other."

"I'm glad you feel like that."

"Don't you?"

"Yes I do, but then, I've never been a cop."

"Well I didn't leave and create this team in order to drown in red tape and police rules. We play by different rules. We'll get the team together tomorrow.

Tonight you and I work out how we can use it," Rachel picked up a small photograph, "I mean Emily, to progress our investigation."

***

The pub was busy this evening with all the tables and chairs taken. There was a buzz of excitement in the air as teams discussed tactics amongst themselves. Alfred, Ronnie and Margaret had managed to claim a tall table, giving them a good view of the competition. The quiz compere was tucked up at one end of the bar, with a microphone ready next to her pint. She was chatting to one of the bar staff.

"Busy tonight," said Ronnie.

"There's not been a quiz for yonks," said Alfred, "drags all manner of folk from the woodwork." Margaret sipped on a brandy and Babycham. The men were drinking pints, foregoing the whisky chasers when in the presence of a lady. "There'll be some stiff competition."

"We'll wipe the floor with the lot of them," joked Ronnie. He looked towards the old pool table. "Who's the young 'uns over there?" He nodded towards the table.

"Bottom villagers. Couple are locals and they look like they've drafted in some ringers. Typical cops. Law unto themselves."

"Cops?"

"Young lad with the lady with dyed hair. He's called Jamie. He's a cop in the city. I'm guessing the two imposters with him are probably cops too." Jamie looked up, as if sensing he was being spoken about, and waved across to Alfred who returned his greeting with a raised hand. "Wouldn't trust him as far as I could throw him," Alfred muttered under his breath whilst continuing to smile.

"Seems friendly enough."

"Aren't they all? Until they slap the cuffs on." Margaret looked at Alfred in astonishment. Jamie looked away and laughed aloud at something that he had shared with the group. A girl with blonde hair glanced across to their table. *Cop*, thought Ronnie, *And the lad next to you*. He looked away, wondering whether she would think the same about him.

"Enough of your chequered past, Alf. How's tonight work then?"

"Four rounds, well five I suppose, but five's a picture round. Break halfway through for a pie and pea supper, then on we go."

"What's first prize?" asked Margaret, "I've not been to one of these in years." Alfred leaned in towards Margaret.

"Is Ronnie leading you astray?" Margaret blushed. "Only joking, love. First prize is a bottle of champagne and a free round of drinks. Second, a bottle of wine, third, four cans of beer." Alfred looked up to a young man approaching their table. "Here comes the picture round." The youth placed a sheet containing twenty images before them.

"We'll mark these at the end of the quiz. Good luck guys," said the youth.

"Thank you, young man," said Margaret. Ronnie stood up.

"Same again? I'll get the next round in. You two do your best. I'll finish it off when I get back." He winked at them and walked off cockily to the bar. Margaret and Alfred studiously reviewed the picture images, determined to try and complete all the answers before Ronnie returned.

The bar was busy as customers tried to get their orders in before the first questions were asked. Ronnie stood second in line when he was jostled from behind as a man's voice called out,

"Four pints please, love." An arm extended over his shoulder with its hand holding a twenty-pound note. The barmaid ignored the man and served the person in front of Ronnie. "Deaf cow," a male voice behind mumbled. Ronnie looked over his shoulder and, raising his chin, looked into the face of Jamie Hyatt.

"We're all queueing, son. She'll get to us in turn."

"They should have more staff on," said Jamie, "they knew that it was going to be busy. It should be locals first." The man at the bar turned with two pints. Ronnie stepped to one side, allowing the male to move past, and Jamie tried to fill the gap. Ronnie stepped back in, barring Jamie's way and smiled at the barmaid. Jamie tried his request again and was ignored once again by the barmaid, who smiled at Ronnie.

"What can I get you, Ronnie?"

"Two pints of Landlord please, love."

"Coming up." Jamie's arm retracted as a gap came present next to Ronnie. Jamie filled the gap and leaned his elbows on the bar, looking across at Ronnie.

"You local? Don't think I've seen you before."

"Recently moved in." Two pints were placed before Ronnie. "Thanks, and a brandy and Babycham, please" The barmaid went to prepare the drink.

"Which house?" asked Jamie.

"Renting a shepherd's cottage in the top village."

"I live down the bottom end." The barmaid returned. Ronnie gave her a twenty-pound note.

"Four pints of lager," said Jamie to the barmaid.

"Hang on, love. I'll have two packs of crisps, please. One plain and one cheese and onion." interrupted Ronnie. The barmaid reached for the requisite packs and placed them on the bar. Ronnie could feel Jamie's eyes boring into him with impatience.

"That all,?" Ronnie winked at the barmaid who knew exactly what he was doing.

"You got any pickled eggs?"

"Yes. Normal or —" she reached under the counter producing a large jar, which she wiped with the bar cloth, "curried?" The barmaid and Ronnie squinted at the contents as she gave them a swirl.

"I think normal," said Ronnie, who pointed at the curried eggs. "You sure that they shouldn't be in a lab?"

"In the bin maybe," she laughed and placed the jar to one side. "Pickled egg coming up." The barmaid returned with an egg nestled in a small bun case. Ronnie opened the plain crisps and dropped the egg in.

"Thanks, that's me." Ronnie waited for his change. He turned to Jamie. "Lived here long?"

"Long enough to get served first," he replied. "I'm the local cop round here." Ronnie grimaced.

"Well, someone has to be." The air was cut with the piercing whine of a microphone held too close to a speaker. The room silenced.

"Well, that's one way of doing it," said the announcer over a speaker. "Quiz starts in one minute."

"I'd better get back to my team. Nice to meet you …" Ronnie paused.

"Jamie."

"Jamie. Good luck in the quiz." Ronnie grabbed his purchases and walked away, Jamie turned to the bar where the barmaid had produced two pints of lager and was pulling two more. He looked across to the table that Ronnie had walked to and noted whom he was with.

***

Sunday, two o'clock, and the team had gathered in the office at Rachel's request. Ronnie looked in reasonable shape, despite his night out at the pub. His team had managed an admirable second place. Both gents had gallantly given their prize to Margaret, who had proven herself to be a formidable team member. First prize went to a team who were clearly professional quizzers. Jamie's team appeared to drift into the ether as he and his partner got absolutely sozzled.

Usually, the team would not work weekends. However, a text had gone out last night from Rachel requesting everyone's presence at the office. They all knew that she wouldn't have called them in unless it was urgent. They now all waited in anticipation. Rachel returned from the loo and joined them.

"Come on, Rach. Spit it out," said Sarah. Rachel looked around the room, gauging the tension. She leaned forwards in her armchair.

"Something of interest has come up which undoubtedly will affect the investigation. Positively or negatively, we will have to wait and see." Postures altered faces alert as the team waited. "I've been told to keep the information to myself but that's not how we work. So here we go." Rachel then explained her meeting with Jamal Kaur and the information that had been passed to her.

"We got a photo of her?" asked Ronnie. Matt passed Rachel a file and she removed the photo, passing it to Ronnie.

"I could have told you last night, but I still wasn't sure how I was going to handle it all."

"That's OK," said Ronnie, "It wouldn't have made a difference. She was there last night, though. Sitting in a group with Hyatt."

"Doing her job then," said Joe.

"Certainly looks like it."

"Does she know we have Ronnie and Joe in the village?" asked Tom. Ronnie passed the photograph to his right.

"No, and she won't be told."

"An informant," said Jim, "what have they got on her?"

"Misuse of police computers. Checking out her partner. Apart from that she's as clean as a whistle."

"Poor lass," said Sarah. "She can't enjoy it."

"At the moment she has no choice, but to our benefit, we now have someone close to Hyatt. He's corrupt and they want to nail him."

"Is he Victoria's murderer though?" asked Jim.

"I met him last night," said Ronnie.

"What did you think of him?"

"Sure of himself, arrogant. He's a big lad."

"Sounds like you in your younger days," joked Rachel.

"Cheeky but true," replied Ronnie. "But that doesn't make him a murderer."

"He is corrupt though," said Tom. "Happy to blur some lines."

"We'll need to tread carefully when we interview him, guys," said Rachel.

"True," said Tom.

"A taskable informant can be priceless," said Jim. "She's on our side, which is what counts."

"I'll let you all mull that over for a while. Meanwhile, let's go round and get everyone's updates. We have a busy week ahead of us."

***

Roger Melthrop had enjoyed his sermon this morning, even if his audience had only comprised five people. He felt that he had delivered his important message, and God's, to the group and they had appeared to have been absorbed by his delivery. Melthrop was slightly perturbed that the new member of the village, Ronald, had not been in attendance, but he had dropped a note at the house reminding him of choir practice tomorrow. Melthrop was now taking his weekly sojourn to the bottom village as he felt it important to show his face regularly. Spotting PC Hyatt outside of his house he wandered over.

"Good afternoon, Constable."

"Father," replied Jamie, who quickly tucked his lit cigarette behind his back, as if hiding a mortal sin.

"How are we today?"

"Fine, though I have a bit of a headache. Heavy night at the quiz night last night in the pub."

"That explains why church attendance was light this morning. Heavy heads cause heavy hearts. A period of reflection can sometimes be the best hangover cure."

"I'm sure." A young lady walked out of Jamie's house and dumped her holdall near Jamie's feet.

"Ready to go when you are," said Emily, "Apparently, Ross is peeling himself out of his bed." Emily noticed Melthrop. "Oh, sorry. I didn't mean to interrupt."

"Not at all, not at all. Toyah, isn't it? You must be busy." Jamie interrupted.

"No, Father. This is Emily. One of my work colleagues." Melthrop looked confused. Jamie clarified. "Tanya with the red hair is my partner. This is Emily. She's a police constable." Jamie stepped past Emily. "I'll go and check on Ross." Jamie entered the house, leaving Emily with Melthrop. He looked her up and down, his eyes lingering on her chest, then smiled.

"I'm the pastor at the church."

"Pleased to meet you." Emily hadn't failed to notice his wandering gaze and slipped on her coat, which she zipped up.

"You look too young to be in the force. Where are you stationed?"

"Fenchurch."

"A nice city but it can have its rough areas."

"All places do."

"That they do. Now, don't let the job go spoiling you."

"I won't." Emily picked up her bag. "I'd better check on the others." She turned towards the house.

"Don't let me hold you up." Emily walked away. *I won't be letting you anywhere near me.* She entered the house where Tanya was in the front room.

"He's a bit creepy," said Emily.

"The vicar with the wandering eyes," said Tanya laughing. "He's harmless but desperate. You would be too if you saw his wife."

"Well, you're welcome to him." Emily looked out the window and watched as Melthrop turned away and continued his walk. He headed towards the shop. *Well, they are recruiting them young*, he thought. *What an attractive young lady though.*

***

Emily had been dropped at Sterndale Railway Station and had caught the train back to Fenchurch. She walked out onto the railway platforms, and considered getting a taxi home but decided that the walk would do her good.

Although it was a Sunday, the city remained busy with the ebb and flow of traffic, and also tourists, who wandered around the city admiring its historical sites. Emily nipped left, cut through a hotel car park heading for an alleyway which would take her down to the riverside. The walk was the prettiest route into the city as long as the river wasn't high. Reaching the footpath running adjacent to the river, she zipped up her coat, blocking a cold breeze that cut from the water.

Trimble wasn't expecting an update until later today which would give her time to organise her thoughts and put them down on paper. He did not consider that this was her day off. She received no financial remuneration for effectively working on her days off. The job simply expected it of her. *I could resign*, she thought, not for the first time. In reality, Emily didn't know what else she could do. Her wage was good. It was her circumstances that weren't. *Get a grip, Em.* She halted by an empty bench which was sheltered by a tree and rested there.

Reaching into her bag, Emily took out a small notebook and jotted down the times and dates of her deployment in the village. Detailed the names of persons she had met. She had found Ross to be OK, Tanya a laugh – and Jamie? What did she honestly think of him? In the pub, he acted like he was a celebrity who was well-known and well-liked. He appeared to wear the pants in his relationship with Tanya. Though Tanya was strong-spirited, she still hung on all his words. He treated her a bit like a trophy. They seemed happy, though. Boy, could they drink, and Jamie wasn't afraid to splash his cash.

Although she'd had a sociable night, Jamie hadn't let anything slip. Work had been mentioned by them all but only in passing. Emily got the impression that she had simply been invited so that Jamie could demonstrate how popular he was. When they got back to the house they'd all had a nightcap and gone to bed. The house itself wasn't that special but Jamie and Tanya loved their gadgets. Top of the range of everything. Emily knew that she couldn't afford that on her wage.

The last thing Emily jotted on her pad was 'vicar'. He was probably harmless but he had given her the creeps. It wouldn't do Trimble's department any harm to do some intelligence checks around him. Emily needed to know if they had anything on him, especially if she was going to get deployed in the village again.

She packed away her notebook, stood up, and headed in the direction of home.

***

"I don't care what job anyone does, Monday is always a crap day," explained Matt. Rachel and Matt were sitting in a small café in Fenchurch. Matt picked up a small cake from the selection before him and took a bite.

"Looks like your day has started well," said Rachel. "Sure you don't need another coffee to help you get those cakes down?"

"You know what I mean. The team's had most of the weekend off. Monday has returned and now they're back, noses to the grindstone for five days. Think of the teachers, council workers and the average Joe Bloggs. It's the same for them."

"There's no average about them, Matt. What about all the shift workers? Cops, nurses, care staff? I think our Mondays are looking good compared to most." Matt looked at her guiltily. "I'll take that as an agreement. Now, eat up, we have an appointment to keep."

Rachel and Matt slowly walked up to and entered the bank. The queue for the teller kiosks was short, however, they were clearly expected. As they entered, a member of staff approached them.

"Good morning, Miss Barnes. If you'd like to follow me Mr Fothergill is expecting you." Matt raised a brow. Unphased, Rachel smiled at the lady.

"Thank you." Rachel acknowledged that there wouldn't be too many middle-aged ladies, walking with a stick, who would have an appointment with the bank manager this morning. They were led through a security door and down a short corridor where they paused as the lady knocked on an office door, opened it and stepped in.

"Miss Barnes and her colleague, to see Mr Fothergill."

"Thank you, Janet. Do show them in." The door opened wider and Janet gestured for them to enter. A smartly dressed lady, with greying hair tied up in a bun, was standing behind a desk. Balanced on her nose was a pair of spectacles which she peered over as she examined Rachel and Matt. Seemingly satisfied, her austere features broke into a smile as she walked around the desk.

"Please take a seat, officers. I'm Cynthia, Mr Fothergill's secretary. I'll inform him that you are here." Cynthia disappeared through an adjoining office door as Janet also left the room. Matt and Rachel took a seat, Matt with a smirk on his face.

"I feel that I'm waiting to see the headmaster."

"It does feel a bit like that doesn't it." They both then remained silent. A minute later, Cynthia reappeared.

"Mr Fothergill is free to see you now." She gestured towards the open door, they entered, and the door was closed softly behind them.

"Good morning, officers. Please take a seat." Charles Fothergill gestured towards two chairs which had been placed opposite his desk. Both were straight-backed, evenly spaced apart, and couldn't be more dissimilar to his grand ox-blood and oak, leather-cushioned throne.

The office was his domain. Matthew held the back of one chair as Rachel lowered herself into it, then took the other chair himself. Fothergill smiled, noting Matt's gentlemanly conduct. Fothergill sat himself down and rested back in his chair, with one leg crossed over the other at the knees. His suit jacket hung up on a clothes hanger and was suspended from a coat stand. He was dressed impeccably in pinstriped trousers, a matching waistcoat and a neatly pressed shirt and tie.

"Cynthia will bring in some tea for us in a minute." Fothergill checked his watch. "You've got me for half an hour. How can I help you?" *Extremely sure of yourself,* thought Rachel. *Bravado disguising nerves? Let's see.*

"Mr Fothergill, thank you for taking the time to see us. It's much appreciated."

"Not at all. Jonathan advised me to expect you at some point, though I'm not exactly sure how much use I will be." There was a light knock on the office door and Cynthia walked in carrying a tray holding three mugs. She placed it on the desk and quietly left the room.

"Don't know what I'd do without her. Please," Charles extended a hand towards the cups and each selected a drink.

"You're reviewing Victoria's disappearance, I believe."

"Yes, we are," said Rachel. "I've been going through your statements, which you provided during the initial enquiry." Rachel pulled out a thick green file from her briefcase. Charles looked at the file, his eyes widening.

"That's not all about me?" asked Charles.

"We like to be thorough," said Matt, taking a small notepad and pen from his pocket.

"You don't mind if I take notes, do you? It helps us keep on track." Charles uncrossed his legs and rolled his seat forward towards the desk, resting his elbows upon the writing surface.

"Not at all," said Charles, "I have nothing to hide."

"We have files on everyone, Mr Fothergill," clarified Rachel. "People's statements, phone records, bank records, everything you'd expect."

"I shouldn't be surprised."

"Can I ask what your relationship was with Victoria?"

"She was a friend."

"Only a friend?"

"We were considering getting married." Rachel looked through her papers.

"You weren't engaged though?"

"No, but that would have been the next logical step. Our families were talking."

"Talking?"

"Both felt that we could be a good match."

"And what about you? Did you feel that you were a good match?"

"Yes. I had good prospects. Victoria needed looking after. It would have worked."

"And how did Victoria feel about it?"

"She was keen."

"Interesting." Rachel sifted through the papers in her lap and pulled one out. "Can you tell me who Megan Renwick was to you at the time?" Fothergill looked startled.

"Renwick? Megan Renwick? I have a faint recollection of a Megan. No, that was Mary. Now who —"

"It was a long time ago, to be fair. However, we have been to see Megan. She advises us that she used to work as a sex worker, back in the day." Charles shot bolt upright in his chair. He pointed at Rachel.

"Stop there. How dare you." Rachel raised a hand.

"Mr Fothergill, I'm not here to judge you. I have little interest in your private life, apart from where it may have affected Victoria. Did Victoria know that you were seeing Megan?" Charles was flustered.

"Well, well — it would have been none of her business anyway."

"Not the business of your prospective fiancée? Forgive me, but she may have thought differently." Charles looked suitably chastised. "And you're married now?" Rachel nodded to Charles' wedding ring.

"Yes, for fifteen years."

"Children?"

"Yes, but Victoria is none of my family's concern. We met after her disappearance and anyway, they are on holiday abroad. They are not accessible."

"Noted," said Rachel. "Are you happily married?" Charles paused and then spat out his reply.

"Yes. Indeed I am. What a silly question?" Matt looked up at Charles.

"That's good to hear," said Rachel. "I've read the statements from the event of the night. By your own admission, you were drunk and, on entering the pub, upon seeing Victoria, you effectively started a fight."

"I'm not proud of that."

"I'm sure that you're not. Can I ask, when you were together, did you ever harm Victoria?" Fothergill's eyes turned steely. He looked at Rachel with disgust.

"I did not." Fothergill checked his watch and stood up. "I believe that that is the end of our interview, thank you. I have an appointment to attend." Fothergill removed his suit jacket from the hanger and pressed an intercom button upon his desk. "Cynthia, please could you show our guests out." He smiled at Rachel, who reciprocated as she packed away her paperwork. The door to the office opened.

"Thank you for your time, Mr Fothergill." Rachel stood up and Matthew followed suit. "I'll be in contact should we need to speak to you again." Fothergill smiled stiffly.

"Any appointments can be made through Cynthia who will advise you when or if I am available." He gestured towards his open office door. "Thank you kindly, Cynthia." Rachel and Matt walked out of the office, guided by the secretary. Cynthia led them out to the foyer, towards the front doors of the building.

"I hope that your meeting went well," said Cynthia, "Charles is always busy. He can be a bit abrupt at times." Rachel wondered whether Cynthia had been listening in to some of the conversation. "He has a lunch appointment at twelve." Cynthia giggled nervously. "That's when I'll take my break too.

I wonder whether you will still be around?" Rachel looked at Cynthia in confusion. Matt stepped in. "We will, Cynthia. Can we take you for a coffee?"

"That would be lovely, Mr — ?"

"Matthew, Cynthia. Do you know Cabrelo's?"

"The little café on Junnergate?"

"That's the one. We'll see you there at twelve."

"I'll be there." Cynthia left them at the bank doors and swiftly walked back towards her office.

"What the hell was all that about?" asked Matt.

"Not sure. I think we rattled him a little bit though."

"A little bit? He was seething."

"Quick to anger. Supports Megan's statement."

"Certainly does."

"Let's take a slow walk to Cabrelo's. If you check in with the office, I'll make a quick call to Jamal."

Chapter 12

Cabrelo's was filling up with the lunchtime trade but Matt had managed to secure a table at the back. Detached enough to be private but with a good view of the door.

"Here she comes." Matt nudged Rachel's knee, then stood up and walked to the front of the cafe. Cynthia had entered wearing a raincoat, collar up, and a scarf half obscuring her face. She looked around nervously and spotted Matt as he approached her. Rachel watched as Matt gently guided her to their table. She smiled as Cynthia approached, seeing that Matt had gone to the counter to order.

"Thanks for coming," said Rachel as Matt returned to the table. Cynthia took a seat, still wrapped in her scarf and coat. Rachel held back a laugh at the drama of Cynthia's demeanour, appreciating that it was not every day that Cynthia would hold a clandestine meeting. "You're safe with us. I've got a view of the door and Matt will look after us."

"Are you sure?"

"I am. Where's Mr Fothergill's lunch meeting?"

"With a client at The Hilton."

"Good. Well he's busy, so enjoy your tea," A waitress placed a cup and saucer down and walked away "and relax." Cynthia lowered her scarf and collar. "Now, what can we do for you?" Cynthia reached into her handbag.

"Now, I don't want to get into trouble. I'm not a snitch."

"You won't," reassured Matt.

"I like my job and I wouldn't like to see Mr Fothergill get hurt," Cynthia pulled some folded white papers from her bag and slid them across the table, "but I think he's in some sort of trouble." Rachel took the paperwork and opened it. "They are photocopies." She read them and handed them to Matt, who took an involuntary sharp intake of breath.

"Where did you get them?" asked Rachel.

"Mr Fothergill had them in his desk." Cynthia took a sip of tea.

"In his desk?"

"I was worried. He's been strange recently, nervous. I have the spare keys for all of his lockers and his desk. I like to keep an eye on things. I thought you should know about this."

"You did right," reassured Matt.

"I don't want anything more to do with it though. I've done my bit." Cynthia pulled her collar up and pulled up her scarf. Rachel and Matt did not try to stop her as she stood up. "Thanks for the tea." Cynthia turned and furtively left the shop. Matt handed the paperwork back to Rachel with a smile on his face.

"What a day. I am loving this," said Matt. Rachel placed the paperwork in her bag.

"Can you pay the bill and we'll get going."

"Already done, in case we needed to get a quick getaway." Matt stood up. "Come on Marps. We haven't got all day." The couple left the shop and walked the five minutes to their car. Matt climbed into the driver's seat.

"What's the decision then, house or office?" asked Matt.

"Office first. Let's drop off the file and the notes with Jim. Then we can head back to Evesham."

"It's all starting to bubble." Matt started the engine and headed off.

"Yes, the investigation seems to be gaining some momentum. We need to control that though. Move forwards at our own pace. More interviews to do this week then we can assess where we are."

***

"When a knight won his spurs in the stories of old," boomed Ron's voice from the bathroom. He walked out, drying his hands on a towel, continuing to sing a hymn remembered from his childhood. He draped the towel over the bedroom radiator, checked his watch and headed downstairs to the kitchen, singing as he went.

Tonight was Ron's first choir practice and he wanted to impress. He grabbed his coat from the back of a kitchen chair and shrugged it on. Next, he donned his flat cap and, to protect his vocal cords, wrapped a scarf around his neck. Lastly, a quick nip of malt whisky, to lubricate his throat, and then he was ready. Ron stepped out of the house into the night and quickly sparked up a cigarette.

The air was cold and darkness had set in. With no street lights to illuminate his route, Ron took out his mobile phone and flicked its torch on. A penumbra of light illuminated his way as he headed to the church, passing houses with yellow slits of light pushing through curtain gaps. He walked up to the church and pushed gently on the gate which creaked as it swung back. Ahead, the church stained glass windows threw out a welcoming light and the sound of the church organ penetrated the air. Ronnie laughed.

"It's like the scene from a bloody horror film." Closing the gate behind him, he took out his handkerchief and dabbed some sweat from his forehead. *I need to lose some weight*, he thought. He continued up the path glancing at flowers, which were fresh upon Reginald Chiswick's grave, and entered the church through its arched weighty oak door.

The inside of the church was slightly warmer than the outside air. Ronnie stepped onto large stone flags and, looking right, saw a small gathering of people standing in the front pews. He looked around, admiring the oak-beamed ceiling, complimented by aged rows of pews, which were stationed on either side of the nave. The organ notes bounced from the interior architecture as the vicar beckoned frantically for Ron to join them. Ron removed his cap and, taking a deep breath, entered the lion's den. His heart was pounding. *Calm yourself*, he thought, *it's only choir practice*. He smiled, and with a forced air of confidence, approached the group. The vicar turned and tapped the organist on the shoulder, causing her to stop playing. Melthrop scooted forward with his arms outstretched.

"Welcome, Ronnie, welcome. The six other choir members turned in anticipation. "Everyone, this is Ronnie, our new member." They smiled in greeting. "If you could take your places, please." The choir moved into position as Melthrop guided Ronnie. "We'll do introductions afterwards. Need to get started. I'll put you next to Tim, he'll keep you right." Ronnie looked at Tim who had thinning hair tied back in a ponytail and a smell of dampness about him. He smiled in greeting. "Here's your music. I trust you are OK with Latin. You are on the tenor part." Melthrop walked to the front of the choir.

"Latin?" Ronnie checked with Tim.

"Oh yes. It's a lovely piece." Melthrop rapped on his lectern with a baton.

"OK, everybody. We'll start with Dona Nobis Pacem to warm us up."

"Shit," mumbled Ronnie, as he looked to the heavens for forgiveness.

An hour later, practice had finished and Ronnie was safely at home. He had found the whole event stressful but despite what he believed to be his woeful attempts, the vicar had seemed happy with him. Ronnie supposed that the choir was so depleted that they would accept anyone and everyone. However, his head was pounding, so he took a couple of paracetamol, swallowed with some cool water. It appeared that the evening had been a success.

Tim was a nice young chap who loved the human race and his place within it. Ronnie had failed to discover what Tim did for a living but he gave the impression of being a full-time student. Ronnie had spoken with most of the members and reassured the vicar that he would return. However, he wasn't sure about Melthrop, he seemed a bit 'wet', but on the other end of the scale, Mrs Melthrop was as hard as steel. Ronnie had complimented her on the flowers within the church but when he asked if anyone tended the ones within the graveyard, he was given a hard stare and nothing in the way of a reply. He realised that he would have to tread carefully with her.

Ronnie switched the television on and settled watching an old rerun of The Bill. *A good night's work done. I could do with this headache to go*. He picked up his cigs and withdrew one, ready to light it when the ad break started.

***

Jamal parked his car and walked towards the entrance of the Holiday Inn, stopped at the doorway and scanned the area before he entered. He was dressed in his suit and carried a briefcase. The meeting room had been booked by Trimble, using a false name and company, for a business meeting which was due to start in twenty minutes.

"All clear." Jim's voice announced over the covert radio. "Kaur has entered the hotel. All cars in the car park are empty. Rachel, you are good to go."

"Received." Matt and Rachel drove into the car park and parked away from Kaur's car. The team observation van was parked in a parking bay near the main entrance to the hotel. Jim was sitting inside, watching the area. The team were being overly cautious but the more they practised, the slicker their operating procedures would become. They therefore took any opportunity to hone their skills. Jim watched Matt and Rachel climb out of their vehicle and enter the hotel lobby.

"Good morning," said the male receptionist, beaming at them with an iridescent smile and tanned complexion. "How can I help?"

"We have a meeting. Benson Industries." The receptionist typed into the keyboard before him and checked the data on his computer screen.

"I see. Yes, there it is. Meeting room two. Left down the hallway and second door on the left. I believe that some of your colleagues have arrived. There is coffee and tea already prepared in the room."

"Thank you." Rachel followed the receptionist's directions.

"A man happy in his job," said Matt.

"Yes," said Rachel. They approached the closed meeting room door, knocked and entered. Jamal was helping himself to coffee from a jug. He turned his head as they entered.

"Leave some biscuits for us," said Matt.

"Custard creams and Jammy Dodgers, mate. No expense spared."

"That'll do me."

"Only the three of us?" asked Rachel.

"Yes, it seems that I am now C&D's go-between. Honestly, I'm spending more time out of the office dealing with this shit than I am in, dealing with my own."

"The lofty heights of rank," said Rachel.

"I can see why you left," replied Jamal with a laugh. "Grab a drink and help yourselves to biscuits," he winked at Matt. "We only have the room for an hour."

"I'll pour," said Matt to Rachel. "You two get cracking." Rachel updated Jamal on their enquiries to date.

"Progress," said Jamal. "You seem to have stirred something up. Why now though? Why not when I reviewed it all?"

"Different tactics? More time has passed? Sometimes people clam up when the cops get involved. We're not the cops."

"Well, as long as it's progressing then it doesn't matter. Next moves?"

"We need to speak with Jamie and Tanya Hyatt. I want to speak with them separately. Can you facilitate me seeing him at work? I'd like to see how he acts in his own environment."

"Certainly can. A favour for a favour?"

"Go on?"

"We already have some tracking equipment on his car."

"Nice," said Matt, leaning forward with interest. Jamal and Rachel glanced at him, almost having forgotten he was there. Matt had a grin on his face and was nodding. He loved the secret side of policing. Jamal raised an eyebrow and looked back at Rachel. "We want to get a listening device into his house."

"And you want us to do it?"

"It'll save us from breaking in. You are speaking with Tanya anyway and I believe your team has the requisite skills to deploy a device."

"We do."

"I have a copy of our authority for you to read." Jamal reached into his briefcase and retrieved a typed and completed Regulatory of Investigative Powers Act (RIPA) application form. The form detailed the police's intelligence case and reasons for recording the Hyatts' private conversations. "I've also taken the liberty of bringing the listening device for you."

"Confident I'd accept then?"

"Let's say hopeful. We are in this together."

"That we are," Rachel accepted the device. "When can I see Jamie?"

"He's on late shifts Wednesday."

"Wednesday then. Is Miss Dutton aware of the devices?"

"No, and that's how it stays. She's a good cop but she's still an informant. It's only a need-to-know basis."

"Fair enough. Let me have a read through this," Rachel lifted the paperwork, "then we can sort out the plan."

"Another coffee, Jamal?" asked Matt standing up and walking to the side table where the pot waited.

"Yes, mate." Jamal joined Matt as Rachel read on.

***

Tanya had spent half the morning in bed with Jamie, both lazing around before he headed off to work. The first of two late shifts meant that she would have the evenings to herself. Jamie's working days dragged on for Tanya. She often spent long hours alone whilst he worked prolonged shifts, overtime, or went for a 'drink with the lads' after work. Sometimes she felt like a second choice to the police service which dominated Jamie's life. She looked around the lounge though and couldn't complain about her possessions. Jamie knew how to treat her and frequently did. She wanted for nothing.

Unexpectedly, Victoria's smiling face popped into her mind. Her friend who, in her youth, wanted for nothing either. A friend with whom she had parted on bad terms, if parted is what she could call it. Victoria had wanted for nothing. *Except my man.*

"Look where that got you," she said aloud. There was a knock at the front door. Tanya looked out of the living room window and saw a dark car that she didn't recognise parked outside of her house. She frowned, walked to the front door and opened it. Tanya was confronted by a man and a woman, neither of whom she knew.

"Can I help you?" The man smiled warmly. He wore casual clothing and carried a backpack. The lady wore jeans and a heavy-knit pullover.

"I certainly hope so. We're here on behalf of Lord Fanshaw, conducting some enquiries concerning the disappearance of Victoria," said Tom.

"Victoria?"

"Yes, his daughter. I believe that you and her were close friends. You are Tanya aren't you."

"Well, yes but — Are you with the police? It's only that my husband —"

"Jamie," said Sarah, "is a copper. No, we're not with the police. We're a private company. Nothing to do with the cops."

"We do some cold case review work. Mr Fanshaw has asked us to review Victoria's disappearance and, as her best friend, we thought that you'd be a great person to talk to."

"We'll be doing other enquiries in and around the village. You're not the only one. You have nothing to worry about." Sarah smiled. "Half an hour of your time?" Tanya stepped back in the doorway. *We're in,* thought Tom. "Is it OK if we come in?" Tanya opened the door fully.

"Certainly. Anything I can do to help." Tom and Sarah entered the house as Tanya gestured to the right. "The lounge is through there." They entered the room as Tanya closed the door behind them. She followed them in. "Jamie's at work. Would this be better when he is around too?"

"Did he know Victoria?" asked Sarah.

"No. He met her only once."

"We can catch up with him later then."

"Grab a seat," said Tanya, "I'll stick the kettle on."

"I'll help you," said Sarah, following Tanya into the kitchen.

Tom quickly scanned the room as the ladies walked into the kitchen. He knew that Sarah would keep Tanya busy and this may be the only opportunity that he'd get to deploy the device.

A large flatscreen television dominated one wall with a sound bar below it. Any noise from the television would drown out a listening device so that was a definite no-go. The positioning of the sofas and the log burner demonstrated where conversations would likely be held within the room. Ceiling light, side table, PlayStation, footstool, bookcase. He reached into the backpack and retrieved a hardback book. A faded title adorned the spine. The book was nondescript, a blender which would go unnoticed on the shelf. Tom opened the front pages and within he placed the battery pack which would power the audio feed. A slim wire threaded through a series of tiny holes punched into the spine. He flicked the device to sleep mode, closed the cover and slid it into place on the shelf. Tom could hear Sarah returning. He swiftly took a seat and as she entered, gave a slight dip of his head.

"Here you go, Tom." Sarah handed the drink to Tom, knowing that his nod indicated a successful deployment. Tanya followed her in. Both ladies took a seat as Tom took out a small pad from his backpack.

"Right, let's start with how you met Victoria."

***

Fenchurch Station loomed over Matt and Rachel as they walked to the front doors and entered. Jamal Kaur waited behind the visitor's desk and buzzed both of them straight through.

"If you can put these on, please," he said, handing them both a visitor pass and lanyard. "This way." They followed Kaur down a short corridor and waited with him as he pressed a button to summon a lift. The doors opened and all three stepped inside. Kaur pressed the button for floor two. "I've booked a private room within the intelligence suite. Hyatt's skipper will be bringing him now. We have left it fairly relaxed so that he doesn't get jumpy." The lift pinged and the door opened. The men stepped aside to let Rachel out and then Kaur showed them to the room. Kaur seemed more nervous than anyone. "I'll leave you to it. Flick me a text when you're finished." Kaur swiftly left the room.

The room comprised a round table with four chairs. To one side a single desk with a computer on it. A single window, with mirrored sheen, allowed daylight to enter. Matt placed a briefcase on the table.

"No coffee?" asked Matt.

"Times are tight," said Rachel, nudging the chairs out. There was a knock at the door.

"Come in," said Rachel. A balding head, followed by uniformed shoulders, poked around the corner.

"Rachel?" said the uniformed sergeant.

"That's me." she smiled.

"Young Jamie's here."

"Great, show him in." The door opened wide and Jamie Hyatt strode in, standing tall, a commanding presence. Rachel smiled and held her hand out.

"PC Hyatt, thanks a lot for coming." Jamie shook her hand reflexively and looked beyond her to Matt, who raised a hand in greeting.

"Matt," he said, in clarification. Rachel looked to the sergeant.

"Thank you. I'm sure PC Hyatt will escort us out when we are finished."

"He will," said the sergeant, closing the door as he left.

"Take a seat, Jamie. Sorry, but no one supplied drinks." He looked at Rachel suspiciously.

"Are you Complaints and Discipline?" Rachel laughed.

"We certainly are not."

"Do I need the federation or a solicitor?" Rachel was not surprised that he was demonstrating the natural suspicion of every police officer.

"You don't. We're hoping that you can help us. We're not cops. I used to be a DI though. I resigned a couple of years ago, and set up my own investigation team. Still have the contacts though and thought you'd be easier to track down at work."

"Where were you stationed?"

"Barnston." Jamie's frown eased.

"The cop who was run over?"

"That's me," Rachel held her stick up, "still suffering the consequences. Enough about me though, Jamie. I want to pick your brains and get your opinion about Victoria Fanshaw's disappearance." Jamie's shoulders relaxed. He pulled a chair out. "We've been asked to independently review the case. Not by the cops, but by Lord Fanshaw. Any light you can shine on that night in question would be a great help." Jamie took a chair and straddled it.

"Ask me anything you like." He smiled.

***

"Do you think that Victoria was happy with her life?" asked Sarah. Tanya pondered the question.

"I think she was frustrated."

"Go on."

"She was a free spirit. Not a woman to be controlled. The family were keen for her to marry Charles."

"Charles?"

"Charles Fothergill. She felt that they were pushing her into it and she certainly didn't want that."

"Who is 'they'?"

"Her father and Jonathan, her brother. She didn't like Charles though. Didn't trust him. Jonathan was trying to get her out of the way so that he could run the estate."

"Which is what he is doing now."

"Funny that, isn't it?"

"Did Victoria get on with her family? Not everyone does."

"Doted on by her father. Not so much her brother. Sibling rivalry, I suppose."

"Was she jealous of Jonathan?" Tanya laughed as she reached forward to the coffee table for a pack of cigarettes.

"Not at all. As far as she was concerned he could have the estate. All she wanted was a regular income from it all."

"For doing nothing?"

"Yep, that was Victoria for you."

"I can imagine that didn't impress Jonathan."

"I suppose not, but when you're rolling in money what does it matter?" Tanya took a cigarette from the packet, "You fancy a cig?"

"Yeah."

"Outside I'm afraid. Jamie doesn't like me smoking in the house. You?" she asked Tom.

"Not for me, thanks. I'll collect the cups."

"Fill your boots," said Tanya as she walked towards the front door, with Sarah following. Tom heard the front door open and the women started talking. He picked up his backpack and moved swiftly into the kitchen.

***

"You only met her that once?" asked Rachel.

"I'd say met is stretching it. She was in the pub with her own mates."

"Who were?"

"Tanya, Mark and a bloke called Danny. I was out having a laugh. The pub was busy. I was playing pool and she kept looking over at me."

"What did you think?"

"Think? Nothin'."

"She was a good-looking woman."

"You get used to it, if you know what I mean?" Jamie winked at Rachel.

"I'm sure you do. What next?"

"Well you can see it in my statement. Some pissed up bloke walked in and bang …" Jamie lifted his arms to either side, "the pub explodes. Danny gets attacked. Tanya and Victoria start scrapping. It was a right mess." Jamie chuckled.

"You didn't step in to sort it out? You are a copper."

"Fuck, no. You're having a laugh, aren't you? Anyway, the landlord quickly got a grip."

"Thank goodness someone did." Jamie missed the sarcasm in Rachel's response. "The pub got closed. Where did you go?"

"Back to Tan's"

"With Mark?"

"No."

"Only you and Tanya?"

"Correct. I told him I'd check if she was OK and to give me an hour." He winked at Rachel again. *What a sordid little man you are*, thought Rachel.

"Where did Mark go?"

"No bloody idea."

"And Victoria?"

"Left her with her brother, it turns out, at the pub."

"You didn't see her again?"

"Nope."

"And Mark?"

"Next morning at Tanya's. I stayed the night. He was having a cig by the front door when we came down to make a coffee."

"How'd he seem?"

"Quiet, but let's face it, he's never gonna be the one to set the world on fire."

***

Sarah walked back into the kitchen followed by Tanya, dragging in cool air tinged with cigarette smoke behind them.

"Kettle's boiled," said Tom, who had now rinsed the cups and placed them on the work surface. He smiled at Sarah. *Another device deployed*, she thought. Tanya moved to the kettle and started spooning out coffee.

"It's a nice place that you've got here," said Tom.

"I like it," said Tanya, "we haven't got any kids so it's big enough for us."

"You work at all?"

"Nah, I hardly get to see Jamie as it is. He works all funny hours, so I fit in around him. I'm a kept woman." Tanya laughed and handed them both a drink.

"And he's keeping you in style," Sarah joined in.

"Yeah, I don't want for much. He's a good man to me."

"Must be a high flyer if he can afford all this?" Tanya laughed again.

"Jamie? A high flyer? Never. He's only a PC. Likes it like that. Says it keeps him flexible and free. Luckily, he had a bit of inheritance when we got together, and he dabbles in stocks and shares. We've been lucky."

"Well, you make your own luck, Tanya. Good on you," said Tom. They walked back into the living room. "Can we cover off the end of the night in the pub?"

***

"When you've left the pub you see Victoria with her brother?" asked Rachel.

"Yes. Charles Fothergill was nearby too. I didn't know him then but it was him that started the fight."

"Anyone else?"

"Danny must have been there as well. He had been scrapping with Charles. No idea where he went though. We were keen on getting away."

"You get on with them all?"

"Don't have much to do with them. I'm too busy working and I suppose they do what they do."

"Fair enough," Rachel paused. "I appreciate that it was all a long time ago but you're older now, with a honed copper's instinct. If you were me, who would you be looking at?" Jamie flexed his shoulders and looked contemplative.

"For murdering Victoria?"

"Yes. Who would be your top suspect?" Jamie leaned forwards.

"Danny."

"Why?"

"Jealousy. Look at the state of him now. He's a piss-head. From all accounts he fancied Victoria. He knew he didn't stand a chance, so he decided no one could have her. Bumped her off and turned to the bottle. Can't see how we never caught him." There was a knock at the door. Rachel turned and said,

"Come in." Jamie's shift sergeant poked his head around the door.

"Apologies but we need Jamie. We're short on the ground and it's getting busy."

"That's OK. We're about finished." Jamie stood up.

"Great." The sergeant stepped in and held the door open for Jamie.

"Thanks, Jamie," said Rachel. "We'll be in contact if we need anything else."

"No problem." Jamie left the room.

"I'll show you out," said the shift sergeant to Rachel and Matt.

***

"Everyone has been kicked out of the pub," said Sarah.

"Yeah. To be fair, we were all pissed. The fight had happened and the landlord had had enough."

"You've gone off to one side with Mark. Victoria's with her brother and Charles Fothergill is nearby. Everyone else starts heading home?"

"Yeah."

"What did you do?"

"Mark and I stumbled our way back to mine. He was staying over."

"You never saw Victoria again?"

"No."

"No messages, texts, calls?"

"None. The first I heard she was missing was when Jonathan called at mine the next day."

"He called down to see you?"

"Yeah. Mark, Jamie and I were having a coffee when he knocked on the door."

"Jamie was at yours too?"

"Yeah, he'd stayed the night."

"You said you'd walk back with Mark."

"I did. Jamie turned up at the house thirty minutes later. Asked if he could crash for the night. Daft idiot had been wandering round the village, trying to find my house." Sarah glanced towards Tom, who was taking notes.

"How was Jonathan?"

"Annoyed. He wanted to speak with Victoria and claimed she hadn't come home. He wanted to search my house."

"And did he?"

"No. Jamie told him to fuck off."

"Bet he took that well," said Tom.

"No, but Jamie showed him his warrant card and he soon shifted."

"You miss her?" asked Tom. Victoria looked sad but resolute.

"Time moves on. It was a long time ago," she replied.

***

Tom and Sarah walked away from the Hyatt's house, turned a corner and approached their car. Sarah opened the driver's door.

"What do you think?" she asked, as she climbed into the car. Tom opened the passenger side and climbed in. They closed the doors.

"She's a nice lady. Appears to have nothing to hide." Sarah started the engine and pulled away.

"She can't be totally naive to Jamie's activities though, can she?"

"Maybe she chooses not to know. He provides her with the lifestyle that she wants. Maybe that's all that matters to her."

"She never said that she missed Victoria either."

"No. That was interesting. Deflected the question. We have the listening devices in place now though. They may give us something."

"That's why I didn't want to push too much. Providing that we get the access that Kaur has said we will."

"They'll keep their word," reassured Tom. "We've successfully deployed the devices for them. I'm sure they'll play ball. I'll give Rach a call." The car headed up the hill and out of the village. Tom dialled Rachel using the car hands-free. She answered promptly.

"Tom."

"Hi, you're hands-free. Successful deployment."

"Great, I'll let Kaur know. How was your visit?"

"It went well. Yours?"

"Same. Meet at the office for a debrief?"

"On our way."

"See you soon."

***

"Afternoon, mate," said Tom as he walked into the office.

"Hi, guys. Kettle's boiled." Jim was sitting behind his desk, tapping away on a keyboard.

"You getting stir crazy yet?" asked Sarah.

"Just about coping," replied Jim. "With, effectively, four teams out on the ground you all keep me busy. The picture is building though. It feels like we are getting somewhere." He looked across to a monitor on the wall. "Here's Rach and Matt." A CCTV image showed their car entering the compound. Sarah walked over to the kettle and started making a brew. Jim stopped typing and walked over to the sofas with a pad and pen in hand. A couple of minutes later, Rachel and Matt entered the office.

"Kaur's message has been passed on," said Rachel, placing her bag down and gratefully accepting a drink. "They'll let us know the quality of the audio when they get some conversation. It appears that Tanya is still home alone."

"Cheers," said Matt to Sarah, as he accepted a drink and took a seat. Rachel took a seat as well.

"You start us off, guys. Then we'll give you the low down on Jamie." The team spent the next forty minutes debriefing each other's meetings as Jim took notes.

"A good afternoon's work," said Rachel. "We also have the devices in place. Thoughts?"

"I think we can use the discrepancy in the Hyatts' account of the evening," said Jim. "He tells you that he left the pub with Tanya and yet she tells us that he arrived thirty minutes later."

"Does that make him a suspect?" asked Matt.

"Everyone's a suspect at the moment," said Rachel, "we haven't ruled anyone out."

"We need to know what his account is for that thirty minutes," said Sarah.

"How about making a phone call to Tanya when we know Jamie's at home?" said Jim. "Kaur's team can monitor the listening devices when we do it. Use the call as a trigger and they can monitor their reaction afterwards."

"It might give us something," said Tom.

"I like it," said Rachel. "It could help both our investigation and the police one. I'm sure Jamal will go for it. Nice one, Jim."

"Neither party has mentioned receiving any note like the others have," said Jim. "Have they received one? If not, why not? If they have, why haven't they told us?"

"Apart from Sir David, no one else has told us either," said Matt.

"It's gotta be key to the enquiry though. Someone knows, or suspects certain individuals. Who is it? Who is sending them?" said Jim.

"Has Joe checked in?" asked Matt. "He was going to try and see if he could get any further with Danny."

"Not yet."

"I'll call him this evening if he hasn't made contact," said Matt. The team went silent and all looked to Rachel for direction.

"We get the result of our enquiries written up and fed into Jim this afternoon. Jim's already identifying some investigative opportunities for us. I'll speak with Kaur and we'll aim to get the call made to Tanya this week. We need updates from Joe and Ronnie. I'm going back to the hall this evening and will talk to Sir David tomorrow. This week is all about rattling some cages and getting reactions. We build slowly and see where we are by the end of the week."

Chapter 13

Emily closed her room door behind her, chucked her bag onto her bed, removed her coat and threw it over a chair. The shift had dragged today, with most of it being spent on file preparation. Working in the city was OK but she preferred her previous posting. Even better she would sooner work within an intelligence role but it seemed that she was more use to the force working in uniform. Maybe when she finished this job they would consider a transfer to another department. Emily felt that she had suffered enough for her previous misdemeanours. As if on cue, her telephone rang. She looked at the screen, sighed and answered.

"Hi, Heather. Can you talk?" said Trimble.

"Yes, a bit late isn't it."

"Needs must. How's it going?" Emily flumped into the chair.

"Steady away. Quiet day today. I haven't seen much of him. He got sent out on a job. I'm in with him though. He's comfortable with me."

"Good. You've got a day off tomorrow."

"Yeah, can't wait."

"Good. I'll need you to visit the village." Emily frowned and shook her head.

"I'm due to be off. He's working on earlies anyway. It would be pointless."

"I'll be the judge of whether it is pointless or not. Take a visit to Evesham House, they have a lovely café there."

"But —"

"No buts. I want you to be there at two o'clock. I've put some money into your account to cover your expenses."

"I'll have to cancel my plans."

"Cancel them then. This takes precedence."

"What am I supposed to do at the café?"

"Tanya Hyatt should be there. Get chatting to her. See where it takes you. I need to know what their relationship is like. See if you can dig up any shit on our target. I want her phone number too."

"Anything else? Who's gonna win the two-thirty at Newmarket?"

"Now, now, no need for that. You knew what this game was about when you got into it." *I had no bloody choice,* thought Emily.

"I'll be there."

"Good girl." Emily terminated the call and looking at her handset said,

"Condescending bastard." She chucked the phone on her bed. "Another day ruined."

***

Joe knocked at the door of Danny's house and waited for a reply which was not forthcoming. He walked back to the gate and, checking left and right, couldn't see anybody around. He turned back to the front door, tried the handle and smiled when he realised that it wasn't locked. He cracked the door open.

"Dan, you in? It's Joe," he called out. Joe knew that Danny's car wasn't outside and he could sense that the house was empty. He checked behind him, then took his chance. Joe entered and eased the door back behind him, leaving it cracked open in case he needed a quick exit.

An armchair was positioned facing the television and a PlayStation. A couple of empty cans of beer stood on the carpet by the foot of the chair. To one side of the chair, an abandoned pile of envelopes. Joe crouched down and examined them, quickly realising that Danny had some outstanding debts. Standing back up, he scanned the room. A thin veil of dust covered most surfaces. In-built shelving housed a small number of books and above the Playstation a row of old PS game sleeves and DVDs. One small box caught Joe's attention, as did a discarded crumpled envelope which looked to have been thrown into the cold fire grate.

"I've lived in worse," said Joe as he walked towards a door. He opened it and peered into the kitchen. "Maybe not". The kitchen was a tip with unwashed dishes, numerous empty cans and bottles, and a bin overflowing with refuse. An insidious odour of stale food and alcohol crept towards him. He closed the door quickly. "Poor bastard." Joe understood the lows of life and would be the last person to judge a man battling addiction.

He returned to the living room and bent down, recovering the discarded envelope from the grate. Unravelling the envelope he pulled a sheet of paper from within. *Bingo*, he thought. Taking out his phone, he snapped a quick picture before replacing the note and envelope back into the fire as he had found it. Joe heard a car, a door open and close, then footsteps. He moved to the window. The blind was drawn. Someone approached the door and paused. Joe waited. Heart pounding. Breath held. *Think, think, think*.

"Hello," called a woman's voice. *Not Danny.* The person waited. Joe waited. He looked towards the door. An envelope appeared within the crack, was flicked through the air and dropped to the floor. Footsteps retreated. Joe carefully parted the blind and caught a flash of red. *Postie*, thought Joe, the hammering in his chest starting to calm. He took a breath and moved towards the letter. Red typescript adorned the front. Another bill for Danny.

Joe looked back at the room. One last thing to check. One last risk. He moved back to the bookshelf and the box. Opening it carefully, he peered in. A jewellery box placed upon some folded newspaper. He took both items out. Beneath the paper a plain white envelope. Danny unfolded the newspaper and was confronted with the headline.

Sir David Fanshaw's Daughter Reported Missing!

He retrieved the envelope and removed the note from within.

WE KNOW SHE WAS MURDERED

He reached for the small jewellery box. Opened it. Within, a golden necklace with a single golden teardrop pendant.

"What the fuck." With shaking hands, Joe photographed each item, then returned them before replacing the box in its original position. He moved to the front door, and scanned the room, ensuring that it looked the same as when he entered. With a glance outside and, checking it was clear, he left the house, closing the door gently behind him. The street remained empty. Joe returned to his van, started it up and pulled gently away. He knew he needed to call this in, having no idea what to do with his discovery.

***

Ronnie put his coat on.

"Thanks for the game."

"I was lucky tonight," said Alfred.

"Made your own luck, mate. I crumbled under your pressure." Alfred laughed. Ronnie placed his cap on. "I meant to ask. Do you get up to the church much?"

"You're not roping me into your bloody choir. Been avoiding it for years."

"I wouldn't put you through it." Ronnie chuckled. "Beautiful building though. Whoever is keeping the grounds is doing a grand job."

"Audrey's brother covers that. You know, Audrey, the vicar's wife."

"Plays the organ."

"That's her. Does all the flower arranging too."

"She looks like a fearsome woman."

"Not one I'd like to cross." Ronnie fastened his coat and reached for the door handle.

"Had a wander round the headstones the other day. There are some old ones. All well kept. Grass short, fresh flowers. Some you can't read but the Fanshaws are there, Molesworths, Chiswick. Nice chrysanths on his."

"Reg Chiswick?"

"Could be. Passed twenty years ago."

"He was a good lad. Died in a car crash. Surprised at the flowers though. Don't think he has any living relatives."

"Maybe I got the wrong one. No matter." Ron opened the door. "Right, I'm off. Afternoon nap?"

"I expect so. See you in the pub later?"

"Not tonight. I'll be in tomorrow though. See you later, mate." Ronnie stepped out, closing the door behind him.

Twenty minutes later, Ronnie had climbed the hill, feeling slightly puffed having done so. He stopped to catch his breath, removed his cap and wiped away the beads of sweat that had formed on his forehead. He continued, deciding to call at Margaret's on the way past. He rapped on her door and waited. There was no reply. Ronnie peered through the front window and saw that the room was empty. *Oh well, another time.* He continued on and, with a niggle in his mind, headed towards the church.

The sound of a strimmer permeated the fresh cold air as he ascended the road and silenced as he approached the church gates. Now oiled, they opened silently, and with no resumption of machine noise, birds started calling to each other. Ronnie startled a strutting pigeon as he walked the path and watched it take off in a frantic flap to land on a nearby fir tree. He breathed deeply, enjoying the clean air, and allowed the bird to settle. The red chrysanthemums remained clearly in view by Reginald's grave. Ronnie looked thoughtful. *What's your story, Reg?* He took out a cigarette and lit it, allowing his eyes to wander through the stones and grasses. The church stood resolutely, overseeing its affairs. Stained glass windows observed the silent flock and the man who sought answers.

***

Sir David walked into the lounge at Evesham. The fire blazed within the hearth and Rachel was sitting comfortably, typing on her laptop. She looked up as he entered.

"Aagh, Rachel. Fletcher told me you were in here. How are you?" He walked to the sideboard and poured himself a hot coffee, looked at Rachel, then nodded towards the pot. "Refill?"

"I'm good, thanks."

"Making progress?"

"Yes." Sir David's eyebrows raised. He quickly took a seat opposite her.

"I knew I could trust you."

"Don't get too excited. It's slow going but I do believe we are establishing new lines of enquiry."

"Does DI Kaur know?"

"He's overseeing us from a police perspective, so yes."

"Not creating any obstacles?"

"Far from it."

"Good, good. Anything you can share?" Sir David leaned towards her.

"With respect, I'd prefer not to. Early days." Sir David leaned back.

"Naturally. I understand. Keeping one's powder dry." His face looked disappointed.

"It's not a matter of trust," clarified Rachel, "I don't wish to get your hopes up. You've faced enough disappointment and I don't wish to add to it."

"Are you going to find her killer?"

"I'm going to try my damned hardest."

"Then that will do for me." Sir David took a sip of coffee. Rachel closed her laptop.

"Can I ask you about Charles Fothergill?" He looked over his cup at her.

"You can?"

"You were keen for Charles and Victoria to marry?"

"At the time, yes. He was a man with good prospects and came from a respected family. I felt that he would look after her."

"You said 'at the time'?"

"Yes, but now I think that she may have had a lucky escape."

"And why's that?"

"You know, you hear things. Word is that he's become a bit of a player."

"A player?" Sir David looked embarrassed.

"With women. Can't keep it in his pants. That sort of thing."

"Oh!" Rachel feigned shock. "But he's married with kids."

"Yes he is. That's what I mean. A lucky escape." Sir David paused. "Still, I'd prefer that she was here even if it was with him." Sir David gave Rachel a weary smile.

"You have nothing to do with Charles now?"

"No. He spends some time with Jonathan. I'm always polite when I see him."

"Naturally." Rachel paused. "Do you recall one of your farmhands called Daniel?"

"Daniel?" repeated Sir David.

"He doesn't work for you now but did when Victoria was with you."

"Daniel? There's been so many staff through the years."

"Still knocking around the village. He's a bit of a drinker. I think Jonathan sacked him."

"No surprise there. We would have no staff if he sacked every person that he wished to. It's not a name I recall personally. Jonathan's your man, or maybe Kaur. Should I know him? Is he a suspect?"

"Everyone is a suspect, David." He chuckled.

"I suppose they are. Keep your cards close to your chest. I must say that you are a breath of fresh air around here. I'm used to getting my way. Everyone here says yes to me. Not you though."

"Happy to oblige, David."

"Do you fancy a trundle around the estate?" Sir David stood up. Rachel remained sitting.

"No." Sir David looked confused. Rachel smiled. "Honestly, that would be pleasant." Sir David laughed.

"You got me there. Remind me never to play you at Bragg." Rachel placed her laptop to one side and carefully stood up, collecting her walking stick.

"I always play to win," said Rachel.

***

Jamie headed through the city with a determined stride, his confident demeanour camouflaging his inner turmoil. He'd caught a train yesterday and travelled to London where he stayed overnight in a city centre hotel. He wanted a clear head this morning. Not visiting the city for pleasure, today he had been called to a meeting. Tickets had been paid in cash, as had his hotel room. Nobody needed to know about this journey, and if he wished to save his career it was better that nobody found out.

He'd been careful on the way down. His car was parked outside of Fenchurch and he'd booked his journey from a mainline substation. As a seasoned copper, Jamie understood the capabilities of the police. Although not formally trained, he had studied anti-surveillance from online resources and did his best to put measures in place to protect himself. Now entering Soho, he checked his pocket again, comforting himself that he still held the items. Jamie identified the building, scanned the street and approached. With the best will in the world, he had no idea if he was being watched. Soho was busy and any person could be working for the syndicate. Jamie stood at a door and pressed the bell. He waited. Then pressed it again. The door opened. He was faced by an elderly Asian male.

"Do not be so impatient," he said. "It takes me time to get to the door these days. You have an appointment?" Jamie looked nonplussed. "I'm only joking. Mr Jamie, please come this way." Jamie entered a small corridor, which was illuminated by a single strip light. The man closed the door behind Jamie and then shuffled past him, indicating for Jamie to follow. The building was quiet, the volume of commuters outside deadened by the architecture. "Mr Li is waiting." The men turned right at the end, then left, and then started descending some stairs.

"Where are we going?" asked Jamie, in his most authoritative voice.

"The offices are downstairs. Don't worry. All is fine." The male kept moving, giving Jamie no option but to follow. At the bottom of the stairs was a further corridor with a single door on either side. The male stopped at the right-hand side door and knocked, before pushing it open. He indicated for Jamie to enter and waited for him to do so. Jamie moved tentatively forward and walked into the room.

The sparsely furnished office contained a single desk and three chairs. Li was sitting behind the desk and looked Jamie up and down as he entered. Next to Lee, a large portly white male with receding curly hair was standing. He wore a poorly fitting suit with a tie pulled loosely to the neck. His shirt buttons clung desperately to the shirt, which stretched tightly across his abdomen.

"Constable Hyatt, thank you for coming," said the man in a Scottish accent, "please take a seat." Jamie automatically reached for a seat and lowered himself into it. *Who the hell are you?* He thought. As if reading his mind the male spoke.

"For the record, I am Cameron Noble, representing Mr Li, as his lawyer. I am merely here to ensure that you fully understand our, and your, position in these proceedings. To make sure that things are clear, if you know what I mean." Noble took a seat in the remaining chair and sighed with the strain of doing so. Jamie frowned at Noble and addressed Li.

"Mr Li, we need —"

"To get this back on track," interrupted Noble. "Mr Li is a busy man and wishes me to make things crystal clear." Li stared silently at Jamie. "You are employed, and have been so, for several years, by Mr Li."

"But —" Noble held a hand up, halting Jamie's speech.

"You have been fairly remunerated, and will continue to be so, providing that you continue in this work."

"And —" said Jamie. A further raised hand.

"If you don't, then Mr Li, regrettably may I say so, will be forced to expose you as the corrupt officer that you are and, to boot, the murderer of the man in Barnston. We have the images, we have the murder weapon."

"Who the hell do you think you are?" Jamie shouted. The door behind him opened and two stocky Asian males entered. Mr Li's expression did not change. "I am a bloody police officer, I'm not some little dickhead that you can push around." Jamie reached into his pocket and pulled out a USB stick. "I have here every record, of every call, of all your numbers, locations of grows, people trafficked. Enough to hang you." He threw the stick at Li. A man behind Jamie moved forward. Li held his hand up, halting him.

"And we have the records of all your payments, your car purchases, your wife's beauty treatments, your house, your parents, their house. Photography of you attending our houses, our takeaways, our restaurants, and even your hotel last night. Do we make ourselves clear?" said Noble. Jamie looked visibly shaken. He'd come here on a mission, to walk away from it all. How can it have turned so quickly? Noble's voice took on a hard edge. "Now I suggest that you go back to your little city, dickhead. Mr Li will be in contact." Noble stood up, Li stood, fastened his suit jacket, and walked out via a door behind him. Noble said politely, "These gentlemen, will show you out." Jamie's arm was taken firmly and he was guided out of the chair and escorted from the office, leaving Noble behind.

***

Emily entered the café at exactly two o'clock and, looking around, spotted Tanya saying goodbye to another lady. Emily approached the counter and ordered a latte. The lady walked past her and left the room. Emily turned. Tanya was using her mobile phone, then glanced up, as if she could feel eyes upon her. Emily squinted in her direction, her brow wrinkling then smoothing as she feigned recognition. Tanya beamed back and beckoned her over.

"I'll bring it to the table," said the lady making her coffee, realising that she was meeting a friend.

"Thank you," replied Emily. She walked over to Tanya's table and took a seat.

"Hiya, what brings you over here?" asked Tanya.

"A rare day off. Thought I'd take a tour of the house and grounds."

"A day off. What's one of those? Jamie had to go to work this morning. He was out with a mate last night, stayed over in Fenchurch, and then texted me this morning telling me that he wouldn't be back until tea time. Your mob takes the piss, I can tell you."

"I can only agree." Emily doubted that Jamie was at work but Trimble could look into that. The waitress placed Emily's coffee on the table.

"Put it on my tab," said Tanya. She leaned into Emily. "Jamie can pay it off later."

"Thanks."

"A look around the grounds then. Is that what grabs you? Stately homes?"

"I was at a loose end and thought I'd take a wander round, after passing it the other day."

"A loose end eh? Well, I've got a better idea. Why don't you drink up, then we'll bob down to mine, open a bottle and get Jamie to bring in a take-out. You got dinner plans? No. That's settled then."

"I'm driving."

"Leave it at mine. Come on. Life's too short. Stately homes at your age, get a life. Come on. Chop chop." Tanya stood up and walked over to the counter where she spoke to a member of staff. She returned to the table. "Let's go. Where are you parked?" Tanya almost hauled Emily out of her chair and they headed to the car park.

***

"There you go. That'll get us started." Tanya placed a glass of white wine before Emily.

"I love your house," said Emily, "I'm staying in a shitty little flat. You've got some beautiful stuff." Emily noted the Smeg fridge, toaster and kettle. She ran her hand over the fridge surface.

"Hard work, love. It comes with hard work." Tanya walked into the living room followed by Emily.

"I work hard but am way off affording this."

"Jamie's been lucky. Came into some money a few years ago. We got this place and kitted it out properly."

"You've not always been here?"

"Nah, I used to rent a spot down the road. We bought this – I say we, Jamie bought this – and did it all out."

"You're a lucky woman."

"We're looking at getting a spot in Tenerife too." Tanya took out her phone. "We've been eyeing this one up." She handed Emily her phone and Emily scrolled through some images.

"Nice."

"Yeah, we'll be renting it out to his colleagues too, if you fancy it. Mates rates, needless to say."

"Ooh! Can you send me the pics?" Tanya took her phone back. "What's your number?" Tanya drained her glass. "Tell you what, you stick it in and I'll send them. I'll top us up." She handed her phone back to Emily who tapped her number in. "It'll be a great holiday spot," Tanya yelled from the kitchen. She walked back in, carrying the bottle. Emily handed her phone back. Tanya placed the bottle down and, pressing the keys on her phone, sent the images to Emily. *Phone number obtained*, thought Emily.

"I'll take a good look at it. I wonder what Jamie got called in for? I never got a call." Tanya filled her glass and topped up Emily's.

"He never tells me. You lot are so secretive. He's been working a lot recently."

"You don't get lonely?"

"I've plenty of friends. I keep myself busy." Tanya's phone pinged. "Speak of the devil. He's back early. He'll be here in five. So much for the take-out. Frozen pizza it is."

"Honestly, don't go to any trouble. I haven't even had one yet," said Emily, holding up her glass.

"It's no trouble. Let's have a quick cig before his lordship gets home." Tanya grabbed a pack off the coffee table. "Out the back." She stood up and Emily followed her out.

***

Music filtered through the air as Ronnie wandered past the church and down towards his house. He found himself humming along as he tried to identify the hymn being played. Following a restless night, Ronnie had got up late and taken a gentle walk on the lane that headed from the pub and passed the hall. The route that he knew Victoria had taken. He felt that his enquiries weren't progressing any further. He'd formed links in the village and he'd infiltrated well but, without openly talking about Victoria, his chances of gleaning any more information were slim. He hadn't seen Joe for a couple of days and could do with him coming around so that they could compare progress.

Ronnie took out his phone and flicked Joe a text asking him to call round later. Stubbing his cigarette out in the ashtray he'd placed by the front door, Ronnie took out his key and placed it in the lock. The key wouldn't turn. Ronnie frowned.

"I'm sure I locked it." He turned the handle cautiously and the door gently opened. Ronnie paused, withdrew his key and waited silently. No sounds came from within. "You're getting forgetful, old man." He entered the house, closed the door behind him, removed his coat and hung it up. "Time for a brew." Ronnie's phone pinged in his pocket, he looked down, took it out and pushed against the kitchen door raising his head as he did so.

The door gave, stopped, and then shot violently back towards him. Colliding with his forehead and his nose. The phone soared as he fell back. An intense pain pierced his brain and he screamed, hands flying to his head. His shoulder hit a chair, rolled him into a side table which toppled onto the fire grate. Ronnie turned, disorientated, blood streaming from his nose. Lying on his side, he tried to move but his leg and arm wouldn't respond. They wouldn't move. His breathing quickened as he rolled back onto his back. His arm lay limp at his side. A figure moved into the room towards him. Ronnie squinted.

"Help me," said Ronnie, his words slurring in his mouth, at the same time trying to adjust his spectacles with his strong hand.

"Should have kept your nose out," responded the figure peering down at his face. Ronnie's nose was swelling, blood smeared his mouth on lips that lay slack on one side. Ronnie's eyes fluttered as he fought consciousness. The figure blurred before him. A figure whom he recognised. A further pain in his head, Ronnie groaned and lost consciousness.

The person walked to the front door with keys in hand and locked it. They turned and stepped over Ronnie. Saliva drooled from one side of his mouth and his breathing was laboured. The person left the room, entered the kitchen and let themselves out the back door, locking it as they walked down the garden and entered the woodland.

***

"Tanya, where are you?" yelled Jamie, as he walked in the front door, slightly out of breath.

"In the back," Tanya stubbed out her cigarette and walked into the kitchen, followed by Emily. Jamie walked in from the lounge.

"What're you doing here?" asked Jamie.

"We met up at the café. We were having a chat," said Emily.

"And a glass of wine. I was gonna get you to bring in a take-out." Emily could see that Jamie didn't look happy. Tanya leaned in and kissed him on the cheek.

"I could do with getting going anyway. Work busy, Jamie?" asked Emily.

"Work?"

"You got called in. Anything juicy?"

"Oh, that. Nah, something and nothing." He peeled himself away from Tanya who had now draped her arms around him. "Looks like you've been having fun," he said, gently pushing her away. Not wishing to intrude, Emily took her opportunity.

"Right, I'm gonna get off then. Leave you two love birds to it."

"Emily, stay," pleaded Tanya. Jamie looked at Emily, then the door.

"No. No. I'd better get going. You haven't seen Jamie for nearly two days. I'll leave you to it." She walked towards the lounge. "I'll let myself out." Emily left the kitchen and Jamie listened as he heard the lounge and front doors close. He spun on Tanya.

"What you got her round for? What's she been saying?"

"Nothing. I thought she was your mate?"

"Colleague, Tanya, not mate." Tanya's mobile phone rang. She took it from her pocket and looked at the screen.

"Blocked number?" she frowned and answered.

"Tanya Hyatt"

"Hi, Tanya. It's Sarah from the enquiry team."

"Hello," Tanya frowned at Jamie. Jamie silently mouthed to Tanya *Who is it*? Tanya flicked her phone to loudspeaker mode and placed it on the kitchen work surface. "What can I do for you, Sarah?"

"I wanted to clear up a point from our interview yesterday."

"I told you everything that I know." She looked at Jamie, raised her hands to either side and shrugged her shoulders.

"Yeah, I appreciate that. It was only to clear up a discrepancy. You'll know that we also spoke with Jamie."

"He mentioned it."

"Can you clarify for me? On the night that Victoria went missing, you said that you walked home with Mark from the pub and that Jamie turned up thirty minutes later."

"Yeah." Tanya looked at Jamie. The colour had drained from his cheeks.

"It's only that Jamie told us that he had walked you home and that Mark went off for a walk." Tanya's eyes went wide. Jamie started frantically pointing with a finger to the phone and made a T shape with his hands like a basketball coach. He wanted her to stop the call.

"Right, well, I'm not too sure." Jamie started nodding in encouragement. He pointed to the wine bottle and feigned drinking it. "I was drunk. It was a long time ago." Jamie beckoned with his hand to keep going. "I could be wrong. I'm sure Jamie will have remembered it better than me. He is a policeman." Tanya laughed nervously. Jamie gave her a double thumbs up.

"Maybe so," said Sarah. "Simply something we need to clear up. Have a think about it. I'm still going through both of your accounts. I'll probably be in contact again in a couple of days if that's OK?"

"That's fine." Jamie made the time-out signal again. "Anyway Sarah, I need to go. I've got a nail appointment." Tanya winced at her pathetic excuse.

"No problem. Sorry to disturb you. Speak soon." Sarah terminated the call.

"What the fuck?" said Tanya, looking angrily at Jamie.

"You have no idea," reported Jamie. "No bloody idea." His voice rose as his stress breached the surface.

"About what?" she snapped.

"About bloody anything. You've been blabbing to the cops. Blabbing to bloody Emily. What the hell have you told her?"

"Nothing. We spoke about the house, the village, Tenerife. That's it."

"Tenerife. Bloody Tenerife! Why did you tell her about that?" he shouted.

"To show how good you are. How hard you work. To support YOU." Tanya jabbed her forefinger into Jamie's chest. He sank onto a barstool, his anger abated.

"Tanya. It all comes at a price. I can't afford all this," he gestured around the room, "on a shitty copper's wage."

"What about your inheritance?"

"What inheritance? There's never been one." Tanya looked shocked. "We need to talk, Tan. I'm in the shit. I don't know who to turn to."

In a secure room, within Yorkshire Police Headquarters, two members of staff listened intently over their headphones to the conversation being held within the Hyatt's kitchen. Both scribbled notes on their pads as a digital device recorded the event. A staff member turned to Trimble and raised a thumb to him. He gave a satisfied nod in return.

Chapter 14

"Ronnie, you in? It's Joe, the gardener," Joe called out loud. He knocked on the front door again but there was no reply. Joe walked around the back and tried there. Again, no answer. He tried the door which was locked. Ronnie hadn't replied to Joe's texts or calls. His car was out the front, so Joe knew that he must be in the village.

Joe walked around to the front again and peered through the window. He saw a body lying on the floor. "Fuck!" He ran to the front door. Knocked frantically. No reply. He stepped back two paces and booted the door. It shuddered but held fast. Joe ran to his van and retrieved a crowbar. Leaning against the door he wedged the bar where the lock was, leant back, and pulled with all his strength and weight. The door resisted. "Come on." Joe took a breath, braced, and with explosive power, pulled back. The wood groaned. He held firm, pulled with his last strength. The door popped inwards, swung wildly back and smashed into the hall wall. He threw the crowbar down and ran in.

"No, no, no!" Joe recognised the unmistakable body of Ronnie, lying still. He crouched down and looked at his face. His eyes were closed with his mouth drooped at one side, a line of saliva pooling on the carpet beside him. Joe leant in, one hand on Ronnie's chest. Ronnie was breathing. *Recovery position,* thought Joe. He had seen plenty of heroin users in a collapsed state in his former life, and knew that the position could be a lifesaver. Joe reached over, and placed Ronnie's arm on his chest, ready to roll him towards him. He let go and reached for Ronnie's knee. The armed flopped back down to the carpet. *Stroke*, thought Joe. He replaced it, braced it with his body and, reaching for Ronnie's leg, rolled Ronnie onto his side. Ronnie groaned. His eyes fluttered for a second then he was silent.

"It's alright, mate. I've got you. I'm gonna ring for an ambulance. You hold in there." Joe made the call and reported all he could to the call taker. "A first responder is coming, and an ambulance too." Joe looked around the room. "Never saw this coming, mate. The team will be gutted. I'll ring them soon and get someone ahead at the hospital for you. Don't worry I'll sort this spot out." Joe knew that he was rambling but kept on talking to Ronnie.

Five minutes later there was a knock at the door.

"Hello, first responder."

"In here, I think he's had a stroke," shouted Joe. A middle-aged lady walked into the room, carrying a bag.

"Let's have a look. What's his name?"

"Ronnie."

"Ronnie, I'm Fiona. I'm going to take a look at you." Fiona slightly adjusted Ronnie's head, opening his airway further, and then checked his pulse. "Ambulance will be here in a second —" She looked at Joe.

"Joe."

"Thanks, Joe. You've done well. Can you pop out? Make sure that they can find us. I'll look after Ronnie." Joe automatically followed her instruction, left the house, and waited on the road. He could hear a vehicle approach, and on seeing the ambulance, waved his hands frantically. They stopped outside and the passenger climbed out.

"In this house," Joe pointed to the open door.

"Thanks, sir." The passenger entered the house and was followed shortly by his colleague. Joe waited in the front garden, and with shaking hands, rolled a cigarette. He now couldn't see much through the window apart from the medics working around Ronnie. Joe lit a cigarette, got his mobile out and called Matthew.

Thirty minutes later Ronnie was wheeled out of the house on a stretcher. Now with a drip attached to his arm, and wearing an oxygen mask, his eyes remained closed.

"Is he OK?" The first responder took Joe to one side.

"He keeps drifting in and out of consciousness but he's stable at the moment. They're going to get him straight in and assessed by a doctor."

"Is it a stroke?"

"Could be. We'll know more when he's seen. Are you next of kin?"

"No. A friend."

"Right, we'll need next of kin details."

"His boss is going to meet you at the hospital. She'll provide everything that's needed."

"Great. What about locking up here?"

"Leave that with me. I'll sort it."

"Thanks, Joe. For the record, you couldn't have done much more." Joe gave a weak smile. The first responder walked to the back of the ambulance. Joe waited for Jim to arrive.

An hour later, Joe opened the front door, allowing Jim into the house. He had managed to straighten up the room.

"How are you doing?" asked Jim.

"I'm OK. Any update on Ron?"

"He's been assessed. Sending him for a CT scan. Matt's over there with him. What do we need to do here?"

"I've straightened up the room. His phone was over there," Joe pointed to a corner, "must've flown when he fell."

"We'll need that. Anyone been around?"

"No, but I bet the curtains have been twitching."

"I'm sure that they have. Toiletries, clothing? He'll need some in the hospital."

"I'll grab some from his room."

"Good man. I'll take a quick look around here. Check that everything's been switched off. I know you will have but you'll be a bit shaken. I'll double check."

"Cheers." Joe headed upstairs. Jim checked around. He unplugged the TV and grabbed Ronnie's laptop and case.

"Jim," shouted Joe from upstairs. "He's been keeping notes."

"Notes?"

"He's got a book next to his bed. People's names, times and places that he's been to. His thoughts?" *Good man*, thought Jim. *Always the detective, Ronnie.*

"Bring them with his stuff." Joe stepped into the room with a small holdall and a notebook.

"Have done."

"Good. You got the keys?"

"Yes." He threw them to Jim and handed him the bag. "You lock up. I'll go first. Looks like you're a friend of his securing the place. I'm only the gardener. Meet you back at the office."

"Will do." Joe left the house, shortly followed by Jim. They both went to their vehicles and drove out of Evesham.

***

Bob led Jamal into the small reception area of the Complaints and Discipline Department. Kaur had been summoned to a further meeting with Trimble. The area was sparsely furnished, containing one desk and one computer. A further chair was positioned against one wall and a row of small lockers adorned another wall. No one else was present in the room. Bob closed the thick metal door behind them both, which made a whirring sound as the locks set.

"It's like entering Fort Knox," said Kaur, "I take it that you don't get many visitors."

"No. Can you place your mobile phone in a locker please, then place the key on the desk." Kaur did so and, on scanning the room, noted the small CCTV camera in one corner. Bob reached into the desk and produced an RF wand. "A quick sweep," he clarified. Kaur stood still as Bob waved the wand around Kaur's body. The device would detect any other devices transmitting a signal from Kaur. The wand remained silent.

"Do you need me to sign in?" asked Kaur.

"No," said Bob, nodding towards the camera, "the camera will have picked you up and identified you on the facial recognition software."

"Impressive," said Kaur.

"He's waiting for you in there," said Bob, pointing to a further door. Kaur walked to the door, knocked and entered.

Trimble was sitting within the office which was similarly furnished to the reception room, except for a round meeting table with four chairs. Trimble, dressed in a suit and tie, stood up from behind his desk and walked to the meeting table as he addressed Kaur.

"Thanks for coming over," said Trimble to Kaur. "Thought we'd better meet behind closed doors where I know it's safe. You've not visited us here before?"

"I didn't know that this office even existed."

"That's good to know, and we'd like to keep it that way." Trimble looked pointedly at Kaur, who was in no doubt of Trimble's intimation. Trimble took a seat at the table and indicated for Kaur to do so also.

"How's work?"

"Same old, same old. You know how it is. Bouncing from one drama to the next."

"I remember it well. Well, no drama here. I've only called you in for an update and to see where Rachel's enquiry team are. I think we'll be needing some help from you soon."

"OK." Kaur looked confused.

"I want to keep you on board with us. You're my link to Rachel," clarified Trimble. "Where are we at? The call that Rachel's team put in, worked. Hyatt is worried."

"What's he said?"

"Early days, but it clearly rattled him. He hasn't been telling his wife the full truth … no surprise there. We now know he's been to London to see someone and he's not happy with the outcome."

"A criminal?"

"We suspect so. We're doing all the enquiries now. Tanya now knows that Jamie's money, which is funding their lifestyle, is not all coming from his police wages. She also knows that he's made some business deals to earn more money."

"How's she taken it?"

"She seems surprised. We think that she is probably unaware of what he gets up to."

"Has he admitted any criminality?"

"Not yet, but if we keep the pressure on, it will only be a matter of time."

"It's been a good starter for ten then."

"Definitely."

"Any mention of Victoria Fanshaw?"

"Again, not yet. He managed to gloss over that night and get some sympathy from Tanya for his money troubles. He's told her to be careful whom she speaks with. To run everything past him first."

"Will she do that?"

"Let's see. We have our asset out there so we're hoping that Tanya makes contact. However, if Hyatt is up to what we think he is then we'll be pushing to get him in soon. Rachel needs to speed up her side of things. How's she doing?"

"I'm going to a debrief this week. They've hit an issue. Nothing you need to worry about. She tells me that she's developed some strong lines of enquiry."

"Good. Can you encourage her to get a move on?"

"I'll try. Do you have a time frame?"

"Within the next couple of weeks."

"I'll let her know."

"Anything else that you wish to ask me?"

"I think I'd prefer not to know. It means I can maintain my objectivity. You have things in hand here and Rachel seems to have a full grip on her side."

"Simply encourage a degree of acceleration, if you can. Can we speak after your debrief?"

"Yes, I'll text you when it's done."

***

Joe walked along a busy hospital corridor, looking for a direction board. Grey linoleum floors and green pastel walls surrounded him, and the aroma of cleaning solutions assaulted his nostrils. Staff walked by in theatre scrubs, coloured uniforms and white coats. Lines painted on the floors guided patients and families to relevant locations and the hum of muted conversations drifted in the air. Joe didn't like hospitals. The remembrance of a former life, either attending as a patient or stealing, did not sit comfortably with him. He'd deduced that no one wanted to be in a hospital. Neither the staff nor the patients. Sure the staff did a terrific job but they primarily dealt with the traumatic side of the human condition. Hospitals rarely evoked a feeling of joy and when they did it was usually counterbalanced by a sufferance of great pain or anguish.

Joe stopped at a board and read down the list looking for the stroke unit. An arrow pointed him in the direction of the East Wing, which was denoted by the colour dark green. He looked at the floor where a green line directed him on his route. Rachel had been in contact and advised him that Ronnie had been moved to a ward. She'd received a call half an hour ago telling her that Ronnie was awake. His scan had shown that he had suffered a small cerebral bleed and that he would therefore be likely to stay in hospital for some time. Joe headed to the stroke unit with his head down in an attempt to blank out the people around him.

The unit turned out to be in the older part of the hospital. An old nightingale ward with beds down either side, Ronnie had been lucky enough to be allocated a private single room. Joe looked through the window at his friend lying on the bed. Ronnie's eyes were closed and he looked settled. An oxygen mask covered his mouth.

"Visiting?" said a Scottish voice behind him. Joe turned to see a smiling young lady wearing a striped uniform.

"I'm his friend."

"You'll be fine to go in. He's only resting. I'll be doing his obs in a second anyway." She opened the door for Joe to enter. Ronnie had a tube leading to his left arm which was attached to a bag of clear fluid, a pulse oximeter attached to his finger, and a urinary catheter bag hung at the bedside. "He isn't drinking at the moment so the fluid's going to keep him hydrated." The nurse gently touched Ronnie's free hand. "Ronnie, you have a visitor." Ronnie's eyes fluttered and then opened. He squinted at Joe.

"He'll need his glasses. He's blind as a bat without them," said Joe. The nurse reached to the side table, lowered the oxygen mask and placed Ronnie's spectacles on.

"There you go." She turned to Ronnie. "I'll leave you for five minutes. He's struggling to talk but can understand you," she explained, "speak to him normally. He tires quickly and may appear frustrated but it's all part of his illness."

"Will he improve?" The nurse looked towards Ronnie.

"Yes. You will, Ronnie. Won't you?" Ronnie attempted to smile though one side of his face remained slack and unmoving. "Right, I'll be back soon. There's a chair for you there." The nurse moved a chair from the wall to the bedside. "Please don't sit on the bed. I'll be back in five." The nurse left the room and Joe used the offered seat. Ronnie watched him.

"She's nice," said Joe. Ronnie responded with a slight nod. "Bet it's killing you not being able to speak." Joe's attempt at humour brought Ronnie's half smile. "I should take advantage. I can talk without you butting in for once." Ronnie coughed in his throat. Joe leaned forward, concerned. "You OK? Do you need the nurse?" Ronnie's fingers on his strong hand lifted from the bedclothes, halting Joe's panic. "You're OK?" Ronnie nodded.

"Good. I won't stay too long, mate. We need you better as quickly as you can. The team's not the same. We're all worried." Ronnie simply looked at Joe. "I locked your house up." Ronnie's hand started quickly tapping on the covers. Joe didn't notice. "Found your phone in the living room and your notebook upstairs." Ronnie grunted and slapped his hand on the covers. "What is it?" Joe looked at Ronnie who now stared at him intently. "Your phone?" Ronnie nodded. "Jim's got it with your book." Ronnie nodded. "I've got your keys." Joe held up the keys.

Ronnie's eyes widened. Joe frowned in confusion. Ronnie's hand slapped the covers again. He then struggled to raise two fingers. "Two keys?" Joe held up the two keys. Ronnie shook his head, closed his eyes and frowned. He opened them again, stared at Joe, and raised two fingers. "Not two keys," his frown eased. "Two sets of keys?" Ronnie's fingers dropped. He nodded. "There's a second set of keys. Have you got them?" Ronnie shook his head. "Someone else?" Ronnie nodded twice. His head went back. He was getting tired. "Has someone been in your house?" asked Joe in shock. Ronnie's eyes opened, he grunted and nodded.

"Right, time for your obs, Ronnie." said the Scottish nurse, as she entered the room. "Then we'll get you washed when your visitor's gone." Joe stood up.

"I need to go," he said. "I need to speak with Rachel." Another small nod from Ronnie. "I can come back later. Look after him," said Joe to the nurse. He quickly left the room and headed out of the hospital.

***

She'd thought about it, run it through her mind and had come up with no other plausible option. She had nowhere left to turn and so had made the call. Jamie had headed out last night and Tanya had now jumped off the local bus in the middle of Sterndale.

Tanya was worried, her nerves on edge, and still didn't know whether she was doing the right thing. Mark was too close to her, he would be too judgemental. Anyway, he had enough worries, being married to a wife whom he didn't love. Mark thought Tanya didn't know, but she did. She knew him too well. However, Jamie was a different matter. She now knew that he'd been hiding things from her for years. Tanya felt embarrassed. She'd been blind. Could she trust him? Should she? Tanya had searched their bedroom this morning and then had decided to take a chance. She walked into the coffee shop. Emily stood up and waved to her from a table at the back.

Tanya had called Emily two hours ago, asking her if there was any chance at all of meeting up in Sterndale this morning. Emily had agreed to meet at eleven, which she knew would give her time for travel and to check in with Trimble. As she had expected, Trimble wished her to wear an audio device which would record the conversation. Emily always had the kit ready and fitted the wires and recorder to herself before leaving home. She smiled at Tanya and whispered that Tanya had entered the café. Emily beckoned her over.

"I got you a latte. I hope that's right?" Tanya looked nervous.

"Yeah, that's fine. You haven't put a shot of brandy in it, have you?" Emily laughed.

"It's not that bad, is it?"

"Couldn't get much worse." Tanya removed her coat, draped it over a chair and seated herself. She took a sip of coffee.

"Well, I'm all ears." Emily waited.

"I didn't know who else to turn to. We hardly know each other."

"You know you can trust me though, don't you?"

"Can I though?"

"Sometimes you need to leap, Tanya. You wouldn't be here otherwise." Tanya gave Emily an intense stare. Took another sip of coffee and then placed her cup down.

"It's about Jamie." Emily remained silent. "He's been lying to me." Tanya slumped in her chair. Tears formed in her eyes. Emily reached across the table and rested her hand on Tanya's.

"He wouldn't be the first bloke to lie to his partner. Is it that bad?"

"I don't know." Tanya looked distraught. "We argued last night. He's been doing extra jobs, getting extra money in. He's been doing it for years. He's blaming me for spending it all. He's not happy about the Tenerife apartment. He's not even happy with me talking to you. One of his colleagues." Tanya was now crying.

"Other jobs? What other jobs?"

"I dunno. I thought he was always at work with your mob."

"Where'd he go last night?"

"No idea. I kept drinking when he'd gone and then passed out. He's not answering his phone this morning."

"He's maybe simply cooling down. You know that he can look after himself." Tanya wasn't listening.

"I searched our room this morning." She reached into her coat pocket and pulled out a blank envelope. "This was hidden in a drawer with a bag of coke next to it." Emily read the anonymous note not fully believing what it said. She folded it, put it back in the envelope and placed it on the table.

"What the fuck." said Emily. She whispered, "We know she was murdered?"

"I know," said Tanya, retrieving the envelope and putting it back in her coat.

"You need to tell the police."

"He is the police. You're the bloody police. I'm telling you."

"They'll want that note."

"I'll have to put it back. Or he'll know."

"What about the coke?"

"Bloody hell, it's only a bit of coke." Tanya's mobile rang. Both ladies jumped in shock. Tanya looked at the screen. "It's Jamie." She answered it without hesitation.

"I'm in town." She listened to Jamie talking on the other end of the phone.

"Yes, I'll be there." She listened again.

"I love you, too." Tears dripped down Tanya's face. The call ended.

"He's coming to get me." Tanya was smiling as she stood up and put her coat on. "Don't say anything. I'll work it out and let you know." Tanya leaned forward and gave Emily a quick cuddle before walking out of the cafe.

***

Joe walked into the office where everyone had gathered at Rachel's request.

"How's he looking?" asked Sarah.

"Older, and tired. Hooked up to a drip and he can't speak yet. Only groans and grunts."

"It must have been hard to see."

"Not as hard as him having to suffer it all."

"Early days yet," said Rachel, "Ron's a tough cookie. He'll pull through."

"What if he doesn't get his full movement back? Get back to his old self?" asked Sarah.

"Then we'll have to pull together as a team and do what we can for him."

"It's shit," said Joe.

"That it is," agreed Rachel, "However, we now have a job to do. We need to focus and get on with it. Ron's out of play for the moment, but he's left us with some work to do. I feel that we are getting somewhere. Let's keep pushing. Tom, where did you get with Mark Holt?" Rachel felt bad pushing the team but they needed to focus.

"I went down to his office and met with him there. He seems like a nice bloke. Careful with his words, as you'd expect from a solicitor. Practicing in family law, married with kids."

"What are his feelings about Victoria?"

"He was open with them. He used to fancy her. Not that she knew. He was never brave enough to broach the subject with her. Says her disappearance left him shocked and confused."

"And on the night?"

"He remembers the beginning of the night clearly. Talked about who was there. Everyone was drunk. Recalls that there was a fight between Pape and Fothergill."

"What about Tanya and Victoria?"

"That's where he chose his words carefully. He's not clear what happened there."

"What about after? Any clarification about Tanya and Jamie?"

"He says he can't remember the order of who did what. Claims he was too drunk. To be fair, it's in line with his initial statement."

"Is he protecting Tanya?"

"Could be. Maybe Jamie too, now. He is his brother-in-law. That's about it. Nothing to take us forward."

"OK, thanks for that. I'm waiting for an update from Kaur following our phone call to the Hyatts. We should all know where we are with Pape." Rachel ticked off her points on her fingers. "He presents as an alcoholic. He has received the note. He possesses a golden pendant."

"It's all compelling intelligence," said Sarah.

"Yes, but not evidence."

"We need that necklace," said Matt. "There may be a forensic opportunity there. If it's Victoria's?" Rachel smiled at him. *You're learning*, she thought.

"True, but it's important to keep our minds open. Let's not force ourselves down the Pape route and be blind to anyone else. Remember our first priorities. Rule potential people out and that will leave us with our offender."

"But no one has been ruled out?" said Matt.

"I know but if we keep pushing then I'm confident that we'll get there."

"We need to get to the bottom of the notes," said Joe, "someone knows or suspects something. The notes have been received by some of the people whose names are up on that board."

"Not Mark," said Tom.

"Or Jamie and Tanya," said Sarah.

"Charles Fothergill has."

"There's got to be something in them though," said Joe, with a look of frustration on his face.

"Could they be sent by Jonathan? What about Sir David?" asked Matt. The team looked at him in shock for suggesting such a thing. Matt raised a hand. "Bear with me. Both know all the suspects and where they live. Both have lost Victoria, and both are trying to find her killer. Sir David wants closure. Jonathan wants to move on with the estate, settle his father down and take over properly. I'm not saying that I'm right. Purely floating it as possible. They may have sent the notes to stimulate action."

"It may seem unlikely," said Rachel, "but it could still be feasible." The team wasn't convinced. "Thanks, Matt. Note it down please, Jim."

"Already done," replied Jim.

"Where are we with Ronnie's phone and notebook?" asked Rachel.

"I've interrogated both," replied Jim. "He's been working hard, our Ronnie."

"I knew that he would be," said Rachel, smiling.

"As we know he seems to have infiltrated well. He's pally with the shopkeeper, sings in the church choir, and gets to the pub."

"No surprise there," interrupted Joe. The team smiled.

"True," continued Jim. "He seems to have a walking partner called Margaret. He's mentioned her a few times and was getting close to her."

"Do we know her?"

"I've identified her. She lives in the top village near him. We may need to let her know what's happened. She'll be worried."

"I'll sort that," said Rachel.

"In his notes, he mentions red chrysanthemums."

"Is he acting the part of a florist now?" joked Sarah.

"No, he's not comfortable with them. He randomly came across a bunch of them whilst out walking with Margaret. They look to have been deliberately planted on the lane that leads from the pub to Evesham House. Victoria's last suspected route. He photographed them on his phone. Jim turned his computer screen and showed the team the image. He mentions a person with a dog walking on the route. He can't, however, say if that person is of interest."

"He's found a bunch of flowers," said Matt, "So what?"

"He's found the same species of flower in the same colour in the village graveyard." Jim again flipped an image around of the chrysanthemums and the headstone.

"Whose grave?", asked Tom.

"A Reginald Chiswick. He died three weeks before Victoria went missing. A local chap who had lived in the village for years. Ronnie thinks the two are tied."

"Was the lane searched at the time?" asked Tom.

"Yes," replied Jim. "Fingertip search. Nothing found. It's a well-walked area and was back then. Determining anything would have been hard."

"Not a body deposition site then," said Tom.

"No, they wouldn't have missed that," said Jim. "Ronnie can't explain his thoughts at the moment but he clearly has some around this."

"Which brings me to Ronnie's house," said Rachel. "As I let you all know, he believes that someone has been in his house. We don't know who and we don't know why. We can't ask him, or more accurately he can't tell us."

"Someone with a set of keys?"

"Ronnie thinks so. They must have let themselves in," said Joe. "The doors were all locked when I got there. Ronnie had his keys on him."

"Locked himself in?" asked Rachel.

"He was adamant that someone had been there," said Joe. Rachel's mobile phone rang. She walked to her desk and looked at the screen.

"It's Kaur. Take five minutes everyone." She took a seat behind her desk. The team broke up to stretch legs, have a smoke or use the loo. Rachel answered her phone.

"Jamal, what can I do for you?"

Five minutes later Rachel walked back into the room.

"Right everyone, I've been advised that there has been a development." The team turned to look at her. "I've been called to a meeting with Kaur. He hasn't given me any details yet but has said that it will increase the pace of our enquiry. We have two weeks maximum to take some action."

"What?" exclaimed Tom. "Who are they to tell us what to do?"

"He's not telling me what to do. He's advising me that they want to push forward with their side of the enquiry and that we may wish to also."

"But —" said Sarah.

"Typical," interjected Jim. Rachel raised her voice.

"Calm down, everyone. We don't know what they have yet. This could work in our favour. I'll go and meet with him and update you when I know more." Everyone quietened. "Matt," He looked up. "You're with me." He nodded. "Everyone else, start brainstorming. Who is sending the messages? How do we get into Danny's? We need that box and its contents. Someone check in on Ron. Let's collate where we are. The actions we need to complete on each individual. We gather back here after my meeting." Rachel grabbed her bag from her desk. "Malmaison in Fenchurch, Matt. Let's get going." She walked towards the exit. Matt grabbed his coat and followed.

***

Rachel and Matt entered the lift which would take them from the underground car park into the hotel lobby. The doors closed. Rachel received a text. The lift ascended.

"Meeting room five. We can go straight there," said Rachel, relaying the text message. The lift stopped and the door opened. They faced the reception desk, where some visitors were checking in, and turned right down a small corridor, towards the meeting room. The doors on the corridor were numbered. Matt and Rachel stopped outside the door to meeting room five and knocked. Kaur opened the door.

"Rachel, Matt, thanks for coming." He stepped back, allowing them in, and closed the door behind them. "Can I introduce you to John Trimble. I don't believe that you have met." Trimble stood up and walked around the meeting table with his right arm extended. He shook Matt and then Rachel's hands.

"We meet at last, detective. Good to put a face to a name."

"John," replied Rachel in acknowledgement, "likewise, and this is Matt, one of my team." Trimble nodded his head to Matt. "Please take a seat. Coffee is on its way."

"And this is?" asked Rachel, looking at a young lady who was sitting at the meeting table. Trimble smiled, a smile that did not reach his eyes.

"One of mine. Emily, she's in the job." Emily gave Rachel a nervous smile. Rachel smiled back. Matt reached over the table with an extended hand.

"Nice to meet you, Emily." They shook hands. There was a knock at the door, which Kaur opened, and a coffee trolley was trundled in.

"Thank you," said Kaur to the waiter, who promptly left the room.

"Splendid," said Trimble. "Shall we?" Everyone helped themself to coffee and then took seats around the table. Trimble and Emily on one side, Matt and Rachel on the other, with Kaur positioned as umpire at the head. Kaur was about to speak when Trimble stepped in.

"Let's get started. Rachel, I called this meeting as we have had some significant progress in our enquiry, with no small thanks to your team, and to the efforts of Emily." Rachel realised that Trimble clearly saw this as a meeting between him and her, with the other attendees as mere onlookers. Matt thought differently.

"And where do you sit within the investigation, Emily?" asked Matt. *Good on you, Matt*, thought Rachel. Emily looked towards Trimble, who nodded his approval for her to reply. He received a disparaging smile in return. Emily addressed Matt.

"I'm a serving police officer and have been working undercover as an informant." Emily looked embarrassed. Rachel nodded, unsurprised by the admission. Matt smiled reassuringly.

"And I'm a fledgling investigator who is still learning the ropes. Looks like we are both treading in deep water on this one." Emily smiled in return, grateful for his calming presence. Trimble interjected.

"We're all working for the same happy family. Terrific! For clarity, Emily has been working undercover for me. DI Kaur," he looked at Kaur and raised an eyebrow, "has informed me that you are both fully aware that Jamie Hyatt is of interest to my department. The device that you deployed on our behalf has proved invaluable."

"I'm glad that it's helped. Why are we here?" asked Rachel.

"We need to start moving on this one," said Trimble. "Emily has attended a meeting with Tanya Hyatt, the result of which indicates that we need to search the Hyatt's house."

"Covert or overt entry?" asked Rachel.

"Overt would be preferable."

"What are you looking for?"

"Class A drugs. Not large amounts, but enough to bring Hyatt in. We suspect him of so much more. The drugs are our way into him." Rachel grimaced.

"Doesn't help my enquiry."

"Oh, but it will."

"How?" Trimble nodded at Emily who leaned forward in her chair.

"I met with Tanya in a coffee shop in town. She was upset and angry and didn't know where else to turn." Rachel remained silent. Emily continued. "She turned to me cos she knew I was a cop. She showed me a note that she had found hidden next to the coke. It said …"

"We know she was murdered," interrupted Matt. Emily looked shocked.

"It's now the fourth one that we are aware of," said Rachel. "Where's the note now?"

"Tanya kept it. I think she'll put it back where she found it."

"You see," said Trimble, smugly, "we need to get into that house." Rachel leaned back thoughtfully, then spoke.

"Firstly, nice one Emily. If you ever need a job, give me a call." Emily smiled. Matt noted her shoulders relax as if a weight had been lifted. "Secondly, I agree, John. You've been good enough to share your intelligence and Emily's identity. Let me bring you up to speed with my investigation."

"Shall we let the others go?" asked Trimble. Rachel looked him in the eye.

"No, that's not the way we work. You and I need to formulate a plan and, in my experience, we need the experience and resources of everyone around this table to do so." Trimble leaned back, eyebrows raised, forehead wrinkled. Emily looked on at Rachel with admiration. Matt smiled.

"Right, where do we start?" asked Kaur, breaking the thin film of ice that had developed.

Chapter 15

Evesham House towered resplendently, protecting its hallowed grounds, as darkness descended upon the estate. The long drive, illuminated on both verges, guided cars towards the front entrance where Fletcher awaited the guests' arrivals. A thin mist floated across the damp grass, repelled only by the sepia penumbra, cast by the light emanating from both the drive and house. Fletcher stood in the chill air, in full butler suit, inviting the attendees into the house where they would be served canapes and drinks.

Rachel's team had worked tirelessly during the past week, liaising with both Sir David and Yorkshire Police, as well as pulling together all the strands of intelligence gathered to date, so that they could maximise tonight's opportunities. The plan had been formulated, developed, and expounded and tonight it would be executed. The team's only regret was that Ronnie couldn't be present. He was improving and had moments of lucidity, but was struggling with movement, comprehension and vocalisation.

However, Sir David's generosity and the grand house had risen to the occasion. When approached by Rachel and asked to host a black tie dinner for the villagers of Evesham, he had not hesitated. Such events had been held in the past, organised by his wife, but had fallen by the wayside, as Sir David felt that his life had. Fletcher had proved an ally and had produced all the invites, as per Rachel's specification, and with the assistance of Rachel's team, had ensured that they had all been delivered to the invitees. Rachel had reassured Sir David that tonight would strategically forward her investigation and that she would guarantee that it would be compelling. With whisky glass in hand, standing in the unlit first-floor library room, Sir David watched the guests arrive. He raised his glass and said, "Good luck, Rachel," before taking a sip.

***

Matthew zipped up Rachel's dress and secured the fastener at the neck, then rested his hands on her shoulders. They both looked in the mirror at their reflections.

"How are you feeling?" he asked.

"Nervous. We have a lot riding on tonight."

"We do, but the plan is in place. Trust your instincts. You look ravishing by the way." Rachel wore a simple black dress, complimented by a diamond necklace and flat black shoes. Unfortunately, she couldn't afford the luxury of heels. More accurately, her body wouldn't cope with the stress that they would enforce on her legs. Matt picked up his jacket, which had been draped over the back of a chair, and slipped it on. Rachel turned and adjusted his black bowtie.

"Thank you. You are not looking too bad yourself." They both smiled.

"Shall we." He extended a wing and Rachel linked her arm in. She had decided to forgo her walking stick for the evening and had placed it in the lounge, should she require it later in the night. They walked to the bedroom door. Rachel took a deep breath. Matt opened the door. Rachel breathed out and shook her hair. She was ready. They stepped onto the top landing and heard the gentle notes of a piano being played downstairs.

***

Sarah had travelled over to police headquarters and was now sitting within the securest office in the building, the confidential unit. An office hidden within an office which could only be entered by staff with high-level security clearance. The chief constable had authorised her attendance to assist with tonight's operation. Sarah was to be the link between the police and Rachel's team. Alongside her was Gordon, a serving police officer, fulfilling his role as a link to the teams on the ground. Both were sitting sipping coffee as they looked at digital feeds on the screens before them.

"That's Rachel and Matt going downstairs to the party," she said to Gordon.

"Good stuff. My lot haven't entered the village yet, though Jamal is only five minutes away."

"What about the units in Fenchurch?"

"They are ready with their warrants. We'll contact the keyholders if we need to."

"Where's Trimble?"

"Said he would be in his office. I'm sure he'll make an appearance with us at some point."

"We sit and wait then."

"Yep. This job's either all paperwork or sitting patiently. They get all the fun out there." Gordon pointed at the screen. Sarah couldn't disagree, although she knew that 'out there' was sometimes a dangerous place to be.

***

"That's Joe deploying," transmitted Joe over his covert radio set.

"Loud and clear," replied Sarah.

Joe climbed out of the driver's side of his white box van, which he had parked in the visitor car park near the café at Evesham House. He walked around the vehicle and opened the passenger door of his car, extending his hand to assist his passenger. A lady's hand and arm extended, taking hold of it, as Joe helped Emily Dutton out of the car. Emily wore a classy black dress which complimented her slim figure. In full make-up and with coiffured hair, she looked amazing. Joe closed the door behind her.

"It's bloody chilly," said Emily, crossing her arms over her bust and lifting her shoulders.

"Here." Joe slipped his suit jacket off and placed it over her shoulders.

"You're a gent."

"I know." He smiled cheekily. "We go this way." He directed Emily along a path which took them to the front of the house, then climbed the steps to the front door, which Fletcher opened for them.

"I hope we're not late," said Joe.

"Not at all, sir. Most have arrived but I'm sure there will be some more stragglers." Joe didn't know whether to take the comment as comforting or as a telling-off. Emily entered the house, followed by Joe. The air was warm and she handed him back his suit jacket. He placed it on, checked himself in the large hall mirror and followed Emily into the ballroom.

"Keep close," she said.

"I won't leave your side." A waiter approached them, carrying a tray of champagne-filled glasses.

"Can I offer you champagne, madam, sir?" Emily selected a glass.

"Thank you." Joe followed suit.

"Thank you."

"Enjoy your evening, sir." Jim lowered the tray and winked at Joe, then walked away to serve other guests.

"You seen Rachel or Matt yet?" asked Emily.

"Over there by the bay windows. That's Jonathan Fanshaw that they're speaking to."

"Who is the bloke hovering on his right shoulder?" Joe repositioned himself to get a better view.

"I'd say that is Charles Fothergill." Emily nodded, locking his face in her memory. "Shall we move over there?" Joe pointed to an area of the room behind one of the sofas. It looked relatively quiet but would provide them with a good view of the room. They moved over and stood chatting to one another. Joe nudged Emily.

"That's Sir David entering now." Emily turned to see a dapper grey-haired gentleman enter the room. He looked cheerful and comfortable and greeted guests as he weaved through the crowd.

"How'd you get an invite?" Emily heard a raucous voice from behind her. She turned to be confronted by Tanya's bright red hair and lipstick. Standing next to her was Jamie, with a big grin on his face, and Mark, her brother. Obviously, all had been enjoying the free alcohol.

"She came with me," said Joe. Jamie looked at him sceptically. "I've done some work for Sir David, on the estate. The invite said to bring a guest. I brought my friend Emily."

"Small world," said Jamie.

"Well, I'm chuffed to bits," said Tanya, cuddling Emily. "This party is just getting started." *If only you knew*, thought Emily. Joe looked across the room and watched Danny walk in. Despite his height and broad frame, he walked with his head dipped and shoulders hunched. Joe tapped Emily's arm and leaned in.

"Back in a minute. Danny's arrived." He walked away, with Jamie's eyes following him. Jim walked across to the bar and placed a tray of empty champagne flutes down.

"Bet this lot are keeping you busy," said a gruff-voiced male who was sitting by the bar. Alongside him were two other men. The gruff-voiced male and one of the other men were dressed smartly, but not in suits. The third male was older and appeared to be dressed in a vintage black suit and flared bowtie. He held a glass of whisky whilst the two others nursed a pint each.

"Yes, sir," replied Jim, reaching for a full tray.

"Can't stand the stuff meself," said Richard Westbrook.

"I'm with you on that," slurred Patrick Carmichael.

"That's because you are a couple of heathens," Alfred chipped in. Jim smiled graciously, lifted the tray, and walked back out into the room towards the hallway, where guests were also congregating.

"Thank you, I'll have one," snapped a small sour-faced woman behind him. He turned and lowered the tray for Audrey Melthrop to select a glass. "Honestly, that pianist is atrocious," she said to the man on her left. Jim immediately recognised him as Roger Melthrop who, though still wearing black and white, had chosen to attend in his dog collar. Jim smiled in sympathy as Melthrop too selected a glass.

"They should have asked you, dear," said Melthrop.

"They couldn't afford me." Jim left them to their conversation and, as he walked away, pressed a button on his covert transmitter.

"The Melthrops are here."

"Received," replied Sarah.

***

"That's them all," Sarah said to Gordon.

"Jamal has entered the house too," said Gordon. "He's going to head to the library."

"Team ready in the village?"

"Yep, everything's in place." Sarah dialled her phone and waited for it to be answered.

"Sarah," said Tom.

"You in place?"

"Yes. Has Danny arrived?"

"Yes. You are good to go. Let me know when it's done."

"Will do." Sarah looked at Gordon.

"Here goes nothing. You good?"

"Let's roll the dice."

"Sarah to Rach."

"Go ahead."

"You are good to go."
"Received."

***

At Evesham House, Rachel took David to one side. He lowered his head to hear her speak and nodded his understanding. Fletcher watched as this happened and awaited his instruction. Sir David moved away from Rachel and towards the large fireplace. He looked over to Fletcher and nodded. Fletcher approached the pianist, who stopped playing. Fletcher then moved to a large brass gong and struck it with its padded mallet. The note sounded loud and clear, and in shock, the guests silenced. Waiters ushered guests from the hallway into the main room. Sir David stood tall and in his deep resonant voice started,

"Ladies and gentlemen. Thank you so much for attending this evening. It seems a long time since the house has been filled with such liveliness and merriment. I hope that you are enjoying yourselves." There were general calls of agreement from the crowd and laughter from Jamie's side of the room. Sir David looked over patiently and smiled. "Soon, we will be moving through to the dining room where the staff have laid out a wonderful buffet for you all. Please help yourselves. To the food, not the silverware" There was a gentle laugh throughout the room. "Tonight we celebrate Evesham and the wonderful villagers who make it what it is." This generated a round of applause and cheers from the room.

Sir David raised his hands and gestured for the room to quieten, which it did.

"Lastly, for some of you, an extra special surprise. A surprise from which we will all benefit, I hope." Fletcher moved from the doorway, holding some cards in his hands. "Fletcher will now move amongst you all and issue some of you with a further invitation. An invitation to meet with me in the library. If you could kindly gather there before attending the buffet, that would be greatly appreciated. That's it for now. Enjoy your evening."

People in the room started talking quietly, wondering what was happening. Who would be invited? An air of excitement could be felt. Fletcher smiled as he approached Tanya, handing her, Jamie, and Mark a small business card each. The butler then walked away and people parted as he moved through guests who were excited by the intrigue.

"What's going on? How curious! Wonderful, a new party game?" whispered as he passed.

Emily, Joe and Danny were next, followed by Jonathan and Charles. Fletcher then approached the Melthrops. Audrey took her card tentatively and Roger with a smile. He read the invite,

PLEASE ATTEND THE LIBRARY UPSTAIRS

and turned the blank card over, which displayed the image of a single red chrysanthemum.

"A flower, how sweet." Roger showed it to Audrey, "Look Audrey, what flower is that?" Audrey looked at her identical card.

"A chrysanthemum." Audrey looked nervous. She leant into her husband. "What is this all about?"

"Simply a bit of fun, I think. It's thrilling, don't you think?"

"Don't be a fool and stop acting like a child," she sniped. Audrey looked suspiciously around the room at the guests peering at her. Fletcher moved on, handing Rachel and Matt a card, and gave his final card to Sir David. He then moved to the lounge doors and announced that the buffet was open. The guests started moving to the hall with animated chatter buzzing through the air.

***

"Tom to Sarah." Sarah's handset came to life as Tom transmitted. "Items secured and images sent."

"Received, Tom."

Sarah checked the email on her secure laptop and, sure enough, images of the box, news clipping, note and necklace flashed up on a message. The items had been securely removed from Danny's house. She texted Rachel, advising her of Tom's success.

"I'm going to head on over to Evesham now," said Tom.

"Loud and clear. Jim has advised that they're heading to the library now."

"Received."

"So far, so good," said Sarah.

"I'm going to ring the keyholder for the bank," said Gordon.

"Move the search team into the village?" asked Sarah.

"Yeah, I'll send them now. Once we know everyone's in the library, then we'll move them forward."

***

"Come on in, everybody," said Sir David. "I've taken the liberty of providing drinks." Sir David indicated to a table which held flutes of champagne and tumblers of orange juice. "Help yourselves and please take a seat. We'll explain everything."

The library was a long domed room which extended across one wing of the first floor. Wooden bookcases lined each wall, some glass fronted and some open to the air. The room smelled of age, of history, and the aged books positioned on the shelves reflected this. Chairs had been gathered towards one end of the room and the guests filtered in, taking positions.

Fletcher ushered from behind and when everyone was in, gently closed the doors from within. He took his position at the doors and Kaur moved to stand beside him. Unbeknown to the library guests, Jim now took his position outside in the hallway, with two plainclothes officers beside him.

Jamie collected a drink for Tanya and himself, noting that the doors had been shut and were now guarded by Fletcher and another man. *Where do I know you from?* thought Jamie. He scanned the rest of the room, as a copper would, and identified no other exits apart from the windows, which only gave a view of darkness at this time, and the estate grounds during daylight. He nodded to Kaur who gave no indication back. Jamie smiled and took a seat next to Tanya.

"Now that we are all here, I'll hand you over to Rachel," said Sir David, who took a seat to one side. Rachel moved to address the group. Matt texted Sarah '*Move now.*'

"Good evening, everyone." Rachel's voice sounded clear and strong. "I know you will all be wondering why you are gathered here and I am hoping that I can explain that."

"It's all a bit dramatic isn't it, Rachel?" said Jamie, raising his glass to her. "What game are we playing here?"

"No game, Jamie." Rachel addressed the rest of the guests. "We've met before," said Rachel, in explanation.

“She’s a copper,” interrupted Jamie.

“Ex, actually. Now if you don’t mind…” Rachel looked pointedly at Jamie, “then I’ll continue.”

“Please do.” Jamie winked at Rachel. Kaur reached into his pocket for his phone. He had received a text which he read.

“To make you all aware, I used to be a police detective but now, through circumstance, run my own private investigation unit,” continued Rachel, as she noted Kaur giving her a nod. “My team specialise in many areas of investigation, one of which is cold case reviews.” The guests muttered, and realisation dawned on some faces. Rachel continued. “To cut it short we have been employed by Sir David to review the circumstances of the murder of his daughter Victoria. An investigation that we have been conducting over the past few weeks.” Guest reactions were varied; shock, surprise, annoyance. Jamie laughed out loud.

“You think one of us did it, don’t ya?” Rachel looked at Jamie.

“PC Hyatt, either shut up or I will have you removed. You are off duty and drunk, by the looks and sounds of it. Attempt to have some professional courtesy if you can.” Jamie’s visage changed, shocked and angered by Rachel’s response.

“Leave it be,” said Tanya, placing a hand on his arm. He angrily pulled his arm away and eyeballed Rachel, who held his gaze. Jamie looked away first but said nothing. Rachel continued.

“To clarify PC Hyatt’s point, everyone here either knew Victoria or had had some involvement with her. Some of you were present on the night of her disappearance. You lived with her, befriended her, cared for her. You know something.” She looked around. Silence dominated.

“Sir David started all this by providing me with this anonymous letter. Rachel held up the note. Her audience was captivated.

WE KNOW SHE WAS MURDERED

“Do you recognise this? I know that some of you do. Sir David has received this message on several occasions since Victoria’s death. Others in this room have received the same message.” Tanya gasped. The Melthrops looked around in astonishment. Danny drained his glass. “Those who have, rest assured that the notes are currently being seized by Yorkshire Police. Warrants are being executed at homes and workplaces as I speak." Charles Fothergill's face paled. Jonathan looked at him with concern. Danny grabbed his armchair, knuckles whitening. Joe passed him his full glass of champagne, which Danny took without thanks.

"You can't fuckin' do that." Hyatt erupted from his chair, knocking Tanya to one side. Kaur moved forward swiftly. Fletcher opened the doors. The detectives rushed in. Kaur grabbed Hyatt's wrist from behind, pulled his arm back, braced his forearm on Hyatt's tricep and turned him round and down to the floor. Hyatt's body hit the carpet, air dispelling from his lungs with a grunt. The Melthrops screamed.

"Jamie Hyatt you are under arrest for possession of a Class A drug," shouted Kaur. The detectives moved in to assist in restraining Hyatt. Kaur continued the caution.

"Jamie. Jamie," screamed Tanya. Emily moved to her, helping her up. Tanya had tears streaming down her face, with rivulets of mascara smudging her cheeks. "What do I do?"

"Keep quiet," he responded as cuffs were placed on him. "Don't say a word."

"Let them take him," said Emily. The detectives raised Hyatt onto his feet.

"Stick with Emily," shouted Jamie, as he was led from the room. "I love you" echoed in from the corridor as the doors were again closed.

"DI Kaur, Yorkshire Police," said Kaur in explanation to the guests who were transfixed in a state of shock. Tanya was now sobbing.

"Can I take her out?" asked Emily. Kaur looked at Rachel who nodded.

"Yes, there's a small room next door." Emily encouraged Tanya out of her seat and Fletcher allowed them out, closing the door behind them.

"Please continue, Rachel," said Kaur. Rachel held up the note.

"I'm not going to ask you who has received these notes, you already know who you are. But, who sent them? Someone in the know? The killer in a sick taunt at Sir David? A witness? We only identified the sender recently." Jonathan leaned forwards in his chair. Sir David raised an eyebrow and held his breath. Rachel turned to face the doors.

"It was you, Fletcher." He stood silently looking at the group. "Sir David's faithful servant, a protector of the family and a man who watched Victoria grow from a child into a wonderful young lady."

"We needed answers, David," pleaded Fletcher. "The police needed something to push them." Sir David looked dumbfounded.

"How could —"

"He was trying to help Sir David. Only trying to help." She looked back at Fletcher. "It was the typescript, Fletcher. The 'u' printed in small case on both the murder notes and the library invite. All other letters are in upper case. I suspect you have an issue with your laptop and printer. We'll check that later." Fletcher nodded his acceptance. "One man amongst you, who knew you all, suspects it must be one of you, and had all the information that he needed to deliver the notes anonymously to your homes and workplaces." She turned back to Sir David. "Is it an offence to want to help? I don't think so." Sir David did not answer. Rachel turned back to the guests.

"What we don't know and will never know is how Victoria was murdered. All we have gleaned is intelligence. That's all an investigation can do, gather the intelligence and try to turn it into evidence. With that in mind we needed evidence." Rachel held her fingers up as she named the recipients. "The persons receiving notes were Sir David, Jamie Hyatt, Daniel Pape and Charles Fothergill."

Jonathan didn't know where to look, or what to do. His enemy and his best friend. Rachel noted his reaction. "Keep calm, Jonathan. We'll get there." Jonathan stood up and walked away from Charles and took a place behind his father. "All men who knew Victoria adored her, maybe even fancied her. She was a wild spirit, not a lady to be tamed by any man. Charles appears to have moved on, yet Daniel seems stuck in the past." Joe could feel Danny again tensing beside him. There was a knock at the lounge door and Jim walked in, carrying a small wooden box. He handed it to Rachel and walked back out of the door. Rachel looked at Danny.

"We've seized this from your house. I'm sure you recognise it." Danny crumpled in his chair.

"It wasn't me." He started sobbing. Rachel opened the box. She pulled out the note and the newspaper clipping. Kaur moved closer to Danny. All heads turned to face Danny. Jonathan grabbed the clipping, and read the headline.

"You bastard," said Jonathan with a sneer on his face. Matt stood up and placed a restraining arm across Jonathan's chest. Rachel lifted out the gold pendant. "A trophy?" All looked at the pendant.

"I loved her," sobbed Danny, "I would never have harmed her." Kaur moved next to him. Jonathan looked at the pendant. Sir David stood up and looked too.

"It's not hers," said Jonathan, turning to his dad. "She's never owned one like that. She wouldn't wear a crucifix. Hated religion."

"Well I must —" said Roger.

"Shut up," said Audrey, hitting his arm.

"Intelligence," explained Rachel, "not evidence." Jonathan and Sir David stepped back. Kaur placed a hand on Danny's shoulder.

"Stay there, son." Danny barely heard him.

"Which finally brings me to." Matt handed Rachel some photographs. He then handed them out. "Reginald Chiswick."

***

Ronnie woke up feeling thirsty. His room was lit by a small lamp and across his bed, a table was positioned supporting a glass, a jug of water and his phone. He'd been dreaming, and in the warmth of the hospital room, felt sweat beading on his forehead. He'd nodded off whilst watching television, which must have been turned off by a passing nurse. He looked at the far wall, organising his thoughts, then reached for his phone. Frustratingly laborious though it was, he managed to send a text to Joe.

***

"We're struggling with the chrysanthemums you see," said Rachel. "Mr Chiswick died before Victoria disappeared. He's buried in the church graveyard. I'm sure some of you know him." People nodded. "There's a photograph of his headstone. See the chrysanths? Freshly laid. No relatives in the village, but his grave is being tended to. Who usually tends to the flowers at the church, Reverend Melthrop?" Rachel glanced at Melthrop, then continued. "Look at the second picture. The lane Victoria was last seen entering alive. This is a photo taken by one of my operatives at an area towards the top of the lane. Look at the chrysanths." The guests compared the two photographs." Rachel looked at Matt, who stood up and handed out the last photograph. Joe's phone pinged, indicating that he had received a text.

"Our job is to work hard at gathering evidence." The guests received the photo. Joe read his text. Audrey dropped the photograph. Dialled on her phone. Stood up and moved.

"What the heck," exclaimed Roger, looking at the photo of Audrey, bent down and tending the flowers in the lane.

"RUN. RUN. YOU HAVE TO RUN," screamed Audrey down her phone. Joe sprang towards her. Grabbed her phone from her hands.

"Richard," he shouted to Rachel, "It's Richard." He ran to her and showed her Ronnie's text and Audrey's dialled number. "It's her brother." Roger ran over to his wife, who looked shocked by her own outburst.

"What's happening? What have you done?" She looked at him with hatred and started battering him with her fists.

"IT'S RICHARD, NOT ME," she screamed, "DO SOMETHING." Roger stood there transfixed. "OH, FUCK OFF." Audrey pushed him aside and ran towards the doors. Kaur moved and blocked her way. She slapped his face, rocking his head to one side. He grasped her hand, restrained her, and arrested her.

"WHAT FOR?" she screamed.

"Assault, for starters." Joe transmitted quickly over the radio airwaves.

"Jim, Tom. It's Richard Westbrook, the gardener. Get hold of him." Kaur threw Rachel his police radio.

"All units on this channel. Arrest on sight Richard Westbrook," instructed Rachel.

Downstairs in the dining room, Richard swiftly stood up, his chair clattering to the floor behind him. Ferality distorted his face as he spun round towards the door of the room. Richard roared and ran. Paddy watched open-mouthed, unconsciously grabbing his pint from the table to prevent it from falling.

"OUT OF MY WAY," bellowed Westbrook. Richard bowled guests to the side as he forged a path through them. Plates and drinks went soaring, a man tumbled backwards, feet flying in the air. Richard made for the door.

"MOVE" he shouted as he entered the hallway. Looking frantically left and right, he spotted movement on the stairs. A man running. Richard turned left, sprinted and slammed into a door. He passed through, entered another room and slammed the door behind him. Richard bent, seized a desk and hauled it over the door. Fists brayed on the other side.

Richard looked frantically around the room, breathing heavily, with sweat pouring down his face. He saw no other door. Shadows moved across the only window. "Shit. Trapped." Richard looked at the far wall again and smiled. The gun cabinet. He grabbed a chair and smashed the cabinet open.

"Give up. You're cornered," shouted a man outside the door. Richard laughed and reached into the cabinet. He pulled a shotgun from the rack, retrieved some cartridges and loaded the weapon.

"Fuck you," he shouted in reply. He turned. A man screamed outside. The room window imploded and a garden bench flew towards him. Crashed into him. The shotgun exploded. Richard fell back. A body flew through the window space, landed, rolled and pounced on him. He levelled the barrel. Strong hands grabbed it. Another shell exploded. A vicious growl and the gun was ripped from his hands. The butt flew towards Richard's head. Pain and then darkness.

Tom stood hunched over within the room, his burnt hands held protectively under his armpits, the shotgun at his feet. The door shuddered as people outside tried to enter. He turned, and with brute strength, hauled the obstruction away. A uniformed cop forced his way through the gap in the door. Tom pointed at Richard.

"There's your man. Richard Westbrook." The body on the floor groaned. "It'll take more than one of you. He's as strong as an ox."

"Back-up's outside, mate." The officer moved to Westbrook and cuffed his wrist. "And you are?" Tom straightened his black suit and brushed off the front, ignoring the pain in his hands. Another officer entered the room and moved to Westbrook. Tom pushed his dishevelled hair back and smiled.

"Only one of the dinner guests. He's all yours." Tom left the room, enjoying his Bond moment, as the officers cuffed Westbrook.

***

"What a bloody night," said Joe, as he entered the office. The team had gathered there the following morning to write their statements. Jim would add them to the file that he had been collating for Kaur. Joe placed his statement down on Jim's desk. "There you go, mate."

"Cheers. That's the last of them, Rach. I'll scan it and then email the file over to the DI."

"Any update from the interviews?" asked Sarah.

"Thanks, Jim," said Rachel. She turned to face Sarah. "They've got Audrey Melthrop's first account. She's not giving much away at the moment, I'm afraid."

"Trying to protect her brother?" asked Tom.

"In vain though. They've finished with Westbrook." The team was poised, waiting for Rachel's update. She smiled. "Not a full confession I'm afraid, but he's advised us to look in Chiswick's grave."

"Ron was on to something?" asked Joe.

"It seems so," said Rachel. "Westbrook will be arrested for the assault on Ronnie, too."

"Is he pinning it on Audrey?" asked Matt, looking astounded.

"He won't give us any more than that."

"Why'd he run though?"

"Why indeed? They've requested for them both to be kept in custody for a further three days."

"Exhumation order?" asked Tom.

"Yes, an application has been made to open up Mr Chiswick's grave."

"Are we going to find Victoria's body?" asked Joe.

"I expect so. Why else would he send us there? He's always tended the church grounds and his sister the church flowers. They're hoping to do it on Monday. Meanwhile, the cops will keep them both in and see who cracks first."

"Blood can be thicker than water," said Matt.

"Sometimes," said Rachel, "sometimes."

***

Grey skies leaked a drenching mizzle over the umbrella covered group who huddled around the grave of Mr Reginald Chiswick. A mound of turf was piled to one side and hidden behind a white screen. The skeletal remains of Mr Chiswick lay respectfully beneath a black cloth and tarpaulin. A white overalled officer gently scraped a trowel over the earth at the foot of the grave.

Jonathan and Sir David were standing side by side, Jonathan displaying uncharacteristic emotion with an arm placed over his father's shoulders, holding him tight. Rachel leaned forward, Matt moving the umbrella to protect her, and looked into the grave. The SOCO raised a hand, indicating that something had been found. A further officer, armed with a camera, took a photograph. Now reaching with an instrument in one hand, evidence bag in another, the first SOCO reached down and delicately placed the item within the evidence bag, sealed it and placed it on the grass verge above her. Sir David moved forwards and knelt to look. Crestfallen, he looked across to Rachel.

"It's Victoria's." Rachel nodded in acceptance. Within the evidence bag was a single gold pendant. "Thank you, detective. Thank you." Jonathan leant down and helped his father to his feet.

"Come on, dad. This will take some time. Shall we …"

"Take me to the church, please." Rachel and Jonathan turned away in respect. Jonathan led his father to the building where Fletcher waited patiently.

"Back to the hall?" asked Matt.

"Yes, let's go and update them."

***

"Here they come," said Joe, hearing footsteps approaching through the hall. The team waited patiently in the lounge. The door opened, Rachel entered first, followed by Matt.

"It's her," said Rachel. "Sir David's identified her necklace. SOCO are working on retrieving her remains." Sarah, Tom and Joe remained silent, heads nodding in acknowledgement of their success, but respectful of the solemnity of the occasion.

"He wasn't lying then?" said Joe.

"Kaur's done a good job on him," said Tom.

"He has," agreed Rachel, "but whether we ever find out why, who knows?"

"What about Audrey Melthrop?" asked Emily.

"She's got some serious questions to answer. She must have known and covered it up. Assisted him? We all witnessed her outburst. We got lucky with that."

"Made our own luck," said Tom.

"Ronnie helped with that," said Joe.

"He did," said Rachel, "Has someone checked in with him?"

"I rang the ward," said Joe. "Apparently, he has a visitor … Margaret."

"Good for her," said Matt.

"Right," said Rachel, "who is up for a pint?"

"Where?" asked Tom.

"Fenchurch. The hotel is booked, courtesy of Sir David." Rachel received a resounding yes from all.

"Enjoy yourselves," said Emily. Farewells were made, leaving Rachel, Matt and Emily in the lounge.

"Can you give me two minutes please, Matt? I'll see you in the hall." Matt left the room. Emily looked out of a window, watching the team head to their cars.

"You not coming?" asked Rachel. Emily turned to Rachel.

"How easy was it to leave?"

"The job?" asked Rachel.

"Yes."

"It took a lot of thought and a fair dose of bravery. Best thing I did though."

"They've fucking got me though. I hate it. I have to do what they tell me."

"Only if you want to stay."

"What else would I do?"

"Anything you want. Join my team."

"Your team?"

"Why not? You've got some skills. We're still getting established. You may find that you fit in. Discuss it over a pint?"

"You're on."

"Matt's in the hall. We'll give you a lift." Emily took that as her cue to leave.

Rachel looked around the room and wandered to a sideboard where a framed photo of Victoria stood with her looking out to the room. Rachel reached a hand to the frame and gave a sorrowful smile. She heard Matt and Emily talking in the hall, adjusted the photo slightly to give Victoria a view out of the bay windows to the grounds, and quietly left the room, closing the door behind her.

The End

／
Acknowledgements

Thank you to my wonderful editor Amy who keeps me on track, to Jon for his artistry with cover design and to Charles and the whole team at Pen & Sword.

A shout out to anyone who reads my novels, thank you. Writing is a solitary process but feels less so knowing that I can at least entertain some readers. To all readers please consider submitting a review on a platform of your choice. The challenge for all authors is to promote their work to a wider audience. Reader reviews play a large part in achieving this.

Finally, thank you to my tolerant children, my lovely wife Sarah and to Bella (who will remain in all of our hearts forever.)